Clinton Thomas Dent

Above the Snow Line

Mountaineering sketches between 1870 and 1880

Clinton Thomas Dent

Above the Snow Line
Mountaineering sketches between 1870 and 1880

ISBN/EAN: 9783337251611

Printed in Europe, USA, Canada, Australia, Japan

Cover: Foto ©Andreas Hilbeck / pixelio.de

More available books at **www.hansebooks.com**

ABOVE THE SNOW LINE

MOUNTAINEERING SKETCHES
BETWEEN 1870 AND 1880

BY

CLINTON DENT

VICE-PRESIDENT OF THE ALPINE CLUB

> 'Celui qui n'a jamais ses heures
> de folie est moins sage qu'il ne le
> pense'—LA BRUYÈRE

WITH TWO ENGRAVINGS BY EDWARD WHYMPER AND
AN ILLUSTRATION BY PERCY MACQUOID

LONDON
LONGMANS, GREEN, AND CO.
1885

THESE SKETCHES OF MOUNTAINEERING

I DEDICATE TO

T. I. D.

IN THE HOPE THAT A BOOK WITHOUT A HEROINE

MAY, AT LEAST, ACQUIRE SOME FEMININE INTEREST

PREFACE

SOME of the following sketches do not now appear for the first time; but such as have been before published in other form have been entirely re-written, and, in great measure, recast.

To the writer the work has afforded an occasional distraction from more serious professional work, and he cannot wish better than that it should serve the same purpose to the reader.

CORTINA DI AMPEZZO:
September 1884.

CONTENTS

CHAPTER I.

AN EXPEDITION IN THE OLDEN STYLE

Buried records—*Litera scripta manet*—The survival of the unfit—A literary octopus—Sybaritic mountaineering—On mountain 'form'—Lessons to be learned in the Alps—The growth and spread of the climbing craze—Variations of the art—A tropical day in the valley—A deserted hostelry—The hotel staff appears in several characters—Ascent of the Balfrinhorn—Our baggage train and transport department—A well-ventilated shelter—On sleeping out: its advantages on the present occasion—The Mischabelhörner family group—A plea for Saas and the Fée plateau—We attack the Südlenzspitz—The art of detecting hidden crevasses—Plans for the future—Sentiment on a summit—The feast is spread—The Alphubeljoch—We meet our warmest welcome at an inn

CHAPTER II.

THE ROTHHORN (MOMING) FROM ZERMATT

The Alpine dramatis personæ—Mountaineering fact and romance—The thirst for novelty and its symptoms—The first ascent of the Moming—Preliminaries are observed—Rock *v.* snow mountains—The amateur and the guide on rocks and on snow—The programme is made out—Franz Andermatten—Falling stones in the gully—We smooth away the difficulties—The psychological effects of reaching mountain summits—A rock bombardment and a narrow escape—The youthful tourist and his baggage—Hotel trials—We are interviewed—The gushers 31

CHAPTER III.

EARLY ATTEMPTS ON THE AIGUILLE DU DRU

The Alps and the early mountaineers—The last peaks to surrender The Aiguille du Dru—Messrs. Kennedy and Pendlebury's attempt on the peak—One-day expeditions in the Alps and thoughts on huts and sleeping out—The Chamouni guide system—A word on guides, past and present—The somnolent landlord and his peculiarities—Some of the party see a chamois—Doubts as to the peak and the way—The duplicity of the Aiguille deceives us—Telescopic observations—An ill-arranged glacier—Franz and his mighty axe—A start on the rocks in the wrong direction—Progress reported—An adjournment—The rocks of the lower peak of the Aiguille du Dru—Our first failure—The expedition resumed—A new line of ascent—We reach the sticking point—Beaten back—The results gained by the two days' climbing . . 56

CHAPTER IV.

A DAY ACROSS COUNTRY

The art of meteorological vaticination—The climate we leave our homes for—Observations in the valley—The diligence arrives and shoots its load—Types of travellers—The Alpine habitué—The elderly spinster on tour—A stern Briton—A family party—We seek fresh snow-fields—The Bietschhorn—A sepulchral bivouac—On early starts and their curious effects on the temperament—A choice of routes—A deceptive ice gully—The avalanches on the Bietschhorn—We work up

to a dramatic situation—The united party nearly fall out—
A limited panorama—A race for home—Caught out—A short
cut—Driven to extremities—The water jump—An aged person comes to the rescue—A classical banquet at Ried—The
old curé and his hospitality—A wasted life? . . . 96

CHAPTER V.

AN OLD FRIEND WITH A NEW FACE

Chamouni again—The hotel clientèle—A youthful hero—The inevitable English family—A scientific gentleman—A dream
of the future—The hereafter of the Alps and of Alpine
literature—A condensed mountain ascent—Wanted, a programme—A double 'Brocken'—A hill-side phenomenon and
a familiar character—A strong argument—Halting doubts
and fears—A digression on mountaineering accidents—
'From gay to grave, from lively to severe'—The storm
breaks—A battle with the elements—Beating the air—The
ridge carried by assault—What next, and next?—A topographical problem and a cool proposal—The descent down
the Vallée Blanche—The old Montanvert hotel—The Montanvert path and its frequenters 130

CHAPTER VI.

ASCENT OF THE AIGUILLE DU DRU

'*Decies repetita placebit*'

Disadvantages of narratives of personal adventure—Expeditions
on the Aiguille du Dru in 1874—The ridge between the
Aiguilles du Dru and Verte—'Défendu de passer par là'—
Distance lends enchantment—Other climbers attack the
peak—View of the mountain from the Col de Balme—We
try the northern side, and fail more signally than usual—
Showing that mountain fever is of the recurrent type—We
take seats below, but have no opportunity of going up higher

—The campaign opens—We go under canvas—A spasmodic start, and another failure—A change of tactics and a new leader—Our sixteenth attempt—Sports and pastimes at Chamouni—The art of cray-fishing—The apparel oft proclaims the man—A canine acquaintance—A new ally—The turning-point of the expedition—A rehearsal for the final performance—A difficult descent—A blank in the narrative—A carriage misadventure—A penultimate failure—We start with two guides and finish with one—The rocks of the Dru—Maurer joins the party—Our nineteenth attempt—A narrow escape in the gully—The arête at last—The final scramble - Our foe is vanquished and decorated—The return journey—Benighted—A moonlight descent—We are graciously received On 'fair' mountaineering—The prestige of new peaks—Chamouni becomes festive—'Heut' Abend grosses Feuerwerkfest'—Chamouni dances and shows hospitality—The scene closes in 169

CHAPTER VII.

BYE-DAYS IN ALPINE MIDLANDS

1. *A Pardonable Digression.*

On well-ordered intellects The drawbacks of accurate memory—Sub-Alpine walks: their admirers and their recommendations—The 'High-Level Route'—The Ruinette—An infallible prescription for ill-humour—A climb and a meditation on grass slopes—The agile person's acrobatic feats—The psychological effects of sunrise—The ascent of the Ruinette We return to our mutton at Arolla—A vision on the hill-side.

2. *A Little Maiden.*

Saas in the olden days—A neglected valley—The mountains drained dry—A curious omission—The Portienhorn, and its good points as a mountain—The chef produces a masterpiece—An undesirable tenement to be let unfurnished—An evicted family—A rapid act of mountaineering—On the

CONTENTS

pleasures of little climbs—The various methods of making new expeditions on one mountain—On the mountaineer who has nothing to learn, and his consequent ignorance . . 236

CHAPTER VIII.

A SENTIMENTAL ALPINE JOURNEY

Long 'waits' and entr'actes—The Mont Buet as an unknown mountain—We hire carriages—A digression on a stationary vehicle—A straggling start—The incomplete moralist—The niece to the moralist—A discourse on gourmets—An artistic interlude—We become thoughtful, and reach the height of sentiment and the top of the Mont Buet—Some other members of the party—The mountaineers perform—How glissading ambition did o'erleap itself—A vision on the summit—The moralist leaves us for a while—Entertainment at the Bérard Chalet—View of the Aiguille Verte—The end of the journey 266

CHAPTER IX.

A FRAGMENT

An unauthentic MS.—Solitude on the mountain: its advantages to the historian of the Alps—A rope walk—The crossing of the Schrund—A novel form of avalanche and an airy situation—A towering obstacle—The issue of the expedition in the balance—A very narrow escape—The final rush—Victory! —The perils of the descent—I plunge *in medias res*—A flying descent 290

CHAPTER X.

THE FUTURE OF MOUNTAINEERING

Mountaineers and their critics—The early days of the Alpine Club—The founders of mountaineering—The growth of the amusement—Novelty and exploration—The formation of centres—Narrowing of the field of mountaineering—The upward limit of mountaineering—De Saussure's experience—Modern development of climbing—Mr. Whymper's experience—Mr. Graham's experience—The ascent of great heights—Mr. Grove's views—Messrs. Coxwell and Glaisher's balloon experiences—Reasons for dissenting from Mr. Glaisher's views—The possibility of ascending Mount Everest—Physiological aspect of the question—Acclimatisation to great heights—The direction in which mountaineering should be developed—The results that may be obtained—Chamouni a century hence—A Rip van Winkle in the Pennine Alps—The dangers of mountaineering—Conclusion 300

ILLUSTRATIONS

THE BIETSCHHORN FROM THE PETERSGRAT *Frontispiece*

THE AIGUILLE DU DRU FROM THE SOUTH *to face page* 169

A VISION ON A SUMMIT ,, 282

ABOVE THE SNOW LINE

CHAPTER I.

AN EXPEDITION IN THE OLDEN STYLE

Buried records—*Litera scripta manet*—The survival of the unfit—A literary octopus—Sybaritic mountaineering—On mountain 'form'—Lessons to be learned in the Alps—The growth and spread of the climbing craze—Variations of the art—A tropical day in the valley—A deserted hostelry—The hotel staff appears in several characters—Ascent of the Balfrinhorn—Our baggage train and transport department—A well-ventilated shelter—On sleeping out: its advantages on the present occasion—The Mischabelhörner family group—A plea for Saas and the Fée plateau—We attack the Südlenzspitz—The art of detecting hidden crevasses—Plans for the future—Sentiment on a summit—The feast is spread—The Alphubeljoch—We meet our warmest welcome at an inn.

THERE exists a class of generously-minded folk who display a desire to improve their fellow-creatures and a love for their species, by referring pointedly to others for the purpose of mentioning that the objects of their remarks have never been guilty of certain enormities: a critical process, which is about equivalent to tarring an individual, but, from humanitarian considerations, omitting to feather him also. The ordeal, as applied to others, is unwarrantable; but there is a certain odd pleasure in subjecting oneself to it. Now, it is but a paraphrase to say that the more we go about, the more, in all probability, shall we be strengthened in the conviction that the paradise of fools must have a large acreage. The average Briton has a constantly present dread that he is likely to do something to justify his admission into that department of Elysium. The thought that he has so qualified, will wake him up if it crosses his mind even in a dream, or make his blood run cold—whatever that may mean—in his active state. Thus it falls out that he is for ever, as it were, conning over the pass-book of his actions, and marvelling how few entries he can find on the credit side, as he does so. It is asserted as a fact (and it were hard to gainsay the sentiment), that *Litera scripta manet*. No doubt; but how much more obtrusively true is it that printed matter is as indestructible as the Hydra? It has occurred sometimes to the writer, on very, very sleepless nights, to take down from a shelf, to slap the cover in order to get rid of a considerable amount of dust, and to peruse, in a volume well-known to all members of the Alpine Club, accounts written years before, of early mountain expeditions. To trace in some such way, at any rate to search for, indications of a fancied development of mind has a curious fascination for the solitary man. Effusions which an author would jealously hide away from the eyes of his friends, have a strangely absorbing interest to the man who reflects that he himself was their perpetrator.

We most of us, whatever principles we assert on the matter, keep stowed away, in some corner or another, the overflow of a fancied talent. The form varies: it may, perhaps, be a five act tragedy, possibly a psychological disquisition, or a sensational novel in three volumes of MS. It is a satisfaction to turn such treasures out from time to time when no eyes are upon us, even if it be only to thank Heaven devoutly that they have always lain unknown and uncriticised. 'Il n'y a rien qui rafraichisse le sang comme d'avoir su éviter de faire une sottise.' Of work done, of which the author had no especial reason to be proud, a feeling of thankfulness in a lesser degree may arise from the consciousness that, if ever recognised at all, it is now, happily, forgotten. So have these early effusions sometimes amused, not infrequently astounded, and at the worst have nearly always brought the wished-for slumber; and yet in Alpine writings the same accounts were for the most part as faithful representations as the writer could set down on paper of impressions made at the time. It has often occurred to me to ask what manner of description a writer would give of an expedition made many years before. How would the lapse of time influence him? Would he make light of whatever danger there was? Would the picture require a very decided coat of varnish to make it at all recognisable? Would the crudities come out still more strongly, or would the colours all have faded and sunk harmoniously together in his picture? The speculation promised to be interesting enough to make it worth while to give practical effect to the idea. Now the expedition narrated in this chapter was made in 1870, and possibly, therefore, if a description were worth giving at all, it had better have been given fresh. We can always find some proverb tending more or less to justify any course of action that we may be desirous of pursuing, and by distorting the meaning of a quotation manage to serve our own ends. Of all the ill-used remarks of this nature, surely the most often employed is, 'Better late than never;' the extreme elasticity of which saying, in the application thereof, is well evidenced by the doctor who employed it in justification of his late arrival when he came on a professional visit to the lady and found the baby learning its alphabet.

When an aquarium was a fashionable resort, amongst a good many queer and loose fish, we became familiar with a monstrously ill-favoured beast called a cuttle-fish: and may have had a chance of seeing how the animal, if attacked by his physical superior, resorted to the ingenious plan of effusing a quantity of ink, and, under cover of this, retreating hastily backwards out of harm's way. There are some, less ingenuous than the Octopus, who retreat first into obscurity and then pour out their effusion of ink. But it is more common to use the flare of an epigram or of a proverb, as a conjurer does his wand, to distract attention for the moment and divert the thought current from matters we do not wish to be too evident. At any rate, I must in the present instance lay under tribute the author of Proverbs, and add another straw to the already portentous burden that they who wish to compound for literary sins have already piled on his back. Apologising is, however, a dangerous vice, as a well-known writer has remarked. The account, though a sort of literary congenital cripple, has still a prescriptive right to live. Besides this expedition was undertaken in the pre-Sybaritic age of mountaineering, and before the later refinements of that art and science had taken firm hold of its votaries. What would the stern explorers of former time have thought, or said, if they had perceived persons engaged on the glaciers sitting down on campstools to a light refection of truffle pie and cold punch? Such banquets are not uncommon now, though precisians with a tendency to dyspepsia still object strongly to them. In those days, too, mountaineers were not so much differentiated that climbers were talked of by their fellows like cricketers are described in the book of Lillywhite. 'Jones,' for instance, 'is a brilliant cragsman, but inclined to be careless on moraines.' 'Noakes,' again, 'remarkably sure and steady on snow, fairly good in a couloir, would do better if he did not possess such an astounding appetite and would pay more attention to the use of the rope.' 'Stokes possesses remarkable knowledge of the Alps; on rocks climbs with his head; we wish we could say honestly that he can climb at all with his hands and feet.' 'Thompson, first-rate step-cutter; walks on snow with the graceful gait and unlaboured action of a shrimp-catcher at his work: kicks down every loose stone he touches.' Thus different styles of climbing are recognised. 'Form,' as it is called in climbing, was in the old days an unknown term, and yet it is probable that the 'form' was by no means inferior to any that can be shown now-a-days. The reason is obvious enough and the explanation lies simply in the fact that the apprenticeship served in the mountains was then much longer than it is now. People did not so often try to ride a steeple-chase before they had learnt to sit in a saddle, or appreciated that the near side was the best by which to get up. When this particular expedition was made (towards which I feel that I am an unconscionable time in making a start) I had been five or six seasons in the Alps, during the first two of which I had never set foot on a snow-slope. There had always seemed to me from the first, to be so much absolutely to learn in mountaineering: there is no less now, indeed there is more, for the science has been developed, but it seems beyond doubt, that fewer people recognise the fact. Like most other arts, it can only be learnt in one way, by constant practice, by constant care and attention and by always doing everything in the mountains to the best of one's ability. Too many may seem to think that there is a royal road, and fail to recognise that a plebeian does not alter his status by walking along this variety of highway.

Time rolled on. The fascination of climbing spread abroad, and it followed with the increasing number of mountaineers that more and more difficulties were experienced in attempts to diversify the sport in the Alps alone, and in emerging from the common herd of climbers. Then a new danger arose. The sport grew fashionable—a serious symptom to its true lovers. Books of Alpine adventure readily found readers; novels, and other forms of nonsense, were written about the mountains; accounts of new expeditions were telegraphed at once to all parts of the world, and found as important a place in the newspapers as the Derby betting, or the latest reports as to the precise medical details of some eminent person's internal complaint. Still further did the craving for novelty spread, and more strange did the means of satisfying it become. The mountains were ascended without guides: in winter; by people afflicted with mental aberration who wore tall hats and frock coats on the glaciers; by persons who were ignorant of the laws of optics as applied to large telescopes; in bad weather, by wrong routes and so forth. Then, too, set in what may be called the variation craze. This is very infectious. For those who can see no beauty in a scene that some one else has gazed on before it is still a passion. We may still at times, in the Alps, hear people say, 'Oh yes, that is a very fine expedition, no doubt, but I don't think I care much about undertaking it; you see so and so has done it; couldn't we manage to strike out a different line?' The result is a 'variation' expedition. The composer when hard driven, and not strongly under the influence of the Muse, will at times take some innocent, simple melody and submit it to exquisite torture by writing what he is pleased to call variations. Sometimes he will not rest till he has perpetrated as many as thirty-two on some innocent little tune of our childhood. The original air becomes entirely lost, like a sixpence buried in a flour bag, and we may marvel, for instance, as may the travelled American, at the immense amount of foreign matter that may be introduced into 'Home, sweet home.' Even so does the climber sometimes practise his art. But for one who entertains a strict respect for the old order of things, and for the memory of an age of mountaineering now rapidly passing into oblivion, to write in any such strain would be intolerable. And so, even as a theatrical manager when his brilliant play, stolen, or, as it is generally described, 'adapted,' from the French, does not run, I may be allowed to raise the curtain on a revival of the old drama, a comedy in one short act, and not provided with any very thrilling 'situations.' The 'scenarium' lay ready to hand in the leaves of an old journal, which may possibly share, with other old leaves, the property of being rather dry. But we are meandering, as it were, in the valleys, and run some risk of digressing too far from the path which should lead to the mountain in hand. There is a story of a clergyman who selected a rather long text as a preface to his discourse, and finding, when he had read it at length a second time, that his congregation were mostly disposed in attitudes which might be of attention, but which were, at the same time, suggestive of slumber, wisely concluded to defer enlarging upon it till a more fitting occasion, and dismissed his hearers, or at any rate those present, with the remark that they had heard his text and that he would not presume to mar its effectiveness by any exordium upon it. *Revenons.*

In the early part of August 1870, our party walked one sultry day up the Saas Valley. The dust glittered thick and yellow on our boots. Many of the smaller brooks had struck work altogether, while the main river was reduced to a clear stream trickling lazily down between sloping banks of rounded white boulders that shone with a painful glare in the strong sunlight. The more muscular of the grasshoppers found their limbs so lissom in the warmth that they achieved the most prodigious leaps out of sheer lightheartedness; for they sprang so far that they could have had no definite idea where they might chance to light. On the stone walls busy little lizards, with heaving flanks, scurried about with little fitful spurts, and vanished abruptly into the crannies, perpetually playing hide and seek with each other, and always seeming out of breath. The foliage drooped motionless in the heavy air and the shadows it cast lengthened along the dusty ground as steadily as the streak on a sundial. The smoke from the guides' pipes (and guides, like itinerant nigger minstrels, always have pipes in their mouths when moving from the scene of one performance to another) hung in mid air, and the vile choking smell of the sputtering lucifer matches was perceptible when the laggards reached the spot where a man a hundred yards ahead had lighted one of these abominations.

To pass under the shade of a walnut tree was refreshing like a cold douche; and to step forth again into the heat and glare made one almost gasp. Flannel shirts were miserably inadequate to the strain put upon their absorbent qualities. The potatoes and cabbages were white and piteously dusty. Even the pumpkins seemed to be trying to bury their plump forms in the cool recesses of the earth. Everywhere there seemed a consciousness as of a heavy droning hum. All of which may be concisely summed up in the now classical opening remark of a well-known comedy character, one 'Perkyn Middlewick' to wit, 'It's 'ot.'

When within a little distance of the hotel I enquired whether it was worth while for one of the party to push on to secure rooms. The guides thought, on the whole, that it was unnecessary, and this opinion was justified subsequently by the fact that we found ourselves the sole occupants of the hotel during the week or so that we remained in the district. It was the year of the war; ugly rumours were about, but very few tourists. Selecting, therefore, the most luxurious apartment, and having given over to the care of one Franz, who appeared in the character of 'boots' to the hotel, a remarkable pair of cowhide brogues of original design, as hard as sabots and much more uncomfortable, I sat down on a stone slab, in order to cool down to a temperature that might permit of dining without fear of imperilling digestion. So pleased were the hotel authorities at the presence of a traveller that they exerted themselves to the utmost to entertain us well, and with remarkable results. I find a record of the dinner served. There were ten dishes in consecutive order, exclusive of what Americans term 'fixings.' As to the nature of nine it was difficult to speak with any degree of certainty, but the tenth was apparently a blackbird that had perished of starvation and whose attenuated form the chef had bulged out with extraneous matter. Franz, who seemed to be a sort of general utility man to the establishment, had thrown off, with the case of a Gomersal or a Ducrow, the outward habiliments of a boots and appeared now as a waiter, in a shirt so hard and starched that he was unable to bend and could only button his waistcoat by the sense of touch. The repast over, Franz removed the shirt front and unbent thereupon in manner as in person. Assuming engaging airs, he entered into conversation, disappearing however for short intervals at times, in order, as might be inferred from certain sounds proceeding from an adjoining apartment, to discharge the duties of a chamber-maid. Subsequently it transpired that he was the proprietor of the hotel.

We agreed to commence our mountaineering by an ascent of the Balfrinhorn, a most charming walk and one which even in those days was considered a gentle climb. There are few peaks about this district which will better repay the climber of moderately high ambition, and it is possible to complete the expedition without retracing the steps. There is no danger, and it is hard to say to what part of the mountain an enthusiast would have to go in order to discover any: so the expedition, though perhaps prosaic, is still very interesting throughout and quite in the olden style. The solitude at the hotel was somewhat dull, and the conversational powers of the guides soon exhausted if we travelled beyond the subject of chamois hunting. I did indeed try on one occasion to explain to them, in answer to an earnest request, the military system of Great Britain. But, with a limited vocabulary, the task was not easy and, as I could not think of any words to express what was meant by red tape, circumlocution, and short service, my exposition was limited to enlarging on the facts that the warriors of my native country were exceeding valiant folk with very fine chests, that they wore highly padded red coats and little hats like half bonbon boxes cocked on one side and that they would never consent to be slaves. Burgener, anxious for some more stirring expedition, suggested that we should climb the Dom from the Saas side or make a first ascent of the Südlenzspitz. We had often talked of the former expedition, which had not at the time been achieved, and, in order to facilitate its accomplishment, divers small grants of money had been sent out from England to be expended in the construction of a hut some five hours' walk above Fée. In answer to enquiries, the guides reported with no small amount of pride, that the building had been satisfactorily completed and they were of opinion that it was ready for occupation. At some length the process of building was described and it really seemed from their account that they had caused to be erected a shelter of unduly pretentious dimensions. It appeared, however, that the residence was equally well placed to serve as a shelter for an ascent of the Südlenzspitz and we decided ultimately to attack that peak first. Great preparations were made; an extensive assortment of very inferior blankets was produced and spread out in the road in front of the hotel, either for airing or some other ill-defined purpose, possibly from some natural pride in the extensive resources of the hotel. Then they pulled down and piled into a little stack, opposite the front door, fire wood enough to roast an ox, or convert an enthusiast into a saint.

One fine afternoon we started. The entire staff and *personnel* of the hotel would have turned out to wish us good luck, but did not actually do so, as he was engaged in a back shed milking a cow. Laden with a large bundle of fire wood, I toiled up the steep grass slopes above Fée, leading to the Hochbalm glacier. The day was oppressively hot, and I was not wholly ungrateful on finding that the string round my bundle was loose and that the sticks dropped out one after another : accordingly I selected a place in the extreme rear of the caravan, lest my delinquencies should perchance be observed. The sun beat mercilessly down upon our backs on these bare slopes and we sighed involuntarily for Vallombrosa or Monaco or some equally shady place. The guides, who up to that time had spoken of their building as if it were of somewhat palatial dimensions, now began rather to disparage the construction. Doubts were expressed as to the effects certain storms and heavy falls of snow might have had on it and regrets that the weather had prevented the builders from attending as minutely to details of finish and decoration as they could have wished. Putting this and that together, I came to the conclusion that the erection would probably be found to display but indifferent architectural merit. However, there was nothing better to look forward to. 'Where is it?' 'Oh, right up there, under the big cliff, close to where Alexander is.' In the dim distance could be distinguished the form of our guide as a little dark mass progressing on two pink flesh-coloured streaks, striding rapidly up the hill. The phenomenon of colour was due to the fact that, prompted by the sultriness of the day, Alexander had adopted in his garb a temporary variation of the Highland costume. A few minutes later he joined us, clothed indeed, and in a right, but still a melancholy frame of mind. Shaking his head sadly, he explained that a grievous disaster had taken place, evidently in the spring. The forebodings of the constructively-minded rustics we had left below, who knew about as much of architecture as they did of metaphysics, proved now to be true. They had remarked that they feared lest some chance stone should have fallen, and possibly have inflicted damage on the hut. Why they had selected a site where such an accident might happen, was not at the moment quite obvious, but it became so later on. Burgener told us that the roof had been carried away. Beyond question the roof was gone; at any rate it was not there, and the rock must have fallen in a remarkable way indeed, for the cliff above was slightly overhanging, and the falling boulder, which was held accountable for the disaster, had carried away every vestige of wood-work about the place, not leaving even a splinter or a chip. However, to the credit of the builders, be it said that they had tidied up and swept very nicely, for there was no sawdust to be seen anywhere, nor indeed, any trace of carpentering work. The hut consequently resolved itself into a semi-circular stone wall, very much out of the perpendicular, built against a rock face. The chief architect, evidently a thoughtful person, had not omitted to leave a door. But it was easier on the whole to step over the wall, which I did, with as much scorn as Remus himself could have thrown into the action when seeking to aggravate his brother Romulus. So we entered into possession of the premises without, at any rate, the trouble of any preliminary legal formalities.

In the matter of sleeping out, all mountaineers pass, provided they keep long enough at it, through three stages. In the early period, when imbued with what has been poetically termed the 'ecstatic alacrity' of youth, they burn with a desire to undergo hardship on mountains. Possibly a craving for sympathy in discomfort—that most universal of human attributes—prompts them to spend their nights in the most unsuitable places for repose. The practical carrying out of this tendency is apt to freeze very literally their ardour; at least, it did so in our case. Then follows a period during which the climber laughs to scorn any idea of dividing his mountain expedition. He starts the moment after midnight and plods along with a gait as free and elastic as that of a stage pilgrim or a competitor in a six days' 'go-as-you-please' pedestrian contest: for those who have a certain gift of somnambulism this method has its advantages. Finally comes a stage when the climber's one thought is to get all the enjoyment possible out of his expedition and to get it in the way that seems best at the time. Now again he may be found at times tenanting huts, or the forms of shelter which are supposed to represent them. But his manner is changed; he no longer travels burdened with the impedimenta of his earlier days. He never looks at his watch now, except to ascertain the utmost limit of time he can dwell on a view. With advancing years and increasing Alpine wisdom, he derides the idea of accurately timing an expedition. His pedometer is probably left at home; he eats whenever he is hungry, and ceases to consider it a *sine quâ non* that he must return to hotel quarters in time for dinner. Nor does he ever commit the youthful folly of walking at the rate of five miles an hour along the mule path in the valley or the high road at the end of an expedition, gaining thereby sore feet and absolutely nothing else. When he has reached this stage, however, he is considered *passé*; and when he has reached this stage he probably begins really to appreciate to the full the depth of the charm to be found in mountaineering.

But I digress even as the driven pig. A miserable night did we spend behind the stone wall. About 9 P.M. came a furious hail-storm: at 10 P.M. rain fell heavily: at 11 P.M. snow began and went on till daybreak about 4 A.M. At 5 A.M. we got up quite stiff and stark like a recently killed villain of melodrama, when carried off the stage by four supers. By 6 A.M. I had got into my boots. At 9 A.M. we swooped down once more on Franz at the hotel at Saas, persuaded him to relinquish certain scavenging occupations in which he was engaged, and to resume his post of waiter. A day or two later we sought our shelter once more. No luxurious provisions did we take with us. Some remarkable red wine, so sour that it forced one involuntarily to turn the head round over the shoulder on drinking it, filled one knapsack. The other contained slices of bread with parallel strata of a greasy nature intervening. These were spoken of, when we had occasion to allude to them, as sandwiches. The fat was found to be an excellent emollient to my boots.

The Südlenzspitz, though tall, labours under the topographical disadvantage of being placed in the company of giants. Close by, on the north side, is the Nadelhorn (14,876 ft.), while to the south, at no great distance, the Dom towers far above, reaching a height of 14,942 feet. In the Federal map of Switzerland (which is not very accurate in its delineation of the Saas district), the height of the Südlenzspitz is marked as 14,108 ft. North and south from the Südlenzspitz, stretch away well-marked, but not particularly sharp ridges, the northern being chiefly of snow, and inclined at a moderate angle. To the east, a sharper rocky ridge falls away, terminating below, after the fashion of a 'rational' divided skirt, in two undecided continuations which enclosed the Fall glacier. Climbing up by this ridge, Mr. W. W. Graham ascended the mountain in 1882. The 'variation' is described as presenting very serious difficulties. But in our day, the old-fashioned custom of ascending mountains by the most obviously practicable way was still in vogue, and we decided, therefore, to make for the northern buttress. Leaping over the wall enclosing the ground-floor of our bivouac, we descended on to the Hochbalm glacier, made our way across the upper snow basin, and in good time reached the foot of the slope no great distance south of the Nadelhorn. The view during this part of the walk is very characteristic of the range. From almost any point of view, the traveller is surrounded on three sides by a clearly marked amphitheatre of very beautifully formed mountains. On the right, the shapely little Ulrichshorn rises up in a self-sufficient manner, like a single artichoke in a vegetable dish. In front is the mass of the Nadelhorn and Südlenzspitz, while, looking back, the view of the mountains on the east side of the Saas valley is one of great and varied beauty. It must be confessed that these statements are derived principally from a contemplation of the map, for, to tell the truth, the recollection of the panorama we actually saw is rather indistinct. This much, however, I may record with confidence; that in all parts of the Saas district, the views struck me, in a day when I did not very much look at them, as possessing strong individuality and the greatest beauty.

The Zermatt district may be still more striking, and they who have no time to visit both, no doubt do wisely to seek the more hackneyed valley. But for such as do not look upon guide-book statements as the dicta of an autocrat, and can exercise a thousandth part of the independence of judgment they manifest in the ordinary affairs of life, a brief deviation to the Saas country will come as a revelation. After the crowd, dust, and bustle of the highway to the recognised centre of the Alps, to turn aside to this region is a relief, like stepping out of a crowded ball-room on to a verandah, or gliding away in a gondola from the railway station at Venice. Look, too, at the architecture of the great mountains here, and the spectator will perceive how nature has succeeded to perfection in achieving what all artists fail in doing; that is in designing, and in a manner that precludes criticism, a pendant; and a pendant too to the Zermatt panorama. The necessary object in the foreground of the picture—which we all know to be an hotel—is provided. Who but nature would think of framing a pure white picture in a setting of the soft green pastures below, and the deep blue sky above? but here it is, and it is perfect. Yet the blue of the sky is repeated in the picture, for the towering séracs throw azure shadows on the satin-smooth snow slopes at their feet. Rest, strength, eternal solidity above in the mountain forms and crags; repose, softness, and the charm of a brightness below that must yield and fade before long to gather force for fresh development and renewal. No need to seek far for a parallel in our human world. Between the two districts, Zermatt and Saas-Fée, there is but the difference between the man who impresses at once by the force of character, and the man who has to be studied and learned before we recognise that he is something beyond the ordinary run of our fellow-creatures.

Before leaving England we had made tolerably minute inquiries, but had failed to discover any record of a previous ascent of the Südlenzspitz, though, as suggested by Mr. W. M. Conway, the mountain may have been previously climbed by Mr. Chapman. Some uncertainty, therefore, whether we should find any traces of previous climbers, gave the required piquancy to the expedition. We made at once up the slope for a long rocky buttress, and towards a part of the mountain down which the guides asserted stones had been known to fall in the afternoon. This statement was probably made with a view of encouraging their charge to greater exertions, for an old sprained ankle compelled me to the continual necessity of putting my best foot foremost in walking over difficult places. Still, the rocks were at no point very formidable, and progress was rendered somewhat easier by the fact that no critical companion was with me, so I felt at perfect liberty to transport myself upwards in any style that happened to suit the exigencies of the moment. I had not at that time quite passed the stage of believing all that the guides asserted with reference to the climbing capacities of the individual who pays them for assisting his locomotion, and had a distinct idea that I mastered all the obstacles in a particularly skilful manner. They said as much in fact, but reiterated their compliments so often that I somewhat fear now that I must frequently have given occasion for these remarks of approbation; remarks which I have since observed are more frequently called forth to cover a blunder than to praise an exhibition of science. Probably my progress was about as graceful and sure as that of a weak-legged puppy placed for the first time in its life on a frozen pond, or a cockroach seeking to escape from the entrapping basin, for I had not then developed, in climbing rocks, the adhesive powers of—say the chest, which longer practice will sometimes furnish. We were accompanied by a porter of advanced years whose conversational powers were limited by an odd practice of carrying heavy parcels in his mouth. The day before he had carried up a large beam of wood for the camp fire in this manner. I never met a man with so much jaw and so little talk. He had apparently come out in order to practise himself for the mastication of the Saas mutton, for at the end of the day he would accept of nothing but a sum of two francs, for which I was very thankful. Similar disinterestedness in men of his class is not often met with nowadays.

After awhile we left the buttress of rock and turned our attention to a snow slope and made our way up its crest. Here steps were necessary but there was no particular difficulty, for the slope resembled a modern French drawing-room tragedy, in that it was as broad as it was long. We had but to feel that the rope was taut, and could then look about with security. In good time we stepped on to the ridge, and a glance upwards showed that the way was easy enough. We could not but feel that if we were to achieve the honour of a first ascent, such honour would be principally due to the fact that we had subdivided the secondary peaks of the chain more minutely than other travellers. The principle has been carried still further in these latter days, and as any little pale fish that can be caught and fried is considered whitebait, and any article that ladies choose to attach to their heads is termed a bonnet, so any point that can be climbed by an individual line of ascent is now held to be a separate mountain. A considerable snow cornice hung over on the northern side of the arête and great care was necessary, for the ridge itself was so broad and easy, that less careful guides might have made light of it; but Burgener, though he had already acquired a reputation for brilliancy and dash, never suffered himself for one moment to lose sight of the two great qualities in a guide, caution and thoroughness. At each step he probed the snow in front of him with all the diligence of a chiffonnier. It followed that our progress was somewhat slow, but it was none the less highly instructive. The accurate sense of touch in probing doubtful snow with the axe requires and deserves very much more practice than most people would imagine. The unpractised mountaineer may climb with more or less ease a difficult rock the first time he is brought face to face with it, but long and carefully acquired experience is necessary before a man can estimate with certainty the bearing power of a snow bridge with a single thrust of the axe. Indeed many guides of reputation either do not possess or never acquire the muscular sense necessary to enable them to form a reliable opinion on this matter. As a rule, if the rope be properly used and such a mistake be made, somebody plunges through, is hauled out again and no harm is done; but there are occasions when serious accidents have happened, when probably lives have been lost owing to want of skilled knowledge in this detail of snow mountaineering. I have known guides who never failed when they came to a treacherous-looking bridge, to give it one apparently careless thrust with the axe and then walk across with perfect confidence; and I have seen others do exactly the same and disappear suddenly to cool regions below through the bridge; and *vice versâ*. The unskilful prober will make wide detours when he might go in safety, and the man of good snow touch will avoid what looks sound enough : till in returning, perhaps you see that the hard crust concealed but rotten things beneath : as in an ill-made dumpling. It needs no small amount of training to judge between the man who quickly and with certainty satisfies himself of the safety of a particular snow passage, and the man who is too careless properly to investigate it; yet without such experience the amateur is not really able to decide whether a guide be a good or a bad one.

Here and there along the ridge short rock passages gave a welcome relief and at length we stood on the highest point of the ridge which culminates so gently in the actual peak of the Südlenzspitz. Our first care was to scrape about and hunt diligently for traces of any previous party. No relic of conviviality could be found, and as all the flat stones about appeared to be in their natural state of disorder, we piled up some of them into a neat little heap, and came to the conclusion that we had performed very doughty deeds. But we were younger then. The sun was out, there was a dead calm, and we lay for a while basking in the warmth and planning a serious expedition for some future year. It may seem strange in these days of rocket-like mountaineering when the climber, like the poet, *nascitur non fit*, but the peak whose assault we discussed was none other than the Matterhorn. It was no longer thought that goblins and elves tenanted its crags; but although these spectres had not yet been frightened away and turned out of house and home by sardine boxes and broken bottles, some trace of prestige still adhered to the mountain. It had not then, like a galley slave, been bound with chains, or, even as a trussed chicken, girt about with many cords. Nor was the ascent of the peak then talked about as carelessly as might be a walk along Margate pier. Alexander Burgener had never been up the peak, though he was most anxious to get an opportunity of doing so. I can remember well the advice that was given to me on the top of the Südlenzspitz to practise further on a few less formidable mountains before attacking the fascinating Mont Cervin itself. Alas for the old days and the old style of mountaineering! It may be doubted whether such discussions often take place nowadays; but then it was only my sixth season in the Alps. The following year we did hatch out the project laid on the top of the Südlenzspitz to climb the Matterhorn together. To this moment I can remember as I write every detail of the climb and every incident of the day as vividly as if it were yesterday; and what a splendid expedition it was then. The old, old fascination can never come back again in quite the same colours; better, perhaps, that it should not. Is it always true that 'a sorrow's crown of sorrow is remembering happier things'? Surely there is a keenness and a depth of pleasure to be found in recalling happiness, though it may never return in its old form; and the memory of pleasure just toned with a trace of sadness is one of the most profound emotions that can stir the human heart. Go on and climb the Alps ye that follow: nowhere else will you find the same pleasure. But it is changed, and in this amusement the old fascination will never be quite the same to you. It may be, it will be, equally keen, but as there is a difference between skating on virgin ice and that which, though still good, is scored by marks of predecessors, so will you fail to find a something which in the olden days of mountaineering seemed always present. Go elsewhere if you will, and seek fresh fields for mountaineering enterprise in the Caucasus, the Himalayas, the Andes. There you will find the mountains have a charm of their own: the mark is as good, but it is not the Alpine mark. That has been taken by others. *Beati possidentes.*

Judging by the nature of these sentiments it would seem that we must have become pensive to the verge of slumber while on the summit. In descending, we followed our morning's tracks, and scorning the seductive shelter of the hut made straight down for the hotel. On this occasion we found Franz, who was a man of varied resources and accomplishments, hanging his shirt, which apparently he had just washed, up to dry. Our unexpected arrival appeared to disconcert him a little, for the straitened nature of his wardrobe precluded him, to his great disappointment, from appearing at dinner in full costume. He conceived, however, an ingenious, though somewhat transparent subterfuge, and made believe that he had got a bad cold in the chest which compelled him to button his coat up tight round the neck. In honour of our achievements he said he would go down to the cellar and bring us up a curious old wine. The cellar consisted apparently of a packing-case in a shed. Old the wine may have been; curious it certainly was, for it possessed a strong heathery flavour and seemed to turn hot very suddenly and stick fast in the throat like champagne at a suburban charity ball. But nevertheless, with the remnants of the blackbird or some other *rara avis* made into a species of pie, we feasted royally.

A few days later we crossed over to Zermatt by the Alphubel Joch, a heavy fall of snow having prevented any idea of making our contemplated assault on the Dom. A Swiss gentleman of a lively nature and excessive loquacity accompanied us. He was not an adroit snow walker, and disappeared on some five or six occasions abruptly into crevasses. The moment, however, that he got his head out again, he resumed his narrative at the exact point at which it had been perforce broken off without exhibiting the least discomposure. The subject to which his remarks referred I did not succeed in ascertaining. We parted at a little chalet not far from the Riffel, leaving our friend lying flat on his back on the grass contemplating the sky with a fixed expression, with his hands folded over his waistcoat. He may have been a poet inspired with a sudden desire for composition for aught I know, or may have assumed this attitude as likely to facilitate the absorption of a prodigious quantity of milk which he took at the chalet.

As we drew nearer to the odd mixture of highly coloured huts and comfortable hotels that make up the village of Zermatt, a sense of returning home crept over the mind, a consciousness of friends at hand, of warm welcomes, mixed with the half presentiment that is always felt on such occasions, that some change would be found; but happily it was not so. The roadway was in its former state; the cobble stones a trifle more irregular and worn more smooth, but still the same. The same guides, or their prototypes, were sitting on the same wall drumming their heels. The same artist was hard at work on a sketch of the Matterhorn in a field hard by. The same party just returning from the Görner Grat. The same man looking out with sun-scorched face from the salon window and the same click from the self-willed billiard balls on the uncertain table below. Ay, and the same unmistakable heartfelt greetings and handshakings at the door of the Monte Rosa. Churlish indeed should we have been if we had sighed to think that we had met our warmest welcome at an inn.

CHAPTER II.

THE ROTHHORN (MOMING) FROM ZERMATT

The Alpine dramatis personæ—Mountaineering fact and romance—The thirst for novelty and its symptoms—The first ascent of the Moming—Preliminaries are observed—Rock v. snow mountains—The amateur and the guide on rocks and on snow—The programme is made out—Franz Andermatten—Falling stones in the gulley—We smooth away the difficulties — The psychological effects of reaching mountain summits—A rock bombardment and a narrow escape—The youthful tourist and his baggage—Hotel trials—We are interviewed—The gushers.

THE writer of an Alpine narrative labours under more disadvantages than most literary folk—if authors generally will permit the association, and allow that those who rush into print with their Alpine experiences have the smallest claim to be dignified with such a title. One drawback is that their accounts necessarily suffer from a paucity of characters. A five-act tragedy supported, to use a theatrical expression, by two walking gentlemen, one heavy lead and a low comedy 'super,' might possibly pall upon an audience, but in Alpine literature, if I may be permitted to push the metaphor a little further, not only is this the case but the unhappy reader finds the characters like 'barn stormers' playing now comedy, now tragedy, and sometimes, it may possibly be added, dramas of romance.

Again, in all matters absolutely relating to mountaineering in the Alps, the narrator feels bound to stick to matters of fact. The drama of romance must be excluded from his répertoire, or, at any rate, very cautiously handled. I knew a man once, who on a single occasion went a-fishing in Norway and caught a salmon. Naturally he was proud of the achievement, and when in the company of brother sportsmen, would hold up his head, assume a knowing air, and take part in the conversation, such conversation relating, of course, to the size of the various fish those present had caught. Such unswerving and prosaic veracity did my friend possess, that, though sorely tempted as he must have been on many occasions, for ten years he never added a single ounce to the weight of his fish. A writer, an Alpine scribbler at any rate, is perhaps justified if he introduces incidents into an account of an expedition which may not have happened on that particular occasion, but which did happen on some other; and surely he may, without impropriety, romance a little on such part of his work as is not strictly geographical; for example, he may describe a chalet as being dirty, when according to the peasant's standard of cleanliness it would have been considered spotless, or describe a view as magnificent, when as a matter of fact he paid no attention to it, but he would be acting most culpably if he asserted that he got within fifty feet of the summit, well knowing that he was not fifty feet from the base of the peak, or if he stated that rocks were impossible, or an ice-fall impracticable, when the sole reason for his failure consisted in his being possessed with a strong desire to go back home. Of course a writer can only give his own impressions, and these are much tempered by increased experience and the lapse of time, but in taking up old accounts of Alpine work one not unfrequently finds a good deal of description that requires toning down. In these sketches I have striven honestly to render all that relates intimately to the actual mountains as accurate as possible, and would sooner be considered a dull than an unreliable historian.

It is no easy matter to reproduce almost on the spot an account of a climb with absolute accuracy, however strong the desire may be to do so. Besides, a climber does not pursue his pastime with a note book perpetually open before him. If he does, his mountaineering is more of a business than he is usually willing to admit. The guide often, the amateur commonly, fails to recognise exactly from a distance a line of ascent or descent on rocks, though but just completed. Still more difficult is it to work out the precise details of a particular route on a map

D

or photograph. The microscopist knows that the higher powers of his instrument give him no additional insight into the structure of certain objects, but rather mislead. Even so may my readers be asked to employ but gymnoscopic criticism of these sketches.

In September 1872 our party reached Zermatt from Chamouni by the 'high-level' route, a series of walks which no amount of familiarity will ever deprive of their charm, and concerning which more will be found elsewhere in this work. All Alpine climbers were then burning as fiercely as they ever did to achieve something new. They had just begun to realise that the stock of new peaks and passes was not inexhaustible, and that the supply was wholly inadequate to meet the demand. This feeling showed itself in various ways. Climbers looked upon each other with something of suspicion and jealousy, and if any new expedition was being planned by any one of their number the others would quickly recognise the state of affairs. If an Alpine man were found secreted in obscure corners conversing in a low voice with his guides and intent on a study of the map, or if he returned evasive answers when questioned as to his plans, he was at once set down as having, probably, a new expedition in mind. As for the guides, they assumed at once airs of importance, as does a commencing schoolboy newly arrayed in a tall hat, and exhibited such mystery that their intentions were unmistakable. Their behaviour, indeed, may have been partly due to the fact that the natural efforts of their comrades to extract information was invariably accompanied by somewhat undue hospitality, and their brotherly feelings were usually expressed in an acceptably liquid form. As a rule such hospitality did not fail in its object. Whether due to a certain natural leakiness of mind on the part of the guides or not, I cannot say, but certainly the information always oozed out, and the intentions of the party were invariably thoroughly well known before the expedition actually started to achieve fresh glory. Every one of the first-rate peaks in the Zermatt district had been ascended, most of them over and over again, before 1872, but the Rothhorn was still out of the pale of the Zermatt expeditions. Messrs. Leslie Stephen and F. Craufurd Grove, who first climbed the peak, ascended it from Zinal, and descended to the same place. It seemed to us, therefore, that if we could prove the accessibility of the mountain from Zermatt, we should do something more than merely climb the peak by a new route. The rocks looked attractive, and the peak itself lay so immediately above Zermatt that it seemed possible enough to make the ascent without sleeping out or consuming any great amount of time.

We went through all the necessary preliminary

formalities. We assumed airs of mystery at times; why, I know not. We inspected distant peaks through the telescope. At other times we displayed an excess of candour, and talked effusively about districts remote from that which we intended to investigate. We climbed up a hill, and surveyed the face of our mountain through a telescope, thereby wasting a day and acquiring no information whatever. We pointed out to each other the parts of the mountain which appeared most difficult, and displayed marvellous differences of opinion on the subject, owing, as is usually the case, to the circumstance that we were commonly, in all probability, talking at the same time about totally distinct parts of the peak. With the telescope I succeeded in discovering to my own entire satisfaction a perfectly impracticable route to the summit. Finally, in order that no single precaution might be omitted to ensure success, we sent up the guides to reconnoitre—a most useless proceeding. We had new nails put in our boots, ordered provisions, uncoiled our rope and coiled it up again quite unnecessarily, gave directions that we should be called at an unhallowed hour in the morning, and went to bed under the impression that we should not object in the least to turn out at the time arranged.

It is on the rock mountains of Switzerland that the acme of enjoyment is to be found. Not that I wish to disparage the snow-peaks; but if a comparison be instituted it is to most climbers, at any rate in their youthful days, infinitely in favour of the rock. Of course it may be argued that there are comparatively few mountains where the two are not combined. But a mountaineer classifies peaks roughly as rock or snow, according to the chief obstacles that each presents. A climber may encounter serious difficulties in the way of bergschrunds, steep couloirs, soft snow, and so forth; but if on the same expedition he meets with rocks which compel him to put forth greater energies and perseverance than the snow required, he will set the expedition down as a difficult rock climb, simply, of course, because the idea of difficulty which is most vividly impressed on his mind is in connection with that portion of his climb, and *vice versâ*. An undeniable drawback to the snow peaks consists in their monotony. The long series of steps that have to be cut at times, or the dreary wading for hours through soft or powdery snow, are not always forgotten in the pleasure of overcoming the difficulties of a crevasse, reaching the summit of a peak, or the excitement of a good glissade. It is the diversity of obstacles that meet the rock climber, the uncertainty as to what may turn up next, the doubt as to the possibility of finding the friendly crack or the apposite ledge, that constitute some of the main charms. Every step is different, every muscle is called into play as the climber is now flattened against a rough slab, now abnormally stretched from one hold to another, or folded up like the conventional pictures of the ibex, and every step can be recalled afterwards with pleasure and amusement as the mountain is climbed over again in imagination.

But there is more than this; on rocks the amateur is much less dependent on his guides and has much more opportunity of exercising his own powers. It must be admitted that on rocks some amateurs are occasionally wholly dependent not on, but from their guides, and take no more active share in locomotion than does a bale of goods in its transit from a ship's hold to a warehouse. Too often the amateurs who will not take the trouble to learn something of the science and art of mountaineering are but an impediment, an extra burden, as has been often said, to the guides. The guides have to hack out huge steps for their benefit. The amateurs wholly trust to them for steering clear of avalanches, rotten snow bridges, and the like. The amateur's share in a snow ascent usually consists, in fact, either in counselling retreat, insisting on progress, indicating impossible lines of ascent, or in the highly intellectual and arithmetical exercise of counting the number of steps hewn out to ensure his locomotion in the proper direction.

Place the unpaid climber, on the other hand, on rocks. Here the probability is that a slip will entail no unpleasant consequences to anyone but the slipper.

The power of sustaining a sudden strain is so enormously increased when the hands have a firm grip that the amateur can, if he please, sprawl and scramble unaided over difficult places with satisfaction to himself and usually without risk to anyone else; that is, as soon as he has fully persuaded the guides (no easy task, I admit) that the process of pulling vehemently at the rope, possibly encircling his waist in a slip knot, is as detrimental to his equilibrium as it is to his digestion. Guides, however, as has been hinted, do not acknowledge this fact in animal mechanics, and their employers frequently experience as an acute torture that compressing process which, more deliberately applied, is not regarded by some as hurtful, but rather as a necessary accompaniment of fashionable attire. When the amateur has succeeded in overcoming the natural instinct of the guides to pull when there is no occasion to do so, he becomes a unit in the party, a burden of course, and a hindrance to some guides, but nothing to what he was on the snow.

Sentiments similar to the above have not unfrequently been set forth in print: they seldom, if ever, actuate the minds of mountaineers when actually engaged in their pastime or when describing their exploits to less skilled persons.

There is great satisfaction, too, in translating one's self over a given difficult rock passage without other assistance than that provided by nature herself, and without surreptitious aid from one's neighbour in the shape of steps. Then again, snow mountains are as inconsistent as cheap aneroids. One day each step costs much labour and toil, and almost the next perhaps the peak will allow itself to be conquered in one-tenth of the time. Not that the writer seeks to argue that there is no pleasure to be derived from snow mountains. It is to climbing *per se* that these remarks apply. After all, everyone has his own opinion; but he who has not tasted the pleasures of a really difficult and successful rock climb—especially if it be a new one—knows not what the Alps can really do for his amusement.

An expedition of suitable magnitude and difficulty was suggested by the guides, viz. an ascent of the Rothhorn (or Moming) from the Zermatt side. Mr. Passingham of Cambridge was at the time staying at the Monte Rosa Hotel, and it was soon arranged that we should combine our forces. The guides, on being asked their opinion as to the projected climb, reported diplomatically that, given fine weather, the ascent would be difficult but possible. This is the answer that the guides generally do give. We decided to attempt the whole excursion in a single day, considering that a short rest in the comparatively luxurious beds provided by M. Seiler was preferable on the whole to more prolonged repose in a shepherd's hut;

for the so-called repose means usually a night of misery, and the misery under these conditions is apt to make a man literally acquainted with strange bed-fellows. At 2 in the morning we sought for the guides' room, to superintend the packing of our provisions. It was not easy to find, but at last we discovered a dingy little subterranean vault with one small window tightly jammed up and covered with dust. Of this den there were two occupants. One was employed silently in eating large blocks of a curious boiled mess out of a pipkin. The other was smoking a very complicated pipe, and sitting bolt upright on a bench with half a bottle of *vin ordinaire* before him. Why he was carousing thus in the small hours was not evident. From these signs we judged correctly that the apartment was devoted to the guides as a dining, smoking, club and recreation room.

Our staff was already in attendance, and it struck both of us that the success of the expedition was a foregone conclusion if it depended on the excellence of our guides—Alexander Burgener, the embodiment of strength, endurance, and pluck; Ferdinand Imseng, of activity and perseverance, alone would have sufficed, but we had in addition a tough, weather-beaten, cheery companion (for he was always a companion as well as a guide), Franz Andermatten, ever sagacious, ever helpful and ever determined. It would be hard to find a successor adequately to fill our old friend's place.

It is impossible to efface his memory from my mind, nor can I ever forget how on that day he showed all his best qualities and contributed mainly to our success.[1] The prologue is spoken; let us raise the curtain on the comedy.

The guides had already made their usual preparations for packing up—that is to say, they had constructed a multiplicity of little paper parcels and spread them about the room. As to the contents of these little parcels, they were of course uncertain, and all had to be undone to make sure that nothing had been omitted. A good deal of time was thus lost, and nothing much was gained, except that we corrected the error of packing up a handful of loose lucifers and two tallow dips with the butter and honey in a glass tumbler. Then the parcels were stowed away in the knapsacks, the straps of course all rearranged and ultimately replaced by odds and ends of string. Eventually, at 3 A.M., we started, leaving the two occupants of the guides' room still engaged in the same manner as when they first came under observation, and walked up the narrow valley running due north of Zermatt and leading towards the Trift Joch and the base of the mountain for which we were

[1] Franz Andermatten died in August 1883. His name is mentioned elsewhere in these sketches, but I leave what I have written untouched: for I do not hold with those who would efface the recollection of all that was bright and merry in one taken from us.

making. Having journeyed for about half an hour, it was discovered that the telescope had been left behind. Franz instantly started off to get it; not because it was considered particularly necessary, but chiefly on the ground that it is not orthodox to go on a new expedition without a telescope. We stumbled up the narrow winding path, and close below the moraine called our first halt and waited for Franz's return. I selected a cool rock on which to complete the slumber which had been commenced in bed and continued on a tilted chair in the guides' room. After waiting an hour we decided to proceed, as no answer was returned to our frequent shouts. Presently, however, a distant yell attracted our attention, and we beheld, to our astonishment, the cheery face of Franz looking down on us from the top of the moraine. Stimulated by this apparition, we pushed on with great vigour, clambered up the moraine, whose extreme want of cohesion necessitated a treadmill style of progression, and having reached the top passed along it to the snow. Here we bore first to the right, and then, working round, made straight for a sharp-topped buttress which juts out at a right angle from the main mass of the mountain. Arrived at a patch of rocks near the commencement of the arête, we disencumbered ourselves of superfluous baggage; that is to say, after the traditional manner of mountaineers, we discarded about three-fourths of the impedimenta we had so laboriously dragged up to that point, and of which at no subsequent period of the expedition did we make the slightest use. Next, we prepared for such rock difficulties as might present themselves, by buttoning up our coats as tight as was convenient, and decorated our heads respectively with woollen extinguishers like unto the covers placed by old maids over cherished teapots.

It is a grand moment that, when the difficulty of an expedition opens out, when you grasp the axe firmly, settle in to the rope, and brace up the muscles for the effort of the hour: a moment probably the most pleasurable of the whole expedition, when the peak towers clear and bright above, when the climber realises that he is on the point of deciding whether he shall achieve or fail in achieving a long wished for success, or what it may be perhaps allowable to call a cutting-out expedition (for even mountain climbers are prone to small jealousies). The excitement on nearing the actual summit often rather fades away than increases, and the climber lounges up the last few steps to the top with the same sort of nonchalance that a guest invited to drink displays in approaching the bar.

Dividing into two parties, we passed rapidly along the snow ridge which abuts against the east face of the mountain. The cliffs of the Rothhorn seem almost to overhang on this face, and were from our point of view magnificent. On the right, too, the precipice is a sheer one, to employ a not uncommon epithet. Without much difficulty we clambered up the first part of the face of the mountain, taking a zigzag course towards the large gully which is distinctly visible from the other side of the valley, and which terminates above in a deep jagged notch in the ridge not far below the summit. Gradually the climbing became more difficult, and it was found necessary to cross the gully backwards and forwards on several occasions. In so crossing we were exposed to some risk from falling stones; that is to say, some chips and bits of rock on a few occasions went flying by without any very apparent reason. In those days mountaineers were in the habit of considering these projectiles as a possible source of risk. A later generation would pass them by as easily as the stones passed by us, and it is not now the fashion to consider such a situation as we were in at all dangerous. It is difficult to see the reason why. Perhaps people's heads are harder now than they were then. For the greater part of the time we kept to the left or south side of the gully, and reaching the notch looked right down upon the commencement of the Glacier du Durand, a fine expanse of snowfield, singularly wild-looking and much crevassed. Turning to the right, we ascended a short distance along the ridge, and then a halt was called. The guides now proceeded to arrange a length of some hundred feet of rope on the rocks above to assist in our return. The process sorely tried our patience, and we were right glad when the signal was given to go on again. We had now to leave the arête, to descend a little, and so pass on to the west face of the mountain, and by this face to ascend and gradually work back to the ridge. No doubt during this part of the climb we made much the same mistake in judgment as had previously been made on a memorable ascent of the Matterhorn, and crossed far more on to the face than was really necessary or advisable. The mountain has since the time when these lines were originally written passed through the regular stages of gradual depreciation, and it is more difficult now to realise that we considered it at the time very difficult. Probably, however, subsequent travellers have improved considerably on the details of the route we actually followed; at any rate the ascent is now considered quite proper for a novice to attempt, at any rate by the novice himself. We worked ourselves slowly along in the teeth of a biting cold wind, and without finding the fixed rope necessary to assist our progress. Reaching the ridge again, the way became distinctly easier, and we felt now that the peak was at our mercy. Presently, however, we came to a huge inverted pyramid of rock that tried rather successfully to look like the summit, and we had some little difficulty in surmounting it. By dint of strange acrobatic feats and considerable exertion we hoisted our leading guide on to the top. It was fortunate for him perhaps that the seams of his garments were not machine-sewn, or he would certainly have rent his raiment. Finding, however, that the only alternative that offered when he got to the top of the rock was to get down again on the other side, the rest of us concluded that on the whole we should prefer to walk round. The last few yards were perfectly easy, and at 1.30 p.m. we stood on the summit enjoying a most magnificent view in every direction.

It is a somewhat curious phenomenon, but one frequently remarked, that the mountaineer's characteristics seem abruptly to change when he reaches the summit of a peak. The impressionable, excitable person instantly becomes preternaturally calm and prosaic, while those of lymphatic temperament have not unfrequently been observed to develop suddenly rather explosive qualities, and to yell or wave their hats without any very apparent incitement thereto. Individuals whose detractors hold to be gifted with poetic attributes have been heard to utter quite commonplace remarks, and I have even known a phlegmatic companion so far forget himself, under these modifying circumstances, as to make an excessively bad pun and laugh very heartily at it himself, quite an unusual occurrence in a wag. Others find relief for their feelings by punching their companions violently in the back, or resorting to such horse-play as the area of the summit allows scope for. Directly, however, the descent commences the climber resumes his normal nature. The fact is, that in most cases, perhaps, the chief pleasure of the expedition does not come at the moment when the climber realises that he is about to undo, as it were, all his work of the day. There is no real climax of an expedition, and, as has been said, it is quite artificial to suppose that the enjoyment must culminate on reaching the top. But still it is considered proper to testify to some unusual emotional feelings. Some of the most enjoyable climbs that the mountaineer can recall in after life, are not those in which he has reached any particular point. Guides consider it becoming to evince in a somewhat forced way the liveliness of their delight on completing an ascent. But such joy as they exhibit is usually about as genuine and heartfelt as an organ-grinder's grin, or a Lord Mayor's smile on receiving a guest whom he does not know and who has merely come to feed at his expense.

The wind was too cold to permit of a very long stay on the summit, and having added a proper number of stones to the cairn, a ceremony as indispensable as the cutting of a notch in the mainmast when the traditional fisherman changes his shirt, we descended rapidly to the point where it was necessary to quit the ridge. Down the first portion of the steep rock slope we passed with great caution, some of the blocks of stone being treacherously loose, or only lightly frozen to the face.

We had arrived at the most difficult part of the whole climb, and at a rock passage which at that time we considered was the nastiest we had ever encountered. The smooth, almost unbroken face of the slope scarcely afforded any foot-hold, and our security almost entirely depended on the rope we had laid down in our ascent. Had not the rope been in position we should have varied our route, and no doubt found a line of descent over this part much easier than the one we actually made for, even without any help from the fixed cord. Imseng was far below, working his way back to the arête, while the rest of the party were holding on or moving but slowly with faces turned to the mountain. Suddenly I heard a shout from above; those below glanced up at once: a large flat slab of rock, that had afforded us good hold in ascending, but proved now to have been only frozen in to a shallow basin of ice, had been dislodged by the slightest touch from one of the party above, and was sliding down straight at us. It seemed an age, though the stone could not have had to fall more than ten feet or so, before it reached us. Just above me it turned its course slightly; Franz, who was just below, more in its direct line of descent, attempted to stop the mass, but it ground his hands

E

against the rock and swept by straight at Imseng. A yell from us hardly awoke him to the danger: the slab slid on faster and faster, but just as we expected to see our guide swept away, the rock gave a bound for the first time, and as, with a startled expression, he flung himself against the rock face, it leapt up and, flying by within a few inches of his head, thundered down below. A moment or two of silence followed, and then a modified cheer from Imseng, as subdued as that of a 'super' welcoming a theatrical king, announced his safety, and he looked up at us with a serious expression on his face. Franz's escape had been a remarkably lucky one, but his hands were badly cut about and bruised. In fact it was a near thing for all of us, and the mere recollection will still call up that odd sort of thrill a man experiences on suddenly recollecting at 11 P.M. that he ought to have dined out that evening with some very particular people. Had not the rock turned its course just before it reached Franz, and bounded from the face of the mountain over Imseng's head, one or more of the party must unquestionably have been swept away. The place was rather an exceptional one, and the rock glided a remarkably long distance without a bound, but still the incident may serve to show that falling stones are not a wholly imaginary danger.

It would have been difficult, with the elementary

knowledge of mountaineering that I now see we possessed at that day, to have descended without using the attached rope, and quite out of the question for anyone possessed of a proper respect for his suit of dittos to have done so. In this latter respect we had to exercise economical caution: for we had no very great store at the hotel or many changes of raiment. It is generally possible to gauge pretty accurately an Alpine traveller's experience by the amount of luggage he takes on a tour. Some tourists, following the advice given in the 'Practical Guide Book' (a disconnected work written in the style of Mr. Jingle's conversation, but much in favour at one time), were in the habit of travelling with one suit of clothes and a portable bath. The latter, though they took it with them, they seldom took more than once; at the best it was of comparatively little use as an article of apparel, but imparted an aromatic flavour to anything packed up in its immediate neighbourhood. In those youthful days we considered, forsooth, that a little leathern wallet adequately replaced a portmanteau, and in transporting luggage did not always act on the sound commercial maxim that you should never do anything for yourself which a paid person might do equally well for you; consequently a heavy rain shower reduced the traveller to inactivity, and an oversight on the part of the laundress entailed consequences that it is not permissible to mention.

Meanwhile our turn had come to move on. A zigzagging crack, which was too narrow to admit of anything but a most uncomfortable position, afforded the only hand and foot hold on which we could rely. Our gloveless hands, clutching at the rope, cooled down slowly to an unpleasant temperature that rendered it doubtful whether they were attached to the arms or not, and we began to wish we had gone down the Zinal side of the mountain. However, Imseng wormed himself along the rocks, to which he adhered with the tenacity of a lizard, and finally reached the end of our rope and a region of comparative safety. We followed his example slowly, and, having joined him, seated ourselves on some rocks inappropriately designed for repose, and finished off the food we had with us. Climbing carefully down the east face of the mountain, we reached the snow ridge and passed rapidly along it, our spirits rising exuberantly as we looked back on the vanquished peak. As usually happens, the guides had entirely forgotten the place where they had concealed our baggage on the ascent, and in fact had hidden it so carefully that they had some difficulty in finding it when they came to the spot. It is curious to note how often the instinct of guides, so much talked about, is at fault in this matter, and how systematically they are in the habit of carrying up on the mountains superfluous articles, hiding them with entirely unnecessary precautions, and subsequently forgetting the whole transaction.

While they searched about for their cache we enjoyed the use of tobacco, if such an expression be allowable in the case of some curious stuff purchased in the valley. Still, as the packet in which it was contained was labelled 'Tabak,' we considered it to be such. Being indulgently disposed, and not being profound botanists, poetic license alone enabled us to imagine that

> 'We soared above
> Dull earth, in those ambrosial clouds like Jove,
> And from our own empyrean height
> Looked down upon Zermatt with calm delight.'

It may have been so; it gave me a sore throat. Descending rapidly, we reached the Monte Rosa Hotel at 7 P.M., in an exultant frame of mind, a ragged condition of attire, and a preposterous state of hunger. The whole time occupied in the climb was sixteen hours. Of this an hour was wasted while we were waiting for the telescope, and three-quarters of an hour was spent in arranging the rope, by the aid of which we descended. Probably in actual climbing and walking we employed rather under thirteen hours; but the snow was in excellent order, and we descended on the whole very rapidly. Our trials were not over for the day, when we reached the hotel. Two arch young things had prepared an ambuscade and surprised us successfully at the door of the hotel. Sweetly did they gush. 'Oh! where had we been?' We said we had been up in the mountains, indicating the general line of locality with retrospective thumb. 'Oh! wasn't it fearfully dangerous? Weren't we all tied tightly together?' (as if, on the principle of union being strength, we had been fastened up and bound like a bundle of quill pens). 'Oh! hadn't we done something very wonderful?' The situation was becoming irritating. 'Oh! didn't we have to drag ourselves up precipices by the chamois horns on the tops of our sticks?' 'No indeed——' 'Oh! really, now, that guide there' (a driver with imperfectly buttoned garments who was sitting on the wall with a vacuous look) 'told us you were *such* wonderful climbers.' It was becoming exasperating. 'And oh! we wanted to ask you *so* much, for you know all about it. *Do* you think we could walk over the Théodule? Papa' (great heavens! he must be a nonagenarian) 'thinks we should be so foolish to try. Could you persuade him?' 'Well, really——' 'Wouldn't the precipices make us dreadfully giddy?' 'No, no more than you are now.' 'Oh! thank you so much. And you really won't tell us what awful ascent you have been making?' It was maddening. 'After dinner perhaps?' 'Oh! thank you. Oh! Sustie' (this to each other; they both spoke together: probably the names were Susie and Tottie), 'won't that be delightful?' By dexterous manœuvring we escaped these gushing Circes during the evening. Happening to pass later on by the open door of the little *salon*, the following remark was overheard: 'My dear, the conceit of these climbing objects is quite dreadful. They do nothing but flourish their nasty sticks and ropes about: they want the whole place to themselves' (we had been sitting on wooden chairs in the middle of the high street, near an unsavoury heap of refuse), ' and they talk, talk, talk, my dear, all day and all night about what they have been doing in the mountains and of their nonsensical climbs. And what frights they look. I think they are perfectly horrid.' Can the voice have been that of the gusher?

CHAPTER III.

EARLY ATTEMPTS ON THE AIGUILLE DU DRU

The Alps and the early mountaineers—The last peaks to surrender—The Aiguille du Dru—Messrs. Kennedy and Pendlebury's attempt on the peak—One-day expeditions in the Alps and thoughts on huts and sleeping out—The Chamouni guide system—A word on guides, past and present—The somnolent landlord and his peculiarities—Some of the party see a chamois—Doubts as to the peak and the way—The duplicity of the Aiguille deceives us—Telescopic observations—An ill-arranged glacier—Franz and his mighty axe—A start on the rocks in the wrong direction—Progress reported—An adjournment—The rocks of the lower peak of the Aiguille du Dru—Our first failure—The expedition resumed—A new line of ascent—We reach the sticking point—Beaten back—The results gained by the two days' climbing.

ACCOUNTS of failures on the mountains in books of Alpine adventure are as much out of place, according to some critics, as a new hat in a crowded church. Humanly speaking, the possession of this head-gear under such circumstances renders it impossible to divert the thoughts wholly from worldly affairs. This, however, by the way. Now the pioneers of the Alps, the Stephenses, the Willses, the Moores, the Morsheads, and many others, had used up all new material with alarming rapidity, I might say voracity, before the climbing epoch to which the present sketches relate. There is an old story of a man who arrived running in a breathless condition on a railway platform just in time to see the train disappearing. 'You didn't run fast enough, sir,' remarked the porter to him. 'You idiot!' was the answer, 'I ran plenty fast enough, but I didn't begin running soon enough.' Even so was it with the climbers of our generation. They climbed with all possible diligence, but they began their climbing too late. Novelty, that is the desire for achieving new expeditions, was still considered of paramount importance, but unfortunately there was very little new material left. It is difficult to realise adequately now the real veneration entertained for an untrodden peak. A certain amount of familiarity seemed indispensable before a new ascent was even seriously contemplated. It had occurred to certain bold minds that the aiguilles around Chamouni might not be quite as bad as they looked. In 1873 the chief of the still unconquered peaks of the Mont Blanc district were the Aiguille des Charmoz, the Aiguille Blaitière, the Aiguille du Géant, the Aiguille Peuteret, the Aiguille du Dru, and a few other minor points. All of these have since been captured, some of them bound in chains. Opinions differed considerably as to their accessibility. Some hopeful spirits thought that by constantly 'pegging away' they might be scaled; others thought that the only feasible plan would be indeed to peg away, but were of opinion that the pegs should be of iron and driven into the rock. Such views naturally lead to discussions, sometimes rather heated, as to whether mountaineering morality might fitly tolerate such aids to the climber. Of all the peaks mentioned above, the Aiguille du Dru and the Aiguille du Géant were considered as the most hopeful by the leading guides, though the older members of that body held out little prospect of success. It is a rather curious fact that the majority of the leading guides who gave their opinions to us in the matter thought that the Aiguille du Géant was the more promising peak to attack. Subsequent experience has proved that they were greatly in error in this judgment. The Aiguille du Géant has indeed been ascended, but much more aid than is comprised in the ordinary mountaineer's equipment was found necessary. In fact, the stronghold was not carried by direct assault, but by sapping and mining. There is a certain rock needle in Norway which, I am told, was once, and once only, ascended by a party on surveying operations bent. No other means could be found, so a wooden structure was built up around the peak, such as may be seen investing a dilapidated church steeple; and the mountain, like the Royal Martyr of history, yielded up its crowning point at the scaffold. We did not like the prospect of employing any such architectural means to gain our end and the summit, and, from no very clearly defined reasons, turned our attention chiefly to the Aiguille du Dru. Perhaps the prominent appearance of this Aiguille, and the fact that its outline was so familiar from the Montanvert, gradually imbued us with a certain sense of familiarity, which ultimately developed into a notion that if not actually accessible it might at least be worth trying. It seemed too prominent to be impossible; from its height—12,517 feet only—the mountain would doubtless not attract much attention, were it not so advantageously placed. Thousands of tourists had gazed on its symmetrical form: it had been photographed, stared at through binoculars, portrayed in little distorted pictures on useless workboxes, trays and other toy-shop gimcracks, more often than any other mountain of the chain, Mont Blanc excepted. Like an undersized volunteer officer, it no doubt made the most of its height. But in truth the Aiguille du Dru is a magnificent mountain form, with its vast dark precipices on the north face, with its long lines of cliff, broken and jagged and sparsely wrinkled with gullies free from even a patch or trace of snow. Point after point, and pinnacle after pinnacle catch the gaze as we follow the edge of the north-west 'Kamm,' until the eye rests at last on the singularly graceful isosceles triangle of rock which forms the peak. It is spoken of lightly as merely a tooth of rock jutting up from the ridge which culminates in the Aiguille Verte, but when viewed from the Glacier de la Charpoua it is obviously a separate mountain; at any rate it became such when the highest point of the ridge, the Aiguille Verte, had been climbed by somebody else. The cleft in the ridge on the right side of the main mass of the Aiguille du Dru is a very deep one as seen from the glacier, and the sharp needle of rock which is next in the chain is a long way from the Aiguille du Dru itself. North and south the precipices run sheer down to the glaciers beneath. The mountain has then four distinct sides, three of them running down to great depths. Thus, even in the prehistoric days of Alpine climbing, it had some claim to individuality and might fairly be considered as something more than, as it were, one unimportant pinnacle on the roof of some huge cathedral. Perhaps, however, repeated failures to ascend the mountain begot undue veneration and caused an aspiring climber to look with a prejudiced eye on its dimensions.

So far as I know, the mountain had never been assailed till 1873, when Messrs. Pendlebury and Kennedy made an attempt. Mr. R. Pendlebury has kindly furnished me with notes of the climb, which I may be allowed to reproduce nearly in his own words:—
Two parties started simultaneously for the expedition. One was composed of Messrs. Kennedy and Marshall, with the guides Johann Fischer and Ulric Almer of Grindelwald; the other party consisted of the Rev.

C. Taylor, Messrs. W. M. and R. Pendlebury, with the guides Hans Baumann, Peter Baumann, and Edouard Cupelin. The first-mentioned party slept at the Montanvert, while the others enjoyed themselves in a bivouac high up on the side of the Glacier de la Charpoua between the Aiguille du Dru and the Aiguille Moine. This Glacier de la Charpoua, it may be mentioned, is sometimes called the Glacier du Chapeau.

The bivouac appears to have been so comfortable that Mr. Pendlebury and his friends did not take advantage of their start. The Montanvert detachment, who found no such inducement to stay one moment longer than was absolutely necessary[1] in their costly quarters, caught them up the next morning, and the whole party started together. Mr. Kennedy's guides kept to the left of the Glacier de la Charpoua, which looks more broken up than the right-hand side, but apparently proved better going. This, however, it should be observed, was in 1873, and these hanging glaciers alter marvellously in detail from year to year, though always preserving from a distance the same general features. On the same principle, at the proper distance, a mother may be mistaken for her daughter, especially by a judicious person. But on drawing near, however discreet the observer may be, he is yet conscious of little furrows, diminutive

[1] In the old house, be it noted—not the modern luxurious combination of a granite fortress and a palace.

wrinkles, and perhaps of a general shrinkage not to be found in the more recent specimen. Speaking very generally, I should say that these glaciers are, on the whole, easier to traverse than they used to be: at any rate my own personal observation of this particular little glacier extends over a period of some years, and the intricacies—it is hardly proper to call them difficulties—were distinctly less towards the end of the time than they were at the beginning. Of course a different interpretation might be put upon such an opinion: with the evolution of mountaineering skill the complexity of these crumpled up snow-fields may seem to have disentangled, but I am assured that in this particular case it was not so.

This digression must be pardoned. It arose naturally from the circumstance that the route Mr. Kennedy adopted would have proved, at any rate in later years, a digression from the best way. Mr. Pendlebury's party went straight up, keeping, that is, to the right-hand side of the glacier. Towards the upper part the snow slopes became steeper, and soon some step-cutting was required. The object in view was to reach the lowest point in the ridge between the Aiguille du Dru and the Aiguille Verte. It was thought that, by turning to the left from the col, it might be possible to reach the summit by the eastern arête. The col itself from below seemed easily attainable by means of a narrow zigzagging gully, interrupted here and there, that runs down from the summit of the ridge. Ascending by the rocks on the left of the gully the party made for some little way good progress, but then a sudden change came over the scene. After a consultation, it was proposed that the guides Hans Baumann, Peter Baumann, and Fischer should go on a little by themselves and make for the ridge, which they estimated lay about half an hour above them. They were then to examine the rocks above and to bring back a report. The rest of the party remained where they were, and disported themselves as comfortably as circumstances would permit. Hour after hour, however, passed away, and the three guides seemed to make but little progress. They returned at last with the melancholy tidings that they had climbed nearly up to the ridge and had found the rocks very difficult and dangerous. (It should be noted that the line of attack chosen on this occasion—the first serious attempt on the peak—was devised by Hans Baumann, and it says much for his sagacity that this very route proved years afterwards to be the right one.) Questioned as to the advisability of proceeding upwards, the guides employed their favourite figure of speech and remarked that not for millions of francs would they consent to try again. Hans Baumann asserted that he had never climbed more difficult rocks. This opinion, as Mr. Pendlebury suggested at the time, was probably owing to the fact that the cliffs above were covered with snow and glazed with ice, and this condition of the mountain face made each step precarious. The amateurs of the party were of opinion that the ridge would prove attainable later in the season or in exceptionally fine weather. As to the possibility of climbing the rocks above—that is to say, the actual peak—none of the party were able to come to any very positive conclusion. At a rough guess it was estimated that the party halted between two and three hundred feet below the ridge. On the presentation of the guides' report the whole caravan turned back and reached Chamouni safely, but not entirely without incident, for the monotony of the descent and Mr. Taylor's head were broken by the fall of a big stone. This little accident, Mr. Pendlebury remarked with disinterested cheerfulness, was but a trifle. I have not been able to ascertain Mr. Taylor's views on the subject.

When our party first essayed the ascent we knew none of the above particulars, save only that some mountaineers had endeavoured to reach the ridge but had failed to ascend to any great height. Of the actual cause of their ill success, and whether it were owing to the unpropitious elements or to the actual difficulties encountered, we were unaware.

At the time of which I am writing, a somewhat novel mode of ascending mountains was coming into vogue, which consisted in waiting for a suitable day at headquarters, starting at unheard-of hours, and completing the expedition in one day—that is, within twenty-four hours. It was argued in support of this plan, that it was economical and that bivouacking was but a laborious and expensive method of obtaining discomfort. There are, said the advocates of the method, but few mountains in the Alps which cannot be ascended with much greater comfort in one day than in two. The day's climb is much more enjoyable when it is possible to start from sleeping quarters in which it is possible to sleep. The argument that repose in hotel beds, though undoubtedly more luxurious, was of comparatively little use if there were no time to enjoy it, was held to be little to the purpose. Some enthusiasts were wont to state that passing a night in a chalet, or those magnified sentry boxes called cabanes, constituted half the enjoyment on the expedition. This is a little strong—like the flavour of the cabanes—and if it were actually so the whole pleasure would be but small. The camper out arises in the morning from his delicious couch of soft new-mown hay in a spotty and sticky condition, attended with considerable local irritation, and feeling like a person who has recently had his hair cut, with a pinafore but loosely tied around his neck. Porters, like barbers, exhibit a propensity for indulging in garlic immediately before pursuing their avocation, which is not without discomfort to their employers. (And here I may note as a psychological fact that one action of this permeating vegetable is to induce confidential propensities in the consumer. The point may be deemed worthy of investigation, by personal experiment, by botanists and students of materia medica, men who in the interests of science are not prone to consider their personal comfort and finer sensibilities.) Again, in unsettled weather a fine day is often wasted by journeying up in the afternoon to some chalet, or hovel, merely to enjoy the pleasure of returning the following morning in the rain. There is some force too in the argument that but little actual time is gained by the first day's performance, for it is very difficult to start at anything like the prearranged hour for departure from a camp. An immensity of time is always spent in lighting the morning fire, preparing breakfast, and getting under way. On the other side, some little time is undoubtedly saved by discarding the wholly superfluous ceremony of washing, a process at once suggesting itself to the mind of the Briton abroad if he beholds a basin and cold water.

The sum of the argument would seem to be that camping out in some one else's hut is but an unpleasant fiction; that if the climber chooses to go to the expense, he can succeed in making himself a trifle less comfortable in his own tent or under a rock than he would be in an hotel; and that he is the wisest man who refrains from bivouacking when it is not really necessary and is able to make the best of matters when it is: and undoubtedly for many of the recognised expeditions it is essential to have every possible minute of spare time in hand.

We were naturally rather doubtful as to the successful issue of our expedition, at any rate at the first attempt, and we therefore impressed upon the guides the necessity of not divulging the plan. The secret, however, proved to be so big that it was too much for two, and they imparted consequently so much of the information as they had not adequate storage for in their own minds to any who chose to listen. Consequently our intentions were thoroughly well known before we started. There were in those days, perhaps, more good guides, at any rate there were fewer bad ones, in Chamouni than are to be found nowadays. We could not, however, obtain the services—even if we had desired them—of any of the local celebrities. As a matter of fact, we were both of opinion that a training in climbing, such as is acquired among the Oberland and Valais men by chamois hunting and constant rock work, would be most likely to have produced the qualities which would undoubtedly be needed on the aiguilles.

The question of the efficiency of the Chamouni guides and of the Chamouni guide system, a question coeval with mountaineering itself, was burning then as fiercely as it does now. The Alpine Club had striven in vain to improve matters; they had pointed out that ability to answer a kind of mountaineering catechism did not in itself constitute a very reliable test of a peasant's power; they had pointed out too that the plan of electing a 'guide chef' from the general body of guides was one most open to abuse, one sure to lead to favouritism and injustice, and one obviously ill calculated to bring to the front any specially efficient man. But unhappily the regulations of the body of guides were, and still are, entangled hopelessly in the French equivalent for red tape. Jealousy and mistrust of the German-speaking guides, whom serious mountaineers were beginning to import in rather formidable numbers, were beginning to awaken in the simple bosoms of the Savoyard peasants; and our proceedings were consequently looked upon with contemptuous disfavour by those who had any knowledge of our project.

On August 18, 1873, we started. Our guides were Alexander Burgener as leader, Franz Andermatten, the best of companions, our guide, our friend, and sometimes our philosopher, as second string, while a taciturn porter of large frame and small mind, who came from the Saas valley, completed the tale. Of Burgener's exceptional talent in climbing difficult rocks we had had already good proof, and no doubt he was, and still is, a man of remarkable daring, endurance, and activity on rocks. I had reached then that stage in the mountaineering art at which a man is prone to consider the guide he knows best as, beyond all comparison, the best guide that could possibly exist. The lapse of years renders me perhaps better able now to form a dispassionate judgment of Burgener's capacity and skill. Both were very great. I have seen at their work most of the leaders in this department. Burgener never had the marvellous neatness and finish so characteristic of Melchior Anderegg, who, when mountaineering has passed away into the limbo of extinct sports, such as bear-baiting, croquet, and pell-mell, will, if he gets his deserts, even by those who remember Maguignaz, Carrel, Croz, and Almer, still be spoken of as *the* best guide that ever lived. Nor was Burgener gifted with the same simple unaffected qualities which made Jakob Anderegg's loss so keenly felt, nor the lightness and agility of Rey or Jaun; but he united well in himself qualities of strength, carefulness, perseverance and activity, and possessed in addition the numerous attributes of observation, experience, and desire for improvement in his art which together make up what is spoken of as the natural instinct of guides. These were the qualities that made him a first-rate, indeed an exceptional, guide. *Nunc liberavi animam meam.* There is an old saying, involving a sound doctrine, that

> When you flatter lay it on thick;
> Some will come off, but a deal will stick.

The porter proved himself a skilful and strong climber, but he was as silent as an oyster and, like that bivalve mollusc when the freshness of its youth has passed off, was perpetually on the gape.

A hot walk—it always is hot along this part—took us up to the Montanvert. The moonlight threw quaint, fantastic shadows along the path and made the dewy gossamer filaments which swung from branch to branch across the track twinkle into grey and silver; and anything more aggravating than these spiders' threads at night it is hard to imagine. What earthly purpose these animals think they serve by this reckless nocturnal expenditure of bodily glue it is hard to say: possibly the lines are swung across in order that they may practise equilibrium; possibly the threads may serve as lines of escape and retreat after the male spinners have been a-wooing. The atmosphere through the wood was as stuffy as a ship's saloon in a storm, and we were right glad to reach the Montanvert at 3.30 A.M. Here, being athirst, we clamoured for refreshment. The landlord of the ramshackle hostelry at once appeared in full costume; indeed I observed that during the summer it was impossible to tell from his attire whether he had arisen immediately from bed or no. He seemed to act on the principle of the Norwegian peasant, who apparently undresses once a year when the winter commences, and resumes his garments when the light once more comes back and the summer season sets in. Our friend had cultivated to great perfection the art of half sleeping during his waking hours—that is, during such time as he might be called upon to provide entertainment for man and beast. Now at the Montanvert, during the tourists' season, this period extended over the whole twenty-four hours. It was necessary, therefore, in order that he might enjoy a proper physiological period of rest, for him to remain in a dozing state—a sort of æstival hybernation—for the whole time, which in fact he did; or else he was by nature a very dull person, and had actually a very restricted stock of ideas.

The landlord produced at once a battered teapot with a little sieve dangling from its snout, which had been stewing on the hob, and poured out the contained fluid into two stalked saucers of inconvenient diameter. Stimulated by this watery extract, we entered into conversation together. The sight of a tourist with an ice axe led by a kind of reflex process to the landlord's unburdening his mind with his usual remarks. Like other natives of the valley he had but two ideas of 'extraordinary' expeditions. 'Monsieur is going to the Jardin?' he remarked. 'No, monsieur isn't.' 'Then beyond a doubt monsieur will cross the Col du Géant?' he said, playing his trump card. 'No, monsieur will not.' 'Pardon—where does monsieur expect to go to?' 'On the present occasion we go to try the Aiguille du Dru.' The landlord smiled in an aggravating manner. 'Does monsieur think he will get up?' 'Time will show.' 'Ah!' The landlord, who had a chronic cold in the head, searched for his pockethandkerchief, but not finding it, modified the necessary sniff into one of derision, and then demanded the usual exorbitant price for the refreshment, amounting to about five times the value of the teapot, sieve and all. We paid, and left him chuckling softly to himself at our insane idea, as he replaced the teapot on the hob in readiness for the next arrival. That landlord, though physically sleepy, was still wide awake in matters of finance. He once charged me five francs for the loan of a secondhand collection of holes which he termed a blanket.

We got on to the glacier at the usual point and made straight across the slippery hummocks to the grass slope encircling the base of the Aiguille du Dru and the Glacier de la Charpoua. The glacier above gives birth to a feeble meandering little stream which wanders fitfully down the mountain side. At first we kept to the left, but after a while crossed the little torrent, and bearing more to the right plodded leisurely up the steep grass and rock slope. We had made good progress when of a sudden Franz gave a loud whistle and then fell flat down. The other two guides immediately followed his example and beckoned to us with excited gesticulations to behave in a similarly foolish manner. Thereupon we too sat down, and enquired what the purport of this performance might be. It turned out that there was a very little chamois about half a mile off. Knowing that it would be impossible to induce the guides to move on till the animal had disappeared, we seized the opportunity of taking an early breakfast. The guides meanwhile wriggled about on their stomachs, with eyes starting out of their heads, possessed by an extraordinary desire to miss no single movement of the object of their attention. 'See, it moves,' said Franz in a whisper. 'Himmel! it is feeding,' said Burgener. 'It must be the same that Johann saw three weeks ago.' 'Ach! no, that was but a little one' (no true chamois hunter will ever allow that a brother sportsman can possibly have set eyes on a larger animal than himself). 'Truly it is fine.' 'Thunder weather! it moves its head.' In their excitement I regretted that I could not share, not being well versed in hunting craft: my own experience of sport in the Alps being limited to missing one marmot that was sitting on a rock licking its paws. In due course the chamois walked away. Apparently much relieved by there being no further necessity to continue in their former uncomfortable attitudes, the guides sat up and fell to a warm discussion as to the size of the animal. A chamois is to a guide as a fish to the baffled angler or the last new baby to a monthly nurse, and is always pronounced to be beyond question the finest that has ever been seen. To this they agreed generally, but Franz, whose spirits had suddenly evaporated, now shook his head dismally, with the remark that it was unlucky to see a single chamois, and that we should have no success that day. Undaunted by his croaking, we pursued our way to the right side of the glacier, while our guide, who had a ballad appropriate to every occasion, sang rather gaspingly a tremulous little funeral dirge. We worked well across to the right, in order to obtain the best possible view of the Aiguille, and halted repeatedly while discussing the best point at which to attack the rocks. While thus engaged in reconnoitring close under the cliffs of the ridge running between the Aiguille Moine and the Aiguille Verte, a considerable block of ice, falling from the rocks above, whizzed past just in front of us and capered gaily down the slope. Hereupon we came rather rapidly to the conclusion that we had better proceed. Half an hour further on we reached the top of a steep little snow slope, and a point secure from falling stones and ice. Recognising that we must soon cross back to the rocks of the Dru, we tried to come to a final conclusion as to the way to be chosen. As usual, everybody pointed out different routes: even a vestry meeting could hardly have been less unanimous. Some one now ventured to put a question that had been troubling in reality our minds for some time past, viz. which of the peaks that towered above us was really the Aiguille du Dru. On the left there were two distinct points which, though close together, were separated apparently by a deep rift, and some distance to the right of the col which the previous party had tried to reach, a sharp tooth of rock towered up to a considerable height. Evidently, however, from its position this latter needle could not be visible from Chamouni or from the Montanvert. Again, it was clear that the mass comprising the two points close together must be visible from the valley, but which of the two was the higher? Alexander gave as his opinion that the more distant of these two points, that on the right, was the higher, and turned to the porter for confirmation. That worthy nodded his head affirmatively with extreme sagacity, evidently implying that he was of the same opinion. Franz on the other hand thought the left-hand peak was the one that we ought to make for, arguing that it most resembled the Dru as seen from the Montanvert, that there was probably little difference in height between the two, that our ascent would not be believed in unless we were to place a flag on the point visible from Chamouni, and finally that the left-hand peak seemed to be the easier, and would probably be found to conceal the sharper point of the right-hand summit. Having expressed these views, he in turn looked towards the porter to ascertain his sentiments. The porter, who was evidently of a complaisant temperament, nodded his head very vigorously to intimate that these arguments seemed the more powerful of the two to his mind, and then cocked his head on one side in a knowing manner, intended to express that he was studying the angles and that he was prepared to find himself in the right whichever view prevailed. We did not find out for certain till some time after that the right-hand summit, though concealed from view by the Montanvert, is very distinctly visible from Chamouni: excusable ignorance, as most of the Chamouni people are unaware of it to this day. Professor Forbes, as Mr. Douglas Freshfield has kindly pointed out to me, with his usual accuracy distinguished and also measured the two summits, giving their heights respectively as 12,178, and 12,245 feet.[1] Knowing little as we did then of the details of the mountain, we followed Franz's advice and made for the left-hand peak, under the impression that if one proved accessible the other might also, and there really seemed no reason why we should not, if occasion demanded, ascend both.

Leading up from the glacier two distinct lines of attack presented themselves. The right-hand ridge descends to the col very precipitously, but still we had some idea that the rocks did not look wholly impossible. Again, on the left of the Dru the rocks are cut away very abruptly and form the long precipitous

[1] *Travels in the Alps*, p. 119.

ridge seen from the Montanvert. This ridge was so jagged that we could see no possible advantage in climbing to any part of it, except just at the termination where it merges into the south-western face of the main mountain. The choice therefore, in our judgment, lay between storming the mountain by the face right opposite to us or else making for the col and the right-hand ridge; but the latter was the route that Messrs. Pendlebury and Kennedy had followed, and we could not hope to succeed where such giants had failed. Burgener indeed wished to try, but the rest of the party were unanimously in favour of attempting to find a way up the face, a route that at the worst had the merit of novelty. We thought too that if a closer acquaintance proved that the crags were ill arranged for upward locomotion, we might be able to work round on the face and so reach the col by a more circuitous route. With the naked eye—especially a myopic one—the rocks appeared unpromising enough; while viewed through the telescope the rocks looked utterly impossible. But little faith, however, can be rested in telescopic observations of a mountain, so far as the question of determining a route is concerned. Amateurs, who, as a rule, understand the use of a telescope much better than guides, have not the requisite experience to determine the value of what they see, while but few guides see enough to form any basis for determination. Moreover, the instrument we carried with us, though it had an extraordinary number of sections and pulled out like the ill-fated tradesman's trousers in a pantomime, was not a very remarkable one in the matter of definition. Still it is always proper and orthodox to look at a new peak through the telescope, and we were determined not to neglect any formality on the present occasion.

We were now rather more than half-way up the Glacier de la Charpoua. To reach the most promising-looking point at which we might hope to get on the rocks, it was necessary to travel straight across the snow at about the level on which we stood. Now, this Glacier de la Charpoua is not constructed on ordinary principles. Instead of the orthodox transverse bergschrund it possesses a longitudinal crack running up its whole length, a peculiarity that vexed us hugely. Half a dozen times did we attempt to cross by some tempting-looking bridge, but on each occasion we were brought to a stand by impassable crevasses; then had to turn back, go up a little farther, and try again. It was already late in the day and we could ill spare the time lost in this to and fro movement. Eventually we reached a little patch of rocks not far from the head of the glacier. No sooner had we reached these rocks than the guides hunted up a suitable place and concealed some utterly worthless property as carefully as if they expected evil-minded marauders to be wandering about, seeking what they might pilfer.

Having effected the cache with due care, Franz once again burst into a strange carol, the burden of which was unintelligible, but the chorus made frequent allusion to 'der Teufel.' We now saw that, after all, the only feasible plan would be to cut our way still higher up a steep slope, and thus to work right round, describing a large curve. An occasional step required to be scraped, for the glacier is in shadow till late in the morning, owing to the Aiguille Verte intervening and cutting off the sun's rays. Throughout the day our second guide had been burning with a desire to exhibit the good qualities of the most portentous ice axe I ever saw, an instrument of an unwieldy character resembling a labourer's pick on the top of a May pole. Its dimensions were monstrous and its weight preposterous: moreover, the cutting spike had an evil curve and, instead of hewing out blocks of ice neatly, preferred to ram a huge hole in the slope and stick fast therein, while a quiver ran through its mighty frame and communicated itself to the striker, who shuddered at each blow as after taking a dose of very bitter physic. However, Franz was so proud of his halberd that we were obliged to sacrifice rapid progress to the consideration of his feelings, and he was accordingly sent on to cut the steps which were now found necessary. With no little exertion did he construct a staircase of which the steps were about the size of foot baths, and with no slight impatience did we watch his gymnastics and athletic flourishes, which were a sort of mixture of tossing the caber and throwing the hammer combined with a touch of polo. Ultimately we were able to quit the glacier for the actual face of the mountain, at a point probably not very much below that struck by the previous party; but it was our intention at once to bear off to the left.

We blundered a little on the rocks at first after the long spell of snow-walking. A cry from Franz caused us to look round, and we perceived that he had got entangled with the big axe, the spike of which was sticking into the third button of his waistcoat, causing him, as the strain on the rope above and below folded him up in a rather painful manner, to assume the attitude of a mechanical toy monkey on a stick. Fearing that he might be placed in the condition in which cats' meat is usually offered for sale, we slackened the rope and saved him from impending perforation, but with the result that the axe bounded off down the slope, turned two or three summersaults, and then stuck up defiantly in a distant patch of snow, looking like a sign-post. While Franz went off to recover his loved treasure we huddled together on a very little ledge of rock, and sat there in a row like busts on a shelf—if the simile be not considered anatomically inappropriate. But these delays had wasted much time, and already success seemed doubtful. Little time could now be devoted to consultation, and

A START IN THE WRONG DIRECTION

little good would have come of it; now that we were on the rocks the only thing to do was to go straight on and see what would happen. At the same time we had a dim consciousness that we were considerably to the right of the best line of ascent. Our 'general idea'—to borrow a military phrase of which, by the way, it may be remarked that the idea in question is usually confined to the general and is not shared in by the troops—consisted in making for the left-hand side or Montanvert aspect of the final peak. We set our teeth, whatever that may mean, then fell to with a will and for some two hours went with scarcely a check. And a rare two hours' climb we had. The very thought of it makes the pen travel swiftly over the paper, as the scene comes back in every detail. How Burgener led the way without hesitation and almost without mistake; how our second guide chattered unceasingly, caring nought for a listener; how they both stuck to the rocks like limpets; how the big axe got in everybody's way; how the rope got caught on every projecting spur of rock, jerking back the unwary, or when loose sweeping down showers of small angular stones from the little platforms and ridges, thereby engendering ill blood and contumely; how the silent porter climbed stolidly after us, and in the plenitude of his taciturn good-humour poked at us from below with his staff at inconvenient moments and in sensitive places; how at one moment we were

G

flat against the rock, all arms and legs, like crushed spiders, and at another gathered into great loops like a cheese maggot on the point of making a leap; how a volley of little stones came whistling cheerily down from above, playfully peppering us all round; how our spirits rose with our bodies till we became as excited as children: of all these things it boots not to give any detailed description. Those who can recollect similar occasions need but to be reminded of them, and, to tell the truth, the minutiæ, though they are so graven upon the mind that a clear impression could be struck off years afterwards, are apt to prove somewhat tedious. Two facts I may note. One, that the rocks were at first very much easier than was expected; another, that we should have done better had we discarded the rope on this part of the climb: the rocks were hardly a fit place for those who could not dispense with its use. Ever and anon the guides' spirits would rise to that level which may be called the shouting point, and they would jödel till they were black in the face, while the melodious roll of sound echoed cheerily back from the distant cliffs of the Aiguille Moine. And so we journeyed up.

Meanwhile the weather had changed; black clouds had come rolling up and were gathering ominously above us; it was evident that we had no chance of reaching the summit that day, even if it were practicable, but still we persevered desperately in the hope of seeing some possible route for a future attack. Progress, however, on a rock peak is necessarily slow when there are five on the rope, and we should probably have done more wisely if we had divided into two parties. We kept well to the left to a point on the face where a huge tower of rock stands four-square to all the winds of heaven that blow; and above us, as a matter of fact, there seemed to be a good many winds. This landmark, very conspicuous and characteristic of these aiguilles, seemed to be close to the ridge, but on reaching it we found that there was still a stiff passage intervening between us and the point from which we could overlook the other side of the mountain. Now we bore to the right and the climbing became more difficult. We made our way straight up a very shallow gully and finally reached a point on the western ridge overlooking the Montanvert, close to where this ridge merges into the corresponding face of the peak. Here a halt was called, for two reasons. In the first place a few flakes of snow were softly falling around and the gathering clouds betokened more to follow. Secondly, so far as we could judge through the mist, it was apparently impossible to ascend any higher from the place we had reached. So we cast off the rope and clambered separately to various points of vantage to survey the work that lay before us. The summit of the peak, enveloped in thin cloud, appeared to tower no great height above us, but we were too close under the cliff to estimate its elevation very correctly. At the time we thought that if we could only keep up the pace at which we had been going, an hour's climb would have sufficed to reach the top. We found, it may be remarked parenthetically, that we were egregiously in error in this estimate some years later. The shifting clouds made the rock face—that is, the small extent of it that we could see at all—look much more difficult than in all probability it actually was. Through the mists we made out, indistinctly, a formidable-looking irregular crack in the rock face running very straight up and rather to our left, which apparently constituted the only possible route from our position to a higher level. But from where we stood we could not have reached the lower end of this crack without a ladder of about fifty feet in length, and the mist entirely prevented us from judging whether we could reach it by a détour. The choice lay between hunting for some such line or else in trying what seemed on the whole more practicable, viz. working round by the north-east face again, so as to search for a more easy line of ascent. But the latter alternative would have involved of necessity a considerable descent. While we debated what course to take the mists swept up thicker and thicker from below, and in a moment the peak above us was concealed and all the view cut off. A piercingly cold wind began to rise and a sharp storm of hail and sleet descended. Hints were dropped about the difficulty of descending rocks glazed over with ice with a proper amount of deliberation. It was obviously impossible to go up and might soon become very difficult to go down. The question was not actually put, but, in conformity with what was evidently the general sense of the meeting, we somewhat reluctantly made up our minds to return. A dwarf stone man was constructed, the rope readjusted, and half an hour's descent put us out of the mist and snow. We stopped again and stared upwards blankly at the leve line of mist hanging heavily against the peak. Burgener now came forward with a definite resolution and proposed that we should stay where we were for the night and try again the next day. This was referred to a sub-committee, who reported against the suggestion on the ground that the stock of provisions left consisted of a tablespoonful of wine, four rolls, and a small piece of cheese which had strayed from the enveloping paper in the porter's pocket and as a consequence smelt of tobacco and was covered with hairs and fluff. These articles of diet were spread on a rock and we mentally calculated the exact proportion that would fall to each man's share if we attempted, as proposed, to subsist on them for a day and a half. But little deliberation was required. We decided at once to return. The porter gathered the fragments lovingly together and replaced them with other curious articles in his side pocket. By 8.30 P.M. we were back at Chamouni, having been out a little under twenty hours.

A day or two later we made up our minds to start once more. Great preparations were made for an early departure, the idea that we should find it distasteful to start at the hour at which a London ball begins being scouted, as it usually is over-night. We impressed on an intelligent 'boots' with great earnestness the absolute necessity of waking us precisely at midnight, and then went to our repose, feeling about as much inclined for sleep as a child does during the afternoon siesta intended to prepare it for the glories of a pantomime. The 'boots' did not fail; in fact he was extra-punctual, as our departure was the signal for his retiring. At midnight the party assembled in the little courtyard in front of the hotel, but a dismal sight met our gaze. Under the influence of a warm sou'-wester, thick black clouds had filled the valley, and a gentle drizzle reminded us of the balmy climate of our own metropolis in November. Our Alpine tour for the season was nearly at an end, and we gazed despondently around. Ultimately one practical person suggested that if we did not go to the mountain we might as well go to bed, and the practical person endorsed his suggestion by walking off. A scurvy practical joke did the clerk of the weather play on us that night. In the morning the bright sunbeams came streaming in through the window, the sky was cloudless and the outline of every peak was sharply defined in the clear air. A more perfect morning for the expedition could hardly have been chosen. Some ill-timed remarks at breakfast referring pointedly to people who talk a good deal over-night about early starts, and the deep concern of the 'boots' at our presumed slothfulness, goaded us to desperation. We determined to start again and to have one more try the next day whatever the weather might prove to be. Once more we found ourselves in the small hours of the morning on the path leading to Les Ponts. Had it not been for the previous day's lesson we should probably have turned back from this point, for the whole of the mountain opposite was concealed in thick drifting mist. The guides flatly refused to go on as matters stood. We were determined on our side not to give it up, and so a compromise was effected. It was agreed to wait for an hour or two and see if matters mended. So we stretched ourselves out on a damp sloping rock, prepared to resume our journey at the slightest indication of a change for the better. Rest at such a time even under these hard, not to say stony, conditions is seductive, and, as we lay half dozing, strange heretical thoughts came crowding into the mind. Why toil up this mountain when one can rest in luxury on these knobby rocks? Why labour over the shifting moraine, the deceitful glacier, the slippery rock? What is the good of it all? Can it be vanity or—— 'Vorwärts!' The dream vanished as the cheery cry broke out from the guide engaged on outpost duty, and as we rose and stretched ourselves the whole aspect of affairs seemed changed. A distinct break in the clouds at the head of the Mer de Glace gave promise of better things in store, and we felt almost guilty of having wasted an hour or more at our halt. The break became larger and larger, and before long the great cloud banks resolved into one huge streamer flying from the summit of the peak. I fancy that, at any rate in the early stages of mountaineering, many good chances are thrown away on such days, for guides are as a rule somewhat prone to despondency in the early morning hours. Once started, however, they became wondrously keen, complained of our delay, and even asserted with some effrontery that they had predicted fine weather all the time, and this without a blush; still some one rather neatly defined blushing as a suffusion least seldom seen in those who have the most occasion for it, and guides share with politicians a certain power of manipulating their opinions to suit the exigencies of the moment. The traces of our former attempt assisted us materially on the glacier. Our plan of attack consisted in getting on the rocks at our former point, but working on this occasion much more directly up the face. Burgener conceived that by following this line of assault we should be able to ascend, by means of a gully which existed only in his own imagination, to a more practicable part of the peak. Between the two summits of the Aiguille du Dru may be seen, at any rate in photographs, a tempting-looking streak of snow: it seemed possible, if we could once reach the lower point of this streak, to follow its line upwards. The lower peak of the Dru is well rounded on its eastern face, and the rocks appear more broken than in other parts of the mountain.

If we could but once reach the cleft between the peaks there seemed every chance of our being able to reach the lower summit. At the outset progress was fast. We followed our former line till we were in sight of the rock tower and then at once bore off to the right. The climbing was rather more difficult, at least it seemed so to us in those days, than on the other part of the mountain with which we had previously made acquaintance. A series of short flat gullies had to be climbed, but there were exceedingly few inequalities to help us. The rope was of little or no use and might perhaps have been laid aside with advantage. We soon found that we had reached a higher point than at our previous attempt, and as the leader constantly returned favourable reports our spirits rose; so elated in fact did we become that the exact formalities to be observed on reaching the top were seriously discussed whenever the occasion offered for conversation, which was not very often. Old Franz chattered away to himself, as was his wont when matters went well, and on looking back on one occasion I perceived the strange phenomenon of a smile illuminating the porter's features. Howbeit, this worthy spake no words of satisfaction, but pulled ever at his empty pipe. By dint of wriggling over a smooth sloping stone slab we had got into a steep rock gully which promised to lead us to a good height. Burgener, assisted by much pushing and prodding from below and aided on his own part by much snorting and some strong language, had managed to climb on to a great overhanging boulder that cut off the view from the rest of the party below. As he disappeared from sight we watched the paying out of the rope with as much anxiety as a fisherman eyes his vanishing line when the salmon runs. Presently the rope ceased to move and we waited for a few moments in suspense. We felt that the critical moment of the expedition had arrived, and the fact that our own view was exceedingly limited made us all the more anxious to hear the verdict. 'How does it look?' we called out. The answer came back in patois, a bad sign in such emergencies. For a minute or two an animated conversation was kept up; then we decided to take another opinion and accordingly hoisted up our second guide. The chatter was redoubled. 'What does it look like?' we shouted again. 'Not possible from where we are,' was the melancholy answer, and in a tone that crushed at once all our previous elation. I could not find words at the moment to express my disappointment: but the porter could and gallantly he came to the rescue. He opened his mouth for the first time and spoke, and he said very loud indeed that it was 'verdammt.' Precisely: that is just what it was. Having made this short speech, the porter allowed the smile to fade away from his features, shook out some imaginary ashes and proceeded to light some visionary tobacco, sucking at a lighted match through the medium of an empty pipe. It seemed hard to believe at first that we were to be baulked when so near the summit, and it was not till the guides had tried again and again to storm the almost vertical wall of smooth rock and had shown the utter impossibility of turning it either right or left, that we felt we were really beaten. One more forlorn chance remained: we might try the west face of the mountain from the spot we had reached at our first attempt, when the weather had prevented us from making any further progress. Had there been more time at our disposal we should have done better to try another line of ascent more to our right, that is, nearer to the col, and it might be possible to reach the cleft between the two summits by this means. As for the snow streak which looked so tempting at a distance, it is a delusion and a snare, if the latter term be applicable to a place which appears to be much more difficult to get into than it probably would be to get out of. We had already pretty fully realised that the mountain was more difficult to ascend than we had ever contemplated, and it seemed advisable at the moment to make for some definite point which at any rate we felt sure of reaching and to study the peak in detail to the best of our ability; so we made towards our cairn, though with little hope of gaining much knowledge thereby.

Without much difficulty, but not without some little danger from falling stones (though on the whole, the mountain is remarkably free from these annoyances, there being as a matter of fact but few loose stones to fall), we reached our former point and were able to judge distinctly of how much higher we had reached at our second attempt. We saw also that upward progress from the point on which we stood would not be possible, but it must be remembered that we were able only to see a small strip of the mountain lying directly above. Every crag that was not absolutely vertical appeared to overhang, and the few small cracks that might have afforded hand and foot hold led nowhere in particular. Altogether the view was depressing although limited. There was no time to hunt about for other routes, or we should certainly have done so, for we felt that though beaten our discomfiture only arose from the fact that we had chosen a wrong line of ascent. Possibly within a few yards of us lay a feasible route, but we knew not on which side it might be. Here it occurred to the porter for the first time that his pipe was empty and had been so all day: he thereupon made his second remark, which consisted in an audible request for something to put in it. We had dragged up with us (as a matter of fact the porter had carried it the whole time) some 200 feet of rope, thinking it might help us in the descent, but the part of the mountain on which we were presents no more difficulties in this respect than does Avernus.

Arrived on the snow slope opposite the rock face on which we had been climbing during the day, we stopped, extended the telescope, and tried to make out our exact line, and endeavoured also to discover what had been our error; no easy task, as any persons of experience will admit. At any time the appearance of this peak is deceptive, and the outline no more guides you to a knowledge of the natural details than does the outline of a fashionable lady's dress. But as we looked the mountain seemed flattened out by reason of a blue evening mist which obscured all the irregularities. So we turned and resumed our journey down, running hard across the Mer de Glace, for the shades of night drew on apace, and reached Chamouni at 8.30 in the evening, leaving the guides at the Montanvert with half a bottle of thin red wine between three of them. We were overtaken by Edouard Cupelin, one of the best of the Chamouni guides, at any rate on rock mountains, on our way down, and he gave us a rather sensational account of his own adventures on the peak. In justice to him it should be mentioned that he was almost the only Chamouni guide who seemed to think the ascent possible, and in his opinion the general line that we had adopted was the correct one. Our second expedition thus from first to last occupied about $20\frac{1}{2}$ hours, but the halts were not nearly so numerous as on the first occasion. The experience of our two days' climbing led us to the conclusion that Cupelin was right. From the peculiar character of the rocks and the fact that our climbing lay chiefly along short flat gullies we were unable, as already remarked, to get a very clear idea of any part of the mountain except that on which we were actually engaged, and we were led to the opinion that the only plan to find a possible route would consist in trying in succession from below the different parts of the southern face. The final peak, which from this side shoots up clearly defined from the great mass of the mountain, seemed to us tolerably easy of ascent provided one could reach the base. A sort of depression extends three parts of the way round, and the edge of this shallow moat appeared to be defended by an inaccessible belt of vertical rock. The actual rocks were wholly unlike any met with elsewhere in our experience. Great vertical slabs were fitted together with an accuracy which was beautiful in its perfection, but irritating beyond conception to the climber. Progress upwards, when above the level of the col, necessitated a series of fatiguing gymnastics like swimming uphill, but the rocks where they were possible proved invariably firm and good. On both occasions we were stopped by sheer difficulty and probably saw the mountain at its very best. The snow on the rocks, which proved such a formidable difficulty to Mr. Pendlebury's party, had almost entirely disappeared before our assault. The rocks were warm and the weather on the second day was perfect.

Such is the history of our first two attempts to climb this mountain. They served but to whet our appetite for success, but it was not till years after that we were fortunate enough to meet with that success.

CHAPTER IV.

A DAY ACROSS COUNTRY

The art of meteorological vaticination—The climate we leave our homes for—Observations in the valley—The diligence arrives and shoots its load—Types of travellers—The Alpine habitué—The elderly spinster on tour—A stern Briton—A family party—We seek fresh snow-fields—The Bietschhorn—A sepulchra bivouac—On early starts and their curious effects on the temperament—A choice of routes—A deceptive ice gully—The avalanches on the Bietschhorn—We work up to a dramatic situation—The united party nearly fall out—A limited panorama—A race for home—Caught out—A short cut—Driven to extremities—The water jump—An aged person comes to the rescue—A classical banquet at Ried—The old curé and his hospitality—A wasted life?

THE summer season of 1878 was one of the worst on record. Meteorologists, by a species of climatic paradox, might have had a fine time of it; mountaineers had a most wet and disagreeable time of it. The weather prophets easily established a reputation for infallibility—according to the accepted modern standard of vaticination—by predicting invariably evil things. They were thus right five times out of six, which will readily be acknowledged as very creditable in persons who were uninspired, save by a desire to exalt themselves in the eyes of their fellow tourists. But, as in the case of that singularly hopeful person Tantalus, the torture was rendered more artistic and aggravating by sporadic promise of better things. One day the rock aiguilles were powdered over and white-speckled with snow. The climber looked up longingly at the heights above, but visions of numbing cold and frost-bitten fingers caused him to thrust the latter members into his pockets and turn away with a sigh, to put it mildly, and avert his gaze from the chilling spectacle. Then would he follow his daily practice—his thrice-a-daily practice in all probability—of overeating himself. Perhaps, while still engaged at *table d'hôte* in consuming, at any rate in masticating, the multiform dish generically named 'chevreuil,' the glow of a rosy sunset, and the hope of brighter things in store for the morrow, would attract him to the window.

The next day would produce scorching heat, a clear sky, a rising barometer, and a revival of spirits; diet, as the physicians say, as before. The powdered snow would disappear off the ledges and, melting, distribute itself more uniformly over the rocks, which as a result presented a shining appearance, as the morning face of a schoolboy or the Sunday face of a general servant. At night a clear sky and a sharp frost in the high regions, and the next day the mountain would be more impossible than ever. Still, recognising that another few hours

H

of grateful sunshine would cause the thin film of ice glazing the rocks to melt and evaporate, the energetic climber (and we were very energetic that year) would summon his guides and all his resolution, pack up his traps, and start for a bivouac up aloft, to return, in all probability, at the end of twenty-four hours, in a downfall of rain and in the condition of steamy moisture so tersely described by Mr. Mantalini. Such, during July 1878, was our lot day after day in the glorious Alpine climate. We paced up and down, with the regularity of sentries, between our camp on the Aiguille du Dru and Couttet's hotel at Chamouni. Occasionally we ascended some distance up the Glacier de la Charpoua and took observations. Once or twice we proceeded far enough on the rocks of the Aiguille du Dru to prove the impossibility of ascending them to any great height. Still we were loth to depart and run the risk of losing a favourable opportunity of assaulting the mountain with any chance of success. It fell out thus that we had good opportunities of observing our fellow creatures and the various types of travellers, who, notwithstanding the weather, still crowded into Chamouni; for it was only on rock peaks such as the Aiguille du Dru, or difficult mountains like the Aiguille Verte, that climbing was impossible. This condition of things did not affect to any very appreciable extent the perambulating peasants who constitute the vast majority of the body known as guides in Chamouni. These worthies merely loafed a little more than they were wont to do, if that be possible. Perhaps the gathering invariably to be found, during twenty hours out of the twenty-four, at the cross roads near Tairraz's shop was still more numerously attended, and there was some slight increase in the number of sunburnt individuals who found intellectual exercise sufficient to apologise for their existence in wearing their hands in their pockets, smoking indifferent tobacco, expectorating indiscriminately, and uttering statements devoid of sense or point to anybody who cared to listen. The weather had no effect on them; whether wet or dry, cold or warm, they still occupied themselves from June to September in the same manner. Once in the early morning, and once again about five o'clock in the evening, were they momentarily galvanised out of their listlessness by the arriving and departing diligences.

On the arrival of the caravan the contingent was usually reinforced by some of our own countrymen. The proper attitude for the English visitor at Chamouni to assume, when watching the evening incursion of tourists, consisted in leaning against the wall on the south side of the street, and so to pose himself as to indicate independence of the proceedings and to wear an expression of indifference tinged with a suggestion of cynical humour. This was usually accomplished by wearing the hands in the pockets, tilting the hat a little over the eyes, crossing the legs, and laughing unduly at the remarks of companions, whether audible or not. Some few considered that smoking a wooden pipe assisted the realisation of the effect intended: others apparently held that a heavy object held in the mouth interfered with the expression. I have observed that these same onlookers were bitterly indignant at the ordeal they had to pass through on returning to their native shores viâ Folkestone, when clambering wearily with leaden eyes and sage-green complexions up the pier steps. Yet the diligence travellers, begrimed with dust, stung of horse flies, cramped, choked, and so jolted that they recognised more bony prominences than previous anatomical knowledge had ever led them to expect they possessed, were none the less objects of pity. Still human nature is always worthy of study, and those who arrived, together with those who went to see them arrive, were equally interesting under the depressing climatic influences which so often forbade us to take our pleasure elsewhere.

It was curious to note how, day after day, the diligence on its arrival released from the cramped thraldom of its uncomfortable seats almost exactly the same load. As the great lumbering yellow vehicle came within sight, one or two familiar faces would be seen craning out to catch the first sight of an old guide or mountain friend. These *habitués* as a rule secured for themselves the corner seats. We knew exactly what their luggage would be. A bundle of axes like Roman 'fasces' would be handed out first, with perhaps a little unnecessary ostentation, followed by a coil of rope which might have been packed up in the portmanteau, but usually was not; then a knapsack, with marks on the back like a map of the continent of America if the owner was an old hand, and a spotless minute check if he were only trying to look like one. The owners of the knapsacks would be clad in suits that once were dittos, flannel shirts and the familiar British wide-awake, the new aspirants for mountaineering fame decorating their head gear with snow spectacles purchased in Geneva. Very businesslike would they show themselves in collecting their luggage before anybody else; then, with a knowing look at the mountains, they would make their way to Couttet's. Next, perhaps, would follow a party of some two or three spinsters travelling alone and as uncertain about their destination as they were of their age. To attract such, some of the hotel proprietors, more astute than their fellows, despatched to the scene of action porters of cultivated manners and obsequious demeanour, who seldom failed, by proving themselves to be 'such nice polite men, my dear,' to ensnare the victims. Burdened with the numerous parcels and odd little bags this class of traveller greatly affects, the nicely mannered porter would lead the way to the hotel or pension, probably bestowing, as he passed, a wink on some friend among the guides, who recognised at once the type of tourist that would inevitably visit the Montanvert, probably the Chapeau and possibly the Flégère, and recognising too the type in whom judicious compliments were not likely to be invested without satisfactory results. Such people invariably enquired if they could not be taken *en pension*. Somewhat frugal as regards diet, especially breakfast, but with astounding capacities for swallowing *table d'hôte* dinners or such romance as the guides might be pleased to invent on the subject of their own prowess and exploits. Charming old ladies these often were, as pleased with the novelty of everything they saw around them as a gutter child in a country meadow. Their nature changes marvellously in the Alps. Scarcely should we recognise in the small wiry traveller in the mountains the same individual whom we might meet in town—say in the neighbourhood of Bloomsbury. I have noticed such a one not a hundred miles from there whose energy for sight-seeing when in the Alps surpassed all belief. Yet here she seemed but a little, wrinkled, bent-in-the-back old woman, flat of foot, reckless at crossings, finding difficulty on Sunday mornings in fishing a copper out of her reticule for the crossing sweeper, by reason of the undue length of the finger-tips to her one-buttoned black kid gloves, and accompanied on week days, perhaps for the sake of contrast, by a sprightly little black and tan dog of so arrogant a disposition that it declined to use in walking all the legs with which Providence had furnished it. Next, perhaps, the British paterfamilias, who might or might not be a clergyman, most intractable of tourists; ever prone to combine instruction with amusement for the benefit of his bored family, slightly relaxing on week days, but rigid and austere on Sundays beyond conception. And then the foreign sub-Alpine walker or 'intrépide,' clad in special garments of local make and highly vaunted efficiency, garrulous, smoky, voracious, a trifle greasy, and dealing habitually in ecstatic hendecasyllables expressive of admiration of everything he saw. Next the family party, possibly with a courier, with whom the younger members were, as a rule, unduly familiar: the boys wearing tailed shooting coats, consorting but ill with Eton turn-down collars, groaning under the burden of green baize bags containing assorted guide books, strange receptacles for the umbrellas of the party, and with leathern wallets slung around their shoulders, stuffed with the useless articles boys cherish and love to carry with them; the girls awkwardly conscious and feeling ill at ease by reason of the practical dresses, boots, and head gear devised for them at home, looking tenderly after a collection of weakly sticks tipped with chamois horns and decorated with a spirally arranged list of localities; the whole party in an excessively bad temper, which the boys exhibited by pummelling and thumping when 'pa' was not looking and the girls by little sniffs, head tossings, and pointed remarks at each other that they had no idea what guys they looked. It will be observed that the constant bad weather induced a cynical condition of mind.

We made up our minds, notwithstanding the attractions of this varied company, to quit them for a while, to seek fresh snow-fields and glaciers new, and to leave the rocks of the Aiguille du Dru for a time unmolested. At the suggestion of Jaun we betook ourselves to the Oberland for a contemplated ascent of the Bietschhorn by a new route. Under a tropical sun we made our way by the interminable zigzags through the Trient valley down to Vernayaz, where we met again, like the witches in 'Macbeth,' in thunder and in rain. Our project was to ascend the Bietschhorn from the Visp side and descend it by the usual route to Ried. This form of novelty had become so common in mountaineering that a new word had been coined expressly to describe such expeditions, and the climber, if he succeeded in his endeavour, was said to have 'colled' the peak. The phrase, however, was only admissible on the first occasion, and it was subsequently described by any who followed, in more prosaic terms, as going up one side and down the other.

We did not experience any unusual difficulty in

leaving Visp tolerably early in the morning. The chorus of frogs, who were in remarkably fine voice that night in the neighbouring swamps, kept us awake, and the proper musical contrast was provided by the alto humming of some hungry mosquitoes. Our plan of assault was to camp somewhere at the head of the Baltschieder Thal, which is a dreary stony valley with only a few huts that would scarcely be considered habitable even by a London slum-landlord. The living inhabitants appeared to consist of three unkempt children, two pigs, one imbecile old man, and a dog with a fortuitous family. On the whole, therefore, we came to the conclusion that nature would probably provide better accommodation than the local architectural art, and a short search revealed a most luxurious bivouac, close to the left moraine of the Baltschieder Glacier, under the shelter of the Fäschhorn and a little above the level of the ice fall. A huge, flat slab of rock formed the roof of a wedge-shaped cavity capable of holding at least six persons, if disposed in a horizontal position. The space between the floor and the roof, it is true, was not much more than three feet; but the chamber, though well sheltered, demanded no ventilating tubes to ensure a proper supply of fresh air. Having a little spare time and being luxuriously inclined, we decided to sleep on spring beds. First we swept the stone floor, then covered it with a thick layer of dry rhododendron branches, over which were laid large sods of dried peat grass, and the beds were complete. The pointed ends of the twigs showed rather a tendency to penetrate through the grassy covering during the night, but otherwise the mattresses were all that could be desired. About two in the morning we got up—that is, we would have got up had it not been physically impossible to do so by reason of the lowness of the roof. A more correct expression would be perhaps to say that we turned out, rolling from under the shelter of the slab one after another. By the dim light of an ineffective candle, poked into the neck of a broken bottle, we found it no easy matter to collect all the articles which the guides had of course unpacked and stowed away as if they were going to stay a week; indeed, a certain bottle of seltzer water will probably still be found—at any rate the bottle will—by anyone who seeks repose in the same quarters.

We started in the usual frame of mind—that is to say, everybody was exceedingly facetious for about three minutes. In about ten minutes one of the party, who would slake his thirst unduly at a crystal spring near the bivouac the previous evening, found that his boot lace was untied; circumstances which do not seem associated at first sight, but are not, nevertheless, infrequently observed. So again have I often remarked that a good dinner overnight develops in an astonishing manner admiration for distant views when ascending on the subsequent day. Within a quarter of an hour the amateurs of the party ceased to indulge in conversation, their remarks dying away into a species of pained silence similar to that which is induced in youthful voluptuaries by the premature smoking of clay pipes. The guides, however, seldom if ever desisted from dialogue, and never for the purpose of listening to each other's remarks. Still, the respiratory process is governed by the same conditions in the case of guides as in other mortals, and though they would scorn to stoop to the boot-lace subterfuge, and feel that a sudden admiration for scenery would deceive no one, they yet found it necessary before long to distribute their burdens more equally; a process achieved by halting, untying several strings, taking out several parcels and replacing them in the same positions. By these various methods we acquired what athletes call 'second wind' and stepped out more strongly. We crossed a moraine of the usual inconsistency—however, the subject of loose moraines has been, I fancy, touched upon by other writers. The Baltschieder Glacier sweeps at a right angle round a mountain christened, not very originally, the Breithorn. This particular member of that somewhat numerous family blocks up the head of the Baltschieder Thal. We skirted the north base of the Breithorn, passing between it and the Jägihorn, and arriving at the top of a steep little slope came in full view of the eastern slopes of our objective peak. At this point Maurer gave vent to a dismal wail of anguish as it suddenly occurred to him that he had left the bottle of seltzer water down below. With some difficulty did we persuade him that it was not necessary to return for it, although the idea of repose was not wholly distasteful, but we felt that we had probably all our work cut out for us in one sense, and that the days were none too long for such an expedition as the one we had in hand. Two distinct lines of attack appeared to offer themselves. One route, more to our right, led upwards by a gentle curved ridge, chiefly of snow, connecting the Baltschieder Joch with the northern arête of the mountain. In 1866 Messrs. D. W. Freshfield and C. C. Tucker, as we learnt subsequently, attained a high point by this way and were only prevented from accomplishing the actual ascent by bad weather, though they did enough to prove the practicability of the route. However, this way, which appeared the easier of the two, was evidently the longer from our position. The other route had the advantage of lying straight in front of us. Its attraction consisted of a broad long gully of snow enclosed between two ridges of rock. By the dim morning light the snow appeared easy enough and was evidently in suitable condition: howbeit, long snow couloirs, at the summit of which rocks overhang, are not usually to be recommended when the mountain itself is composed of friable material. Now it would be difficult to find in the whole of the Alps a mountain more disposed to cast stones at its assailants than the Bietschhorn, a fact of which we were fully aware. Every ascent of this disintegrating peak so rearranges the rocks that the next comers would not be wholly without justification if they pleaded that the details of their ascent were to a great extent new. Still, mountaineers up to the present have not been quite reduced to such a far-fetched claim to novelty, although in these latter days they have at times come perilously near it. Judging by the direction of the strata, we felt certain that the rock ridges must be practicable, and the problem in mountaineering set before us consisted in finding out how we might best ascend without subjecting ourselves to the inconveniences experienced by some of the early martyrs.

An early breakfast put fresh strength into us. It is a common mistake of mountaineers not to breakfast early enough and not to breakfast often enough. If it be desired to achieve a long expedition when there is not likely to be too much spare time, the wise man will eat something at least every two hours up to about 10 o'clock in the morning, supposing, for instance, he started about 2 A.M. It is astonishing to notice how the full man gains upon the empty one on fatiguing snow slopes. We strode rapidly across the basin of snow called the Jägifirn and arrived at the foot of the gully. But now we could see that our suspicions were more than verified: ugly-looking marks in the snow above indicated falling stones, and the snow itself was obviously in a condition prone to avalanches. This danger must always be present in couloirs to a greater or less extent in such seasons as the one we were experiencing. There had been sufficient power of sun to convert the contents of the gully into what would have been, in fine weather, a glistening ice slope. But much fresh snow had fallen recently. It but rarely can happen, when snow has fallen late in the season or during the hot months, that the new and the old layers can become properly amalgamated. If, therefore, there is too great a thickness of fresh snow to allow of steps being cut through this into the ice beneath, such couloirs are unsafe. The mark of a single avalanche due to the sliding off of the fresh snow on the ice beneath—a mark easily enough recognised—would deter any save an unwise person or a novice from attempting such a line of ascent. The marvellous hereditary instinct so often attributed to guides in judging of this condition really reduces itself to a matter of very simple observation and attention, and one within the reach of anybody. But travellers in the Alps too often appear to treat their reasoning faculties like they do their tall hats, and leave them at home. The question then was, Were the rocks right or left of this snow gully practicable? We all agreed that they were, and proceeded at once to test the accuracy of our opinion.

We crossed the bergschrund—that godsend to writers on mountaineering in search of material to act as padding—and without dwelling on its insecure bridge longer than we need now dwell on the subject made swiftly for some rocks on the left. Scarcely had we gained them when a rush of snow and ice, of no great dimensions, but still large enough to be formidable, obliterated all the tracks we had just made. This settled the point at once, and we felt that by the rocks alone would it be proper to force the ascent. While on the ridge we were safe enough, and had the advantage as we clambered up of a most commanding position from whence we could view the frequent avalanches that swept by. The rain of the previous night, though it had only lasted for an hour or two, had evidently had a great effect on the state of the snow, and the avalanches seemed to pour down almost incessantly: probably some forty or fifty swept by us while we climbed by the side of the gully, and our situation gave rise to that feeling of somewhat pained security which is experienced when standing on a railway platform as an express train dashes by; we certainly felt that some of the downfalls would have reduced our party to a pulp quite as easily and with as much unconcern as the train itself. The guides, who do not perhaps tax their memories very severely for a parallel on such an occasion, asserted, as they generally do, that they had never seen anything like it in the whole course of their lives. They then fell to whistling, laughed very gaily, and borrowed tobacco from each other.

Gradually our difficulties became more pronounced, and conversation on indifferent topics was discarded, the remarks being confined to brief exclamations such as 'Keep it tight!' 'Don't touch that one!' 'Hold on now!' 'You're treading on my fingers!' 'The point of your axe is sticking into my stomach!' and similar ejaculations. Once in a way we ascended for a few feet by the snow, though never quite losing touch of the rocks, and sank waist deep in the soft compound filling up the gully. Then we went back to the rotten rocks for a brief spell, well content to be more out of the reach of chance fragments of ice falling down the shoot. It is wonderful to note how quickly time passes in an exciting climb of this nature; but our progress was actually rather rapid, so fast indeed that we did not fully realise at one period that we were getting into difficulties and that we had without doubt strayed, Christian-like, from the narrow path which was evidently the right one. Throughout the day we were conscious that the climb was too long to be completed if we made any serious mistake involving the retracing of steps. Quite suddenly, our situation became critical: a hurried glance up and down along the line revealed the fact that each member of the party had to do all he knew to preserve his position. The attitudes were ungainly enough to suggest instantaneous photographs at an ill-selected movement of four individuals dancing a 'can-can.' Maurer was engaged apparently in an extremely close and minute inspection of the toe of his right boot. Another member of the party was giving a practical illustration of the fact that he could, by extreme extension of his arms, stretch more than his own height, while a third was endeavouring to find out why the power of co-ordinating his muscular movements was suddenly lost to him, and why he could not persuade his left leg to join his right. For a few moments Jaun, who was leading, hung on by his finger-tips and the issue of the expedition hung in the balance. But our leader, by dint of some complicate sprawls, transferred himself over a passage of rock on which we had no earthly reason to be, and assisted the rest of the party to regain a more promising line of ascent. For those few minutes the situation was dramatic enough, and the thought crossed my mind that the curtain might not improbably descend on it; a solution of the difficulty which commends itself to the playwright when he has involved his *dramatis personæ* in difficulties, but which is not without its objections to the climber. On the whole the rocks on

I

this face of the mountain are much more difficult than on the other, and, writing now after the lapse of some years, I am disposed to think that these are perhaps the most difficult crags of any that I have ever met with to climb properly, that is with a minimum of risk to one's self and to one's companions; as a good proof of this I may say that the ascent would probably have appeared fairly easy to a novice and that it required some little Alpine experience to realise their real difficulty and their treacherous nature. There was scarcely time to test adequately all hand and foothold, and examination of rocks by what surgeons term palpation is a *sine quâ non* in rock climbing. Undoubtedly the mountain was not in the best possible order. We may possibly have rearranged the rocks in our line of ascent in a more convenient manner for those who follow. Certainly we may fairly say that in our actual line of ascent we left no stone unturned to ensure success.

Close below the ridge—within perhaps ten feet of it, for if I remember aright our leader had actually reached the crest—came the climax to what was perhaps rather a perilous climb. The first and second on the rope had met in their upward passage a huge cube of rock whose security they had carefully tested, and to surmount which it was necessary to stretch to the fullest extent in order to gain a respectable hold for the hands. We were all four in a direct line one below the other, and the two last on the rope were placed perforce directly beneath the treacherous crag. By an extension movement which conveyed some notion of the sensation experienced by those on the rack, I had reached a handhold pronounced to be of a passable nature by those above. By this manœuvre I succeeded in getting my feet exactly to a place on which the others, who were much heavier than I, had stood in security; without rhyme or reason the block of stone, which was about the size of a grand pianoforte, suddenly broke away from under me; a huge gap seemed cloven out in the mountain side, and Maurer, below, had only just time to spring aside, enveloped in a cloud of dust, and to throw himself flat against the rock, while the rope was strained to the utmost. Fortunately the handhold above was sound and I was able to hold on with feet dangling in the air, searching in vain for some projection on which to rest. Those above were too insecure to give any efficient help, and in fact possibly viewed my struggles, inasmuch as they were not fully aware at first of what had happened, with as much equanimity as a person inside a boat contemplates the gymnastic performances of a bather trying to climb over the edge. As the cloud of dust cleared off, however, and Maurer's face gradually beamed through it like the sun in a fog, for the excitement had made him the colour of a cornet player giving vent to a high note, they began to realise that something abnormal had happened, while the distant thundering reverberations of the falling mass assured them that it was no ordinary slip. Meanwhile Maurer planted his axe so as to give me some foothold, and with a push from below and a pull from above, fortunately simultaneous, I succeeded in planting my feet where my hands were, and subsequently undoubling found that we were within a few feet of the ridge, that the panorama beyond was undoubtedly magnificent, but was thrown out in strong relief by deep blue-black thunder-clouds advancing towards us.

Jaun now removed his empty pipe from his mouth and replaced it by a lucifer match, which, either as an aid to reflection or possibly for medicinal purposes, he chewed as he contemplated the ridge. A miserably cold wind with a remarkable knack of detecting all the rents in our raiment whistled around; above, the summit of the mountain was enveloped in driving thick mist and cloud. Still the final ridge looked fairly easy, and indeed proved to be so. The snow was deep and soft, and the stones below were so arranged as to remind us forcibly of a newly mended road in our native country; big and little, all seemed loose, and all arranged with their sharpest points and edges uppermost. The ridge is moderately broad, and we were able to flounder along with fair rapidity. Spurred on by the unpromising look of the weather and stimulated by the cold wind, which rendered any halts so unpleasant as to be out of the question, we set to work in earnest and found ourselves at the base of the final little snow and rock cone earlier than the length of the ridge had led us to expect. As we stepped on to the summit we experienced the curious sensation usually arising when climbing through clouds, that the mountain itself was sinking away rapidly from under our feet. The panorama was wholly composed of a foreground consisting of mist, and presented therefore comparatively few attractions.

It was already so late in the afternoon that we could not have afforded to stay in any case, and, as we felt that serious difficulties might possibly be encountered in descending, we set off at once, visions of a warm welcome and a hot bath at Ried rising before our minds. The idea of descending by way of the Baltschieder Joch was negatived without a division. The northern ridge of the Bietschhorn is a counterpart of the one by which we had ascended, with the solitary advantage in our case that we had to go down it and not up. The snow slopes leading down to the Nest Glacier were much broader, and we were strongly tempted more than once to quit the ridge for this western face of the mountain. Ultimately, persuaded that the condition of the snow justified us in so doing, we struck straight down on to the Nest Glacier, skirted round the ridge of rocks dividing the Nest Glacier from the Birch Glacier, and catching sight of a little green patch some way below, threw off the rope and rushed precipitately down to it. Misguided by a few gleams of sunshine breaking out between the driving clouds, we conceived the idea of repose and thought that we might as well be aired and dried. Below, the hotel at Ried was in full view, and it seemed but an hour or two from us: but our troubles were not yet over. The five minutes' halt on such occasions not uncommonly expand into five-and-fifty, and we rather deliberately averted our gaze from the western view of the valley, up which the thunderclouds were advancing steadily in close formation. Eventually we decided to move on, in order to avoid getting once more wet through. Vain hope: rapid though our descent was to the level of the forest it was not rapid enough. We ran furiously down the rough slopes, but, as the storm advanced and we perceived that we should be caught, the agitation of our minds gradually equalled the agitation of our bodies. We seemed to get no nearer Ried, while the darkness increased rapidly around us. Knowing the proclivities of guides on such occasions, my companion and I agreed that nothing should induce us to leave a path, should we perchance find one. Now, in a dim light it is exceedingly easy to discover paths, but extremely difficult to discover that variety of track that leads anywhere. Determined, however, to stick to our resolution, we found ourselves continually pursuing level stretches right and left, only to find that, as routes to any particular place, they were snares and delusions; that there was a path with long zigzags we knew, and indeed, finally, a shout from the guides, who skipped about downhill with an utter disregard for the integrity of their joints, and adopted that curious cantering gait considered on the stage to express light-hearted joy, announced that they had discovered the way. With characteristic inconsistency, they had no sooner found what we had been so long searching for than they proposed to leave it and make short cuts, so called; but we were inflexible, and determined not to leave our path or be seduced by the attractions of a perpendicular descent through an unknown territory. The hotel lights were no longer visible, but we knew that they lay straight below us. The question was whether we should turn right or left. The guides settled the matter by darting off ahead, ostensibly from a perfect acquaintance with their situation, but actually as we suspected to avoid being worried with unpleasant topographical questions. Gradually as we followed the track our stern purpose began to waver, for it was pointed out by some one that the path, though undoubtedly a good one in point of construction and general purpose, had two distinct disadvantages from our present point of view; one being that it led uphill, and the other that it ran in the wrong direction. There are certain contingencies in life in which the Briton finds but one adequate method of relieving and expressing his feelings, such, for instance, as when he finds himself bespattered with mud from the passing hansom on a carefully selected shirt-front and a white tie that would have moved to envy; or when, again, as the last to leave his club at night he finds the only remaining head-gear to consist of a well-worn beaver many sizes too large, with fur under the brim and a decoration of little rosettes and bobstays. It is hard to see why the ejaculation of any particular monosyllable should do him good at such a juncture. Hard words unquestionably break no bones, but neither do they mend the broken collar-stud or the ruptured bootlace; and yet if he swallows the expression down it will certainly ferment within him, and fermentation is characterised by multiplication. If, on the contrary, he articulates his feelings, the whole situation suddenly appears changed, and he can view the most untoward circumstances once more with a calm serenity of temper. But the remedy, though potent, specific almost, is too valuable to be resorted to constantly, and should be reserved, like Thursday's razor, for the most special occasions.

Our situation on the present occasion fully justified us in resorting to the source of relief vaguely alluded to, and we employed it simultaneously with the happiest results. Now the guides triumphed, and such was our accommodating mood that we actually acceded to their counsel and embarked on a perilous descent down a vertical gully. Scarcely had we turned into it when the storm broke and the rain came down in sheets, and very damp sheets too. Some one now suggested that the wisest plan would be to remain under shelter till the rain had passed off. It was argued against this amendment, and with a certain amount of force, first that there was no probability of the rain stopping, and secondly that there was no shelter: so we went on. Gradually, as we became more wet, we grew more desperate, and before long floundered down as regardless of bumps as a bluebottle in a conservatory: at one moment slithering over wet slabs of rock to which damp tufts of moss were loosely adherent, at another climbing carefully over gigantic toothcombs of fallen trees, then plunging head foremost—sometimes not exactly head foremost—through jungle-like masses of long grass and dwarf brushwood. Soaked to the skin, steamy, damp, and perspiring like bridegrooms, we went on, utterly reckless as to our apparel, and haunted by a perpetual idea that we should find ourselves ultimately at some place whence further descent would be impossible.

Within a few minutes the party divided and Jaun and I found ourselves together. By the lightning flashes I saw him from time to time; on one occasion he suddenly disappeared from view, and on joining him cautiously a little while after I found that he had just previously seated himself abruptly on a flat rock, immediately underneath a miniature torrent. The fact that we did not at every ten seconds run against large trees confirmed the idea that we were now almost out of the wood; accordingly we halloaed, as the occasion seemed suitable, but no answer was returned from our companions. Now came the question of how we were to cross the torrent which we knew lay between us and the hotel. Jaun cheerfully remarked that the best plan would be to find the bridge. This was obvious enough, but he confessed that he had forgotten at what part of the river's course the bridge lay. However, keeping close together, we made towards the right, on which side the stream lay. The slopes were here more level and less carelessly laid out. Our hopes revived, for the hotel could only be a few minutes off, and between the peals of thunder we could hear the roar of the torrent and could hear also the hollow sound due to the boulders rolling over its stony bed. Of a sudden we came on to its banks, and formidable enough the stream looked. The idea of searching for the bridge seemed childish, for the whole of the frail wooden structure had probably been carried away long before down to the Rhone valley. The hotel was only a few yards off, and again the situation was exasperating enough to justify a resort to extreme measures, if it were an extreme measure to express forcibly a wish that the torrent might be—well, temporarily stopped up at some higher point. Jaun now volunteered to wade across. It was quite unnecessary for him to divest himself of any clothing for the purpose, and in fact when he had succeeded very pluckily in reaching the other side he was not in the least degree wetter than when he started. He shouted some observations from the other side, which I took to mean that he would go on to the hotel and procure a lantern. Accordingly I seated myself to await his return, selecting unintentionally a little pool of water, which however did just as well as anything else.

Before long a flashing light advancing indicated that Jaun had been successful, and two forms were seen dimly on the opposite side, one with a light. The bearer of the lantern was an aged person in shirt sleeves and a highly excited frame of mind. The aged person, on the distant shore, gesticulated as violently as a marionette doll when its wires have got hitched up wrong, and then, seemingly possessed of a sudden fury, rushed violently down a steep place and beckoned frantically with his lantern. This seemed to mean that I was to descend to a point on the bank opposite to where he stood. It now appeared that there was a bridge within a few yards of us, if a single spiky, submerged, and insecure trunk could be considered such. The old man embraced me warmly when I had made my way across, slapped me hard on the back, and then laughed very loud and suddenly. Then he darted off with the agility and abruptness of movement of an elderly lady from the country crossing in front of an omnibus, or a hen, a foolish animal that always waits to the last moment before running needlessly to the wrong side of the road. Guided by the lantern which the impulsive veteran flourished wildly in every direction, so that no one dared approach him, in another ten minutes we reached the hotel and found ourselves, with the exception of our companions, who had arrived a few minutes before— Heaven only knows how, for they did not—fortunately the only occupants of the hotel. The volatile sexagenarian calmed down, put on his coat, put out his lantern, and retired to repose in an outhouse, a shelter to which I fancy he was relegated owing to certain physical infirmities.

It was eleven o'clock, and we had been pretty actively employed for twenty-one hours. The idea of food and a change of raiment was not, therefore, distasteful. A middle-aged female with an excessively 'rational' and hygienic waist, who said she was the waitress, volunteered to serve the banquet, but the change of raiment necessary was naturally beyond her means, while the idea of borrowing from the aged person's wardrobe did not commend itself to us, so we ordered in a large stock of towels. 'But,' I remarked, 'you can't go about in a bath towel'—the truth of which assertion was immediately evident, for they were so small that it was difficult to fasten them with any degree of security; accordingly blankets were requisitioned, and a very classical effect in costume was thus produced, though what the Romans did when there was a gale of wind I do not know. To keep up the delusion we arranged the chairs after the fashion of couches, and appeased our hunger with a curious repast of stewed apples and mixed biscuits, the sole articles of food that could be discovered. However, to anticipate, we fared better the next day at breakfast; for though Bright Chanticleer proclaimed the morn at 3 A.M. he did not proclaim any subsequent period of time, as he was captured and cooked for our repast. The waitress while we supped was busily engaged in stoking up the stove, and seized upon our damp raiment with avidity to have it ready for the next morning; so energetic was she in fact that we felt it necessary to remonstrate, foreseeing the probability that our clothes might have to be brought back to us in a dust shovel: we remarked that, though sorry for our misdeeds, we would limit for choice the repentant nature of our apparel to the sackcloth we were then wearing and would dispense with the adjunct of ashes. The unreliable nature of the fastenings of our costume prevented us from accompanying our forcible remarks with properly impressive gestures. The remonstrance, however, had the desired effect, and our garments the next day, though somewhat shrivelled and inconveniently tight here and there, still proved that they had resisted effectively the fire as well as the water.

The amount of luxury found in the Lötschthal since those days has materially improved. Time was when the only accommodation for the traveller was to be found at the humble tenement of Mons. le Curé, a worthy old creature as I remember him, who appeared to keep an apiary in his back drawing-room and was wont to produce the most excellent honey and the most uncompromising bread; the latter article, as one might judge, was baked about as often as the old gentleman washed himself. But the milk of human kindness flowed strongly in him (as it may be said to do in those who have been made the subjects of transfusion), though, to tell the truth, it was somewhat decidedly flavoured with garlic, and it needed much resolution to attentively listen to the confidential communications he was in the habit of whispering. A man of education and gentle refinement—at any rate of mind—his was a hard lot, buried away in a squalid little parish, with no earthly being to talk to possessed of more than one idea; yet he slaved on contentedly enough with no thought beyond the peasants in his own district and of how he might relieve their condition, too often at the expense of his own welfare; isolated more than any ascetic, for his mental existence was that of a hermit, from circumstances and not from will. The thought of solitary confinement is terrible, but utter mental isolation is hideous. Yet, while he entertained us hospitably with fare which, though rough, was the very best he could offer, he would not join in the repast: not, probably, from lack of appetite, but from a feeling that, owing to prolonged seclusion and association with the peasants, the more fashionable and accepted methods of preparing food for consumption and conveying it to the mouth, with subsequent details, were somewhat dim to his recollection. Yet his conversation flowed fast and he talked well: the while any reference to friends and fellow-travellers would cause him to pause for a moment or two, look upwards around the room, and fetch a rather long breath before he recommenced. A curiously gaunt old creature he seemed at first sight: with wonderful, bony, plastic hands capable of expressing anything; grotesque almost in his unkempt rustiness; provoking a smile at first, but sadness as one learnt more of him. And how closely are the two emotions associated. In truth Humour was born a twin, and her sister was christened Pathos.

I can recall that he accepted a sum of ten francs when we parted in the morning. His eyes glistened with pleasure as he took the coin and straightway made for a ramshackle hovel on the hill-side, where lay an aged person 'très-malade.' Possibly after his visit there was left a happy peasant in that tumble-down cabin—an emotional object more often described than witnessed. But all this took place years ago, and as we passed the collection of dilapidated tenements in one of which our old friend once lived, I failed to recognise his former dwelling-place. The timbers grew old and worn, the bands rusty, and one day the wheel which had worked steadily for so long stopped. Yet the stream which had moved it ran on as if nothing had happened. Was it a wasted life? Who can say if there be such a thing?

> A few can touch the magic string,
>   And noisy Fame is proud to win them:
> Alas! for those that never sing,
>   But die with all their music in them.

We passed on: in a few minutes the houses were lost to view and there was left but the reflection of how much more, worthy of study, there was in this old curé's nature than in the majority of Swiss with whom mountaineering brings us in close contact.

As we descended the Lötschthal to Gampel the air seemed to thicken. The excessive warmth allowed our garments to stretch once again to their wonted girth, and we became less thoughtful. The vignette of the ancient curé dissolved away and was replaced by a view (mental only, unhappily) of our aiguille at Chamouni, black and bare of snow, inviting another attack. Gampel does not tempt the traveller much to seek repose, and we therefore caught the first train that came crawling along the valley and shaped our course for Chamouni in a second-class carriage tenanted by a *pension* of young ladies out for a holiday apparently, who all chirped and twittered and wrangled for the best places till the going down of the sun, like the Temple sparrows.

CHAPTER V.

AN OLD FRIEND WITH A NEW FACE

Chamouni again—The hotel *clientèle*—A youthful hero—The inevitable English family—A scientific gentleman—A dream of the future—The hereafter of the Alps and of Alpine literature—A condensed mountain ascent—Wanted, a programme—A double ' Brocken '—A hill-side phenomenon and a familiar character—A strong argument—Halting doubts and fears—A digression on mountaineering accidents—' From gay to grave, from lively to severe '—The storm breaks—A battle with the elements—Beating the air—The ridge carried by assault—What next, and next?—A topographical problem and a cool proposal—The descent down the Vallée Blanche—The old Montanvert hotel—The Montanvert path and its frequenters.

It was the summer of 18— and our old quarters at Couttet's hotel knew us once more. As we drove into the village of Chamouni we turned our heads carelessly around to note the various new hotels that might have arisen since our last visit. Observing that they were four or five in number, we rightly conjectured that we should find all the hotel keepers complaining bitterly of the hard times and the want of custom. Also we wondered in how many ways it was possible to build a house without any particular system of drainage, a deficiency which was at that time becoming very marked in Chamouni, but has since, I believe, been improved. Yet the place itself had not altered essentially. New buildings of imposing exterior and little else do not materially alter a place that leads a life like that of modern Chamouni. The population, which throughout the summer appears to pass its time in the streets with its hands in its pockets, was still amusing itself in the same way. The tone of the village was just the same as we had always known it, and even M. Couttet himself had not succeeded in imparting any marine flavour by building an odd little lighthouse with an iron flag on the top which the architect had ingeniously represented as streaming permanently in a direction indicating a wind favourable for fine weather. We knew that we should find the same denizens in the hotel; and they were there.

There was a very young man with a very particoloured face from exposure on the glaciers, who had recently completed the thousand-and-first ascent of Mont Blanc and was perpetually posing gracefully against the door-post or in a lattice-work summerhouse a few steps from the hotel, gazing towards the mountain and rather eagerly joining in any conversation relating to the perils of the ascent. There were three or four young ladies of various periods of life who gazed at him with admiration and enquired at intervals if he wasn't very tired; to which the young man replied carelessly that he was not, and inwardly thought that the discomfort of sunburn and the consequent desquamation was on the whole cheaply bought, the while he wished the expedition had not cost so much and that so many others had not thought of making the same ascent. And then there came a lithe, active lady walker who had been up Mont Blanc and a great many other mountains too, and paid no more attention to the guides' stereotyped compliments than a suspicious dog does to those of a nervous visitor: so the young man's nose was put out of joint and he would have laughed scornfully at the fickleness of hero worship had not the skin of his face been in danger of cracking, and he wished his shirt collar had not been starched and thumped by the village washerwoman into the form of a circular linen saw.

Then there was an excitable Englishman of impulsive habits, with a large family who were perpetually playing a game of follow-my-leader with their parent, and who were under orders to weigh anchor on the following morning at five o'clock for the Montanvert and the Mauvais Pas. The boys were stoking up for the occasion with raw apples, and the girls were occupied, when not pursuing their restless father, in preparing a puggaree for his hat. There was a gentleman who affected the curious untidiness of raiment not unfrequently noticed among Sunday frequenters of the Thames, and who sought to establish a mountaineering reputation by constantly gazing at the peaks around in a knowing manner and wearing a flannel shirt of an obtrusive pattern destitute of any collar. There were guides about, who were on the point of being paid for their services and who were exceedingly polite and obsequious; others whose 'tour' had just passed, were, proportionately, less deferential. There was an elderly lady whose whole soul appeared bent on a little stocking from which she never parted, and who turned the knitting needles to more account for toilet and other small purposes than I could have conceived to be possible. There were two or three mountaineers who appeared anxious only to avoid everyone's gaze and who might be seen in byways and odd corners talking to bronzed guides who looked like business. Finally, there was a gentleman of statistical and scientific tendencies, much given to making quietly astonishing statements of astronomical facts and gently smiling as he rolled over his tongue and enjoyed the flavour of the vast numbers with which it was his pleasure to deal. He absolutely revelled and wallowed in figures. Buttonholed in a corner and compelled to listen with deferential attention, I secretly writhed as he crushed me slowly with the mere weight of his numerals. He shared with others of his frame of mind the peculiarity of always keeping something in hand and skilfully working up to a climax. Such and such a star was so many millions of miles off. We opened our eyes to the proper degree of width and observed, 'Bless me!' or, 'You don't say so?' Instantly he would rejoin, 'Ah, but that's nothing to so and so,' and then favoured us with a still more immeasurable distance. We expressed a slightly greater degree of intelligent amazement. Thereupon he nodded his head, gently inclined it a little to one side, and smiled softly. It gave him such evident pleasure to have a listener that I attended with due reverence to his enthusiastic computations; knowing my man, I felt sure that he was keeping back a real staggerer to finish up with, and was prepared to assume varying degrees of surprise up to the moment when it should come. Unfortunately I misjudged its advent, and feeling that I had somewhat lost in his estimation by evincing undue astonishment at a comparatively small array of figures, I sought to turn the conversation by requesting to know how long he thought it might be before the great rock peaks around us would have crumbled away to their bases. The calculation was too trivial and the number of millions of generations too small to interest him much, but he vouchsafed an approximate estimate.

I let him babble on and fell a-thinking. The peaks were crumbling away bit by bit no doubt, the glaciers shrinking. At a bound the mind leapt into a future which, after all, might be not so very unlike a past. The Alps things of the past! What, I wondered, when the mountains were all levelled down and smiling valleys occupied the troughs of the glaciers of to-day, would some future commentators make of the literature so industriously piled up by the members and followers of the Alpine Club? Imagination ran riot as in a dream, and I fancied some enthusiast exploring the buried city of the second Babylon and excavating the ruins of the 'finest site in Europe.' I pictured to myself the surprise in store for him on digging out the effigies of some of our naval and military heroes, and the mingled feelings with which he would contemplate the unearthed statue of George IV. It seemed possible that in that far-off epoch to which my friend's calculations had borne me, the Alpine Club itself might have ceased to exist. Pursuing his explorations in an easterly direction, the excavator might perchance have lighted on a strange tunnel, almost Arcadian in its simplicity of design, and marvelled at the curious and cheap idols of wax and wood which the people of that ancient day had evidently worshipped. Turning north again, this Schliemann of the future would pass by the ruins of S. Martin's Church, eager to light upon the precious archives of the historic Alpine Club itself. How eagerly he would peruse the lore contained in the Club library, anxious to decipher the inscriptions and discover what manner of men they were who lived and climbed when mountains and glaciers were still to be found on this planet. Human nature would probably not have changed much, and the successful explorer might even have been asked to favour a scientific society of the future with the result of his discoveries, to which in all probability he would have acceded, with a degree of reluctance not quite sufficient to deter the secretary of the society from pressing him.

An abstract of his description of our sibylline leaves I fancied might run somewhat in this style:— After commenting on the fact that the maps and illustrations did not usually correspond in number with the list set forth in the index of the volumes unearthed, he might proceed thus:—'In pursuit of their great and glorious object these ancient heroes appear to have undergone vast personal discomfort. It is difficult therefore to realise fully why so many engaged in this form of exploration. Instances have been given by other learned antiquarians who have studied the habits of this people, of a similar purposeless disregard of comfort, such as the four-wheeled wooden boxes in which they travelled about, the seats in their churches, &c. The outset of their expedition was almost invariably characterised by a display of bad temper, attributed to early rising. After a varying number of hours of excessive toil the travellers were wont to arrive at some fearsome chasm spoken of as a "bergschrund." On this, if the subject-matter of their narrative was insufficient in quantity, they were wont to descant and enlarge at length; sometimes, as we judge, in their descriptions they enlarged the bergschrund itself. They then crossed it. Immediately after this incident they were in the habit of eating, and the minute and instructive details commonly given enable us to form a tolerably accurate opinion as to the nature of the diet with which they supported their exhausted frames. Next they traversed strange localities for which there appear to have been no adequately descriptive expressions in their own language. In fact the difficulty of deciphering these records is greatly increased by the fact that the writers were versatile linguists, for they constantly make use of words of a hybrid character. They were evidently practised meteorologists and took much interest in this subject, as may be gathered throughout from their writings. At length they reached summits, of the nature of which we in our time can have but a feeble conception. So great was their relief at the termination of their self-imposed but toilsome task, that they habitually burst forth into language characterised by a wealth of imagery and a fervour of poetic description which unfortunately conveys but little idea to us in our day of what they actually saw. In descending they were all commonly within an ace of meeting with a violent death. The mode in which the danger attacked them varied within certain restricted limits, but it always occurred and the escape was always narrow. The peril over, they remarked that they breathed freely again, and then at once fell to eating. Arrived at a successful termination of their wearisome labour, they advised others to do the same. They dealt out unsparing satire to their companions, unlimited praise to their guides, and unmeasured ridicule to their porter. They commonly expressed throughout their descriptions grave doubts and uncertainty as to the issue of the expedition: a curious and noteworthy fact, for the heading of the accounts always divulged at the outset their ultimate success. The construction, therefore, of their narratives was in accordance with a well-recognised model and appeared capable of little variation. The only other facts that we can glean are that they were prodigious eaters, were much pestered by some extinct species of insects, and that they make frequent allusions to a substance termed tobacco. The constant repetition of these incidents stamps upon their writings the impress of unexaggerated veracity. Still they were not universally held in favour, indeed were regarded with disapprobation by some individuals of their own race. It would seem indeed from internal evidence that, had it not been for frequent and sharp criticism of their proceedings, their pastime might never have inveigled so many persons with its seductive fascination.'

Now at the time at which these prophetic fancies

were conjured up we had just completed an expedition which it seemed might be worthy of attention, solely on the ground of its very contradictoriness. For the features of this climb were most opposed to those already mentioned, and in fact mention of it scarcely seemed admissible in an Alpine narrative. We took no porter with us to fill the rôle of first low comedy man. We had very little to eat; our stock of wine ran out through a leaky gourd; our tobacco was wet and there was no bergschrund, and yet all this happened on a mountain close to Chamouni.

'Some vast amount of years ago, ere all my youth had vanished from me,' as the poet says, at a date therefore which for obvious reasons it is inexpedient here to mention, I found myself, as already mentioned, at Chamouni. With me was an old mountain friend and fellow climber, J. Oakley Maund. We were both burning with desire to add to the list of the many successful expeditions we had made together, but, as a matter of fact, were somewhat gravelled for lack of suitable matter. Like a ministry on the eve of a general election or a gentleman without a sixpenny-piece at a theatre, we were sorely in need of a programme. The locality was somewhat unfortunately chosen for those in whom the ancient spirit was not yet quite extinct and who wanted to do something new. Ever since the days when Jacques Balmat, Dr. Paccard, and the great De Saussure had donned strange apparel and shown the way—that is to say, for nearly a hundred years—people had been climbing mountains in the district, and it was not to be wondered at if it were hard to find some expedition which nobody else had thought of, or, worse still, had achieved. We gazed at the map and made thumb marks all over it. In every conceivable direction ran little lines indicative of previous explorations. We studied the *carte en relief*, but without much hope of getting any information of value from this inaccurate and lumpy absurdity. Mont Blanc, which, according to this work of plastic art, was modelled out as some eight or ten thousand feet higher than any other point of the chain, had had all the snow worn off its summit by much fingering, so that the component pasteboard showed through. Rivers ran uphill in this map, and lakes were inclined at an angle; bits of sticking plaister represented towns and villages, and the whole article was absolutely bristling with little spikes and points like the old panoramas of London or the docks at Liverpool. Still a considerable number of people seemed willing enough to pay fifty centimes for the pleasure of indicating elaborate expeditions on it with their fore-fingers, and appeared to derive pleasure from gazing on a pasteboard misrepresentation when they could by looking out of window see the real thing for nothing. We abandoned the *carte en relief* and took Jaun and Kaspar Maurer into our confidence. The only suggestions that they could make were the Aiguille des Charmoz and the Dent du Géant. The former of these two peaks we had both tried to ascend in former seasons, without success. Jaun did not think then that it was possible, and without sharing his opinion we gave way to it. With regard to the latter mountain we all thought at the time that an undue amount of what is vaguely termed 'artificial aid' would be necessary to ensure success, an opinion confirmed by subsequent events, for when Signor Sella achieved the honour of the first ascent he was only able to accomplish it by somewhat elaborate engineering appliances. Some bold person of an original turn of thought suggested of course a variation of some way up Mont Blanc, but the utter impossibility of discovering the slightest deviation from any previously ascended route and the utter uselessness of trying to find one caused a general shout of derision, and the bold person thereupon withdrew his suggestion and ordered some coffee. Besides, the weather was fine; every day swarms of tourists could be seen, crawling up the sides of the monarch of mountains, in numbers as many as the flies on a sugar loaf in a grocer's window on a hot day.

One evening we sat in front of Couttet's hotel staring pensively at the familiar outline of the row of aiguilles, and wishing we had lived in the days of Albert Smith, the best friend Chamouni ever had.

At any rate, at that time the natives were unsophisticated and the mountains about were not all done to death. The valley between us and the chain was filled with a light haze, not sufficient to conceal the outline of the mountains but yet enough to blot out their detail and solidity. As the moon rose behind the chain we saw a strange phenomenon. A silhouette was thrown forwards on to the curtain of haze and photographed on it with sharp and clear definition, so that we could recognise, at an immense height, the shadowed peaks looking almost as massive as the actual mountains. Nor was this all; a second curtain of mist seemed to be suspended, in a vertical stratum, in front of the former one, and the shadows were again marked out on this, infinitely more magnified and less distinct, but still perfectly recognisable. As a result we were able to see the semblance of three distinct tiers of mountains one above the other, looking so massive that we could scarcely realise that they were but transparent ghosts of the peaks; and the phenomenon, a double 'Brocken,' must have lasted for more than half an hour. However, we desired something more of the nature of the substance than the shadow, and ultimately came to the conclusion that it was absolutely necessary for our peace of mind to accomplish something on the morrow, and as it really mattered but little what that something might be, provided a good climb was afforded, we must yield to circumstances and perforce adopt the latter-day necessity of all mountaineers. If we could not find the right way up some new mountain we could at least take the wrong way up an old one.

So the next morning we walked up to the Pierre Pointue as a preliminary step—a good many and rather arduous steps—towards the object in view. The exertion of toiling up the zigzags or the more rarefied atmosphere had a remarkable effect on one of the party, whose face when we reached the chalet was found to be wreathed in smiles and wearing an expression of great intelligence. He had in fact become possessed of an idea. Bubbling over with self-satisfied chuckles, he suggested that we should ascend the Aiguille du Midi by the face directly in front of us and then descend on the other side, thus making a col of the mountain. The idea found favour instantly, and the intelligent person was so much pleased that he ordered a bottle of wine, plastered over with a very costly variety of label, and regretted it. Investigation of the cellar revealed only two casks of wine, but the 'carte' comprised a long list of various vintages. Fired with enthusiasm and inflated with *limonade gazeuse*, we left the chalet and strode vigorously up the hill in order to prospect the route and reconnoitre the rocks. The exertion and the pace soon told upon us, the sooner that it was a hot, enervating day; the kind of day that makes one perforce admire the ingenious benevolence of nature in fashioning out on the grassy slopes rounded inequalities, exactly adapted to those of the human figure in a seated or recumbent position. The heated air rising from the ground gave flickering and distorted views of distant objects, like unto marine phenomena viewed through the cheap panes of a seaside lodging-house window. The grasshoppers were extraordinarily busy; the bees droned through the heavy air; the ants, overcome apparently by the temperature, had given up for the time straining their jaws by their foolish practice of carrying large parcels about without any definite object, and had retired to the shady seclusion of their own heaped-up residences; the turf was most inviting. It now occurred to us that there was no absolute necessity for the whole party to ascend on the present occasion, and that perhaps the guides might go up quicker alone. The details of this suggestion were acceded to on the part of the amateurs of the party with astonishing alacrity and unanimity. We laid the scheme before the guides, and they also thought it a very fine one. Thereupon, with much parade and ceremony, they braced themselves up for great exertion, borrowed the telescope, remarked that they expected to be back some time during the night, and started upwards with somewhat over-acted eagerness. My companion and I disposed ourselves comfortably in the shade, and resumed an argument which had originally commenced some days previously. I waxed eloquent on the subject under discussion and with much success, for such was the force of my logic and the cogency of my reasoning that I bore down on my opponent, and reduced him in a short time to absolute silence, from which he did not awake for nearly two hours.

About this time the guides, who in all probability had also been comfortably asleep within a short distance of us, returned and gave a favourable report concerning the mountain. Elated by this news, we climbed a short distance further up, and met there a large party of ephemeral acquaintances who were taking an afternoon's pleasure on the hills. After the manner of people when so engaged, they set forth with great energy and climbed up a steep little rock tump a few hundred yards distant. Arrived at the summit, they roared out unintelligible remarks to us, and we did the same to them till we were hoarse; we waved our hands and hats and they flourished their handkerchiefs as if they were our dearest friends on earth, just setting out on an emigrant ship for the Antipodes. The party then descended; the nearer they came the less friendly and demonstrative were we, and by the time we met the warmth of affection recently manifested on both sides had wholly evaporated, and we conversed in ordinary tones on indifferent topics. Then they set out for another little hill, and we were moved, apparently by some uncontrollable impulse, to go through the same idiotic performance. Emotional behaviour of a similar kind is not infrequently observed in the mountains. We journeyed together back to the Pierre Pointue, viewing each other with distrust and suspicion; and when it was found that we had bespoken the beds—if the exaggerated packing-cases lined with straw bags could be considered such—we parted on terms the reverse of friendly. So frail are the links that bind human affections.

Standing in front of the hut was a type of character very familiar in these tourist-frequented districts. His exterior was unpromising; his beard of a fortnight's growth, or thereabouts, somewhat fitful withal and lacking in uniformity of development. A hard hat, with a shining green veil folded around its battered outline, decorated his head; his raiment was black and rusty, his legs cased in canvas gaiters fastened with many little girths and buckles, and in his right hand he grasped a trusty three-franc pole made of wainy deal, and surmounted at the top by a brown knob similar to those which come out suddenly when we try to open a chest of drawers in a cheap lodging. He fidgeted about for a while, asked questions in a rather loud tone of voice at us, and we felt that it was his intention to enter into conversation. It was even so. After a while he sidled up and requested with much diffidence to be informed what we proposed to climb on the morrow. Now the true mountaineer, however amiable his disposition, always shrinks up into his shell when such a question is put to him on the eve of an expedition. My companion indicated by a sweep of the arm a space of territory extending about from the Mont Buet on the one side round to the Aiguille de Gouté on the other. Our friend surveyed from end to end the extensive panorama suggested, then looked seriously at us and observed that we should probably find it a fine walk. We expressed gravely the opinion that he was quite right, and then went in to dinner, while our composite friend expatiated on the project to his companions as an expedition but little out of the ordinary run, and one that he was perfectly prepared to undertake himself if so disposed; then he resumed his contemplation of a rock some ninety feet or so in height jutting out through the glacier above, which he was under the impression was a lady descending from Mont Blanc. We did not learn his name, but the individual may, nevertheless, possibly be recognised. Some points of the argument were still unsettled when we climbed over the edges of our respective boxes and vanished into the strawy depths below. The clear moonlight streamed in through the window and prevented sleep; so I lay in my wooden box thinking over the recent discussion, but with such a distinct intention—

like little Paul Dombey with Mrs. Pipchin — of fixing my companion presently, that even that hardy old mountaineer deemed it prudent to counterfeit slumber.

In the small hours of the morning we got under weigh. For some time we had been leading a life of sloth in Chamouni, and the delight of finding ourselves once more on the mountain path, and making for a rock climb, entirely precluded that fractiousness which, as all readers of Alpine literature know, ought properly to be described at this period of an expedition. The path was irregular and demanded some equanimity, for the stumbling-blocks were innumerable and artfully placed to trip up the unwary in an aggravating manner. Feeling it unfair that all the work should be thrown on the guides, I had volunteered, rather magnanimously, to bear part of the burden, and selected the lantern as my share. By this means it was not only possible to walk in comfort over a well-lighted track, but the bearer was enabled also to regulate the pace to a speed convenient to his own feelings. Before long, however, we reached the lower snow patches of the Glacier des Pélerins, and the light was no longer necessary.

We made straight across the crisp snow to the base of a promising-looking rock buttress lying to the right of the snow gully that runs up the side of the mountain, feeling sure that either by the rocks or the snow a way up could be found. And now I am painfully conscious of a glaring defect in this Alpine narrative. A mountain ascent without a bergschrund is as tame as a steeplechase without a water jump, but candour compels the admission that no bergschrund was visible. Either we had hit on a spot where the orthodox chasm was filled up for the time, or else this particular glacier was an exception to all others previously treated of in mountain literature. In a few seconds we found ourselves on the rocks, delighted to exchange the monotonous mode of progression compulsory on snow for the varied gymnastic exercises demanded on rocks. The sun had risen, the axes clanked merrily against the stones, the snow was in good condition for walking, everything seemed favourable, and we gazed down complacently on the distance already traversed. Above us the mountain was broken up and easy, and we climbed on rapidly, each in the fashion that seemed best to him. So good was our progress at first, that we were already far up the buttress, and could barely see our morning's tracks in the snow beneath, when a halt was called for breakfast, and we had time to look around. Now, however unconventional this expedition may have been in many respects, the sagacious student of Alpine literature will know that it must be wholly impossible to omit all reference to the weather. As soon might one expect two prosaic persons of slight acquaintanceship to abjure the topic at a chance meeting. The western sky wore a rather ominous look of half mourning, and heavy grey and black clouds were whirling about and forming up in close order in a manner suggestive of rising wind. Even at this stage of the proceedings the thought crossed our minds that the storm which was evidently brewing might possibly overtake us, and that perhaps we ought at once to turn back.

One thing was evident; that we must decide quickly, whatever we did. We determined to push on for a while, and with that intent girded ourselves with the rope and worked our way on to the top of the first buttress. At this point, further progress directly upwards was impossible, and we were compelled to cross the gully and make for the rock on the left-hand side. Considerable care is always necessary in crossing, horizontally, a gully filled with snow, where the rope is rather a source of danger than of security. We had to give all our attention to the passage, and when we reached the rocks opposite, the climbing, though not formidable, was still sufficiently difficult to occupy all our thoughts for the moment, and we had but little leisure, and perhaps but little inclination, for meteorological observations. At the top of the rocks a promising snow slope, stretching upwards with gentle curves and sweeps, seemed to offer a fair prospect of rapid progress. Such snow slopes are at all times a little deceptive. Even when the climber is close to them they look oftentimes much easier than they immediately after prove to be. From a distance, say from under the verandah of a comfortable hotel, when the climber *in posse* indicates the way he would pursue with the end of his cigar, they are absurdly easy. So, too, are obstacles in the hunting-field, such as stiff hedges and uncompromising gates, easy enough when the Nimrod studies them as he whirls along in an express train. Subsequently, when immediately associated with a horse, these same obstacles assume a different guise. Then are the sentiments of the hunter prone to become modified, and compassion for dumb beasts becomes more prominent in the thoughtful votary of the chase, till finally it may be observed that the little wits jump sometimes more than the great ones. Even so does the mountaineer often discover, on a nearer acquaintance that the snow incline up which he proposed to stride merrily is inclined at a highly inconvenient angle. However, at the commencement of our slope we found the snow in good condition, and advanced quickly for some little distance, but before we had got very far it was necessary to resort to the axe, and we had then ample opportunities of looking round. The clouds were lowering more and more, but as they were swept up by a sou'westerly wind, the intervening mass of the mountain prevented us from seeing thoroughly what might be in store for us.

The wind, too, was growing stronger every minute, and my companion, who was still pursuing his argument, and, as it appeared subsequently, making some rather good points, had to exert himself considerably in order to make his voice heard.

Presently we halted for a few minutes on some spiky little rocks, and again looked about. The weather prospects were just in that doubtful state that prompts every member of the party to ask the others what they think. Maurer looked exceedingly vacant and made no remark. Jaun put a bit of snow in his mouth, but declined to give an opinion. We, not to be outdone, assumed very profound expressions, as if prepared to find ourselves in the right whatever happened, but, following the example of Lord Burleigh in the famous tragedy, we said nothing either. At last, some one suggested that we might go on for a little, and then see. Accordingly we went on for a little, but then as a matter of fact the mists swept up around us and we did not see anything at all. It was, no doubt, inconvenient that we were unable to penetrate with our gaze to the regions above, but still we felt that there was one slight counterbalancing advantage, for there was present the haunting consciousness that the gigantic telescope of Chamouni was pointed in our direction, and at least the enveloping mist ensured that privacy which is not always accorded to climbers pursuing their pastime within range of these instruments of science.

In the hope that the condition of the upper snow might be good, and perhaps rather mistaken in the height we had already reached, we made up our minds to push on, with the view of reaching at any rate the top of the ridge before the storm broke. Every now and again a rent in the clouds above, lasting for a few seconds, showed us that the wind was blowing with great force, as thin clouds of loose snow were swept up and whirled along the face in curling wreaths. The spectacle might not, at first sight, have been thought highly diverting: yet as we pointed upwards to the ridge and watched the racing snow-drifts driving over the slopes we were making for, we all laughed very heartily. So universal is the tendency to be amused at the sight of discomfort that it even extends to the contemplation of its occurring shortly to oneself. In the paulo-post-future the experience is exhilarating: in the actual present it is less laughter-moving. Laughter in the presence of events that are, in the true sense of the word, sensational, comes almost as a reflex action (to borrow an expression from the physiologists), and the sympathetic distress that follows takes an appreciable time to develop. I can recall once being a witness with some others of a ghastly accident by which several people were precipitated, together with a mass of broken timbers and débris of all sorts, from a great height. A door was burst open and the ruin met our eyes suddenly. To this day I can remember sounds of laughter at the first view—hysterical if you like to call it so, and not mirthful, but still laughter. In a few seconds the realisation of what had happened came, and then came the distress and with it expressions of horror, as all worked manfully to help and rescue the sufferers. The sequence of emotions was perfectly natural, and only they who have never passed through such an experience would speak of inhumanity. There is no want of humanity in the matter. The suddenness of the impression begets the train of emotions, and the brain grasps the facts but slowly. To take another instance: I have been told by a man whose quickness and presence of mind were remarkable—a man who as a schoolboy won a Royal Humane Society's medal—that on one occasion he witnessed a friend fall over a staircase from a great height. The accident was in the highest degree unexpected: and the witness walked leisurely on as if nothing had happened. But in a few seconds came like a severe blow the sudden realisation of what had taken place. Thought is not always quick. We can no more exert our minds to their fullest capacity on a sudden than we can put forth our utmost physical strength on a sudden. Action when almost instantaneous is independent of the higher mental faculties, and is but a reflex. The experience of those who have been in railway accidents will be of the same nature. In climbing up a very steep or difficult place if a man falls all are prepared more or less for such an accident. The whole attention is given to guarding against a probable contingency, and it follows that the mind can instantly realise its occurrence. And that such is the case I have been unlucky enough to witness, though most fortunately the fall was attended with no serious consequences. On the same principle, to take a more trivial example, on difficult rocks it is the rarest possible accident for a man to sprain his ankle or knee. The muscles are always prepared for a possible slip and kept in tension on the alert. On the loose moraine, when walking leisurely or carelessly, such an accident is a thousand times more likely to occur.

Our leader worked away with a will, but the snow got harder at every step. The growing force of the wind, which in nautical language had increased from that vague degree known as a capful to the indefinite force of a stiff breeze, and the increasing steepness of the slope, compelled Jaun to make the steps larger and larger as we ascended. It soon became evident that the storm would overtake us long before we could hope to get on to the ridge, and that we had deliberately walked into something of a trap. The steps had been cut so far apart that to descend by the same line would have involved the construction of a fresh staircase, and on actually turning, we found that what was a stiff breeze behind us was a half gale when it met our faces. It was certainly easier to go on than to go back; so we went further and fared much worse. The slope became steeper, the ice harder, the half gale became a whole gale, and the delay between each step seemed interminable. Suddenly, as we passed from under the lee of a projecting slope on our right, a tremendous gust of wind, which seemed to have waited for a few moments in order to collect its full forces, swept suddenly down and almost tore us from our foothold. With that a torrent of hail fell, and for a few moments we had enough to do to hold on where we stood. Even my companion's conversation slackened. He had astutely selected a place in the caravan immediately behind me, and as the gale was blowing directly on our backs was enabled to fire off his remarks and arguments without any possibility of response. Anything that I said in answer was audible only to our leader, who took not the smallest interest in the discussion. Unfortunately, too, it was difficult to listen with any attention; for as the gusts came on we were forced to swing all our faces round like chimney cowls instantly in the same direction. The squalls became more frequent and more violent, the thunder and lightning played around merrily, and as the wind howled by we had to throw ourselves flat against the slope, adopting the undignified attitudes of a deer-stalker nearing the brow of a Scotch hill— attitudes which bring somewhat unduly into prominence the inadequate nature of the national costume.

Fortunately, as has been said, we were screened from view; and our poses, though possibly ungraceful, were at any rate uncriticised. The big hailstones, falling softly around, filled up the steps as they were made, and our feet were buried up to the ankles in a moment. In a minute or two the hurricane passed for the time; then we arose, shook ourselves, smiled at nothing in particular, and the leader would find time during the comparative lull to hack out three or four fresh steps. Certain sounds, not accounted for by the elements, coming up from below, may have been suggestions or may have been arguments, but they were knocked out of all intelligible shape before they reached the head of the caravan. Not even the porter at Lloyd's or the captain of a merchantman could have made himself audible in that cyclone. Upwards we went, fighting for each step and for each yard gained as hard as if we were storming a fortress. Even while the leader had his axe in the air ready to deliver a fresh blow a distant roar would betoken another onslaught, and we instantly fell flat down like tin soldiers struck with the well-directed pea, and disposed ourselves at a convenient angle of resistance; and so we went on, when we did go on at all. If the relation is wearisome it is also realistic, for we found that the actual experience was far from being lively; but all things must have an end, including even the *feuilleton* in a Parisian newspaper or the walk up to the Bel Alp on a hot day, and the termination came almost unexpectedly.

We had got thoroughly tired of perpetually clinging on by the simple force of adhesion to the storm-swept slope, and felt almost inclined to give up the struggle against the elements and to go straight on trusting to chance. Maurer, below, wore the expression of frowning discontent best seen in amateur tenors singing a tender love ditty. Jaun had remarked half-a-dozen times that the very next squall would infallibly sweep us all away, and his cheerful prophetic utterances really seemed on the point of being fulfilled, when, almost suddenly, the snow seemed to vanish from under our feet, and we found ourselves on the summit of the ridge; at least directly above us no more ascent appeared to present. It was difficult to realise adequately the exact direction in which we were facing, but I suppose that as the ridge runs about north and south by the compass, we were facing a little south of east. This was an important matter to decide, as the mist was gathered thick around and the idea of descent had to be at once considered now that we had got to a position of some degree of definiteness. At our feet the snow slope fell away in a manner so distinct that we were without doubt really on the top of some portion of the ridge. The difficulty was to estimate how far to our right the summit of the Aiguille du Midi itself lay. However, we felt with relief the truth of somebody's remark that we had at length succeeded in getting somewhere; so far, no doubt, matters were satisfactory. Howbeit, our pleasure was somewhat modified by the discovery that the gale blew with considerably more force on the south-east side than it did on the one by which we had ascended. We looked towards the south and endeavoured to gather our wits together to elucidate the geographical problem that presented. At the foot of the slope must lie the upper basin of the Vallée Blanche and the Glacier de Tacul; unfortunately there seemed to be a prodigious storm going on in that basin, and clouds of loose snow were whirling about in all directions. It was impossible to understand these winds; one might have thought that Æolus had just stepped out to attend a committee meeting of the gods, and that all his subordinates were having high jinks during his absence.

The possibility of actually completing the ascent of the mountain seemed out of the question, and the hope that we might have crept under the shelter of the ridge to the final little rock cone of the Aiguille was literally thrown to the winds. Here again, therefore, this narrative is highly unconventional, for it is impossible to consult M. Roget's 'Thesaurus' and indulge with its aid in any grandiloquent description of the view from the summit, although my account has now reached the stage at which such word painting ought properly to be inserted. We turned to our right, the direction in which the peak lay, and walked some little way along the ridge till we got under shelter of a rock; now we were able once more to stand upright and, huddled together, took the opportunity which had been denied to us for some hours to interchange views. All agreed that the situation was vile; that word, at least, may be taken as the resultant of the various forcible epithets actually employed. All agreed that the cold was intense, the prospect doubtful, and the panorama *nil*. There was but one redeeming feature: extreme discomfort will reveal humour in those in whom that quality would not be expected *a priori* to find a dwelling-place, and to each one of us the spectacle of his three wobegone companions seemed to afford, if not amusement, at least an inkling of complacency. Maurer removed the pack from his shoulders, and it was then perceived that our cup of misery was full, and our sole remaining bottle of wine completely empty. We had originally started with two, one white and one red, of an inferior and indigestible quality, but had left the white wine down below on the snow; we had previously drunk it. The other bottle had broken against some projecting rock in climbing up, and the resulting leakage had led to the formation of a very large circular red patch in the small of Maurer's back, wherever that anatomical region might be situated in our squat and sturdy little guide. After muttering together in patois for a little while the guides seized their axes and suddenly commenced with great vigour to hack out a large hole in the ice. We fell to also, and for some few minutes all worked away with the best of good will; the splinters and little blocks of ice flew around under our blows, and before long we had excavated a flat basin capable of holding water. At the least, the exercise had the effect of warming us, and Maurer, who previously, from the effects of the cold, had been the colour of a congested alderman in the face, gradually assumed a more healthy hue. We now inquired what the object might be of preparing this cavern. Thereupon Jaun gave vent to the ingenious suggestion that we had better remain where we were and sleep in it. The idea seemed too likely to lead to permanent repose to be commendable, and we received his proposition, as befitted its nature, with some coolness, remarking that on the whole we should prefer to go home. This view led to further conversation; ultimately we descended a few feet on the south-east side and then made our way along the face of the slope in a south-westerly direction towards the hut on the Aiguille du Midi. The snow was soft, and we went on for some distance without difficulty, till we again reached the ridge on the south-west side of the Aiguille, having thus passed round the base of the final peak of the mountain, which consists of a

M

comparatively small rocky cone jutting up from the main ridge. We were still of course a long way from the hut, but as in this situation we were much more sheltered, we took the opportunity to review the state of affairs and to consider our position, which for the moment, like that of the pocket of a lady's ball dress, was indeterminate. What were we to do? As with the diners at 'Prix fixe' restaurant, there were three courses for us: we might go down on one side, we might descend on the other side, or we might remain where we were. The latter alternative was as distasteful now as it had been just previously, and it was negatived decisively. 'Very good,' said the guides; 'if you won't stay here we must go down that way,' and they pointed in a direction westerly by the compass. My companion and I were opposed to this plan for two reasons: one that the route would, if it led anywhere in particular, take us down to the Glacier des Bossons, where we did not want to go, the other that by reason of the marvellous fury of the hurricane it would have been altogether impossible to follow at all the line indicated. We were only in fact able to dart out from under shelter of the rock and peer down into the misty depths for a few seconds at a time, for the gale took our breath away as completely as in the 'cavern of the winds' at Niagara. To have climbed down a new and difficult rock cliff in the face of the numbing cold would have been little short of suicidal.

A VISION ON A SUMMIT

It is Artemus Ward, I think, who describes the ingenious manner in which Baron Trenck, of prison-breaking fame, escaped on one occasion from durance vile. For fifteen long years the Baron had lain immured, and had tried in vain to carry out all the sensational methods of escape ever suggesting themselves to his fertile brain. At last an idea occurred to him. He opened the door and walked out. By an intellectual effort of almost equal brilliancy and originality we solved the difficulty that beset us: we turned towards the south-east and walked quietly down the slope for a hundred feet or so. Simplicity of thought is characteristic of great minds. Why, nevertheless, it had not occurred to us before to escape by this line I can no more explain than I can give the reason why all the ladies in a concert-room smile, as one woman, when a singer of their own sex makes her appearance on the platform, or why itinerant harp players always wear tall hats. Immediately the complexion of affairs brightened up. The wind was much less furious than it had been on the ridge, and the hail was replaced by snow. Jaun now gave it as his opinion that the best line of descent would consist in crossing round the head of the Vallée Blanche and the upper slopes of the Glacier du Géant, so as to join the ordinary route leading from the Col du Géant to the Montanvert. But in the thick mist it would have been far from easy to hit off the right track, and we thought it possible to make a short cut to the same end, and to find a way directly down the Vallée Blanche towards the rocks known as the Petit Rognon. We had no compass with us, but the direction of the slope indicated the proper line of descent to follow. In most years it would not be easy to discover the way through the complicated crevasses of the ice-fall situated between the 'Rognon' and the easterly rocks of the Aiguille du Midi; but in 18- so much snow had fallen early in the spring and so little had melted during the summer, that we experienced comparatively little difficulty in descending almost in a straight line. During this part of the expedition the good qualities of our guides showed once more to advantage. Unquestionably while on the ridge they had put forward suggestions which were rather wild in character, and which were proved now to be mistaken. The intense cold and the beating of the storm seemed rather to have paralysed their usually calm judgment, and it is an odd fact that guides, even when first rate, are oftentimes more affected by such conditions than are the amateurs whom they conduct. We could no more, with such experience as we possessed, have led the way aright as our leader did with unerring sagacity, than an untutored person could write out a full orchestra score. We could only insist on a given line being taken if in their judgment it were possible. Once fairly started, we felt that we must push our plan through, employing the same form of argument as the man did in support of a bold statement that a certain beaver, closely pursued by a dog, had climbed up a tree. It was not a question now whether we could do it, or could not do it; we had to do it. The day was far spent, there was possibly much difficult work before us, and the exertion already undergone had been tolerably severe. The temptation was therefore great rather to scamp the work of finding the best and safest track through the ice-fall, but our leader displayed as much care and thoroughness as if he were strolling over snow slopes with a critical Chamouni guide behind him. A momentary glimpse of the familiar form of the Aiguille du Géant right in front of us confirmed the judgment that we were on the right track. In descending the ice-fall we passed to the right of the Petit Rognon, and at the base of the Séracs halted and thought we would have something to eat. Maurer produced our stock of provisions, which consisted of one roll studded with little bits of broken glass and reduced by the action of wine and water to the consistence of a poultice. The refection was, therefore, as unsatisfactory as a meal out of a loosely tied nosebag to a cab horse. And now for another departure from time-honoured custom. All mountain narratives at this period of the day make reference to the use of tobacco, the well-earned pipe, and so forth. But the sleety rain, which for the last hour and a half had replaced the snow, had soaked everything so thoroughly that an attempt to carry out the orthodox proceeding did not, like most failures, end in smoke. So we trudged on again empty and unsolaced.

As the shades of night were falling, four dripping and woe-begone travellers might, to borrow the novelist's common mode of expression, have been observed toiling up the steep path towards the old Montanvert hotel—that is, they might have been observed by anybody who was foolish enough to be out of doors on such a detestable evening. We entered the familiar little room, an ingenious compound of a toyshop and a barrack, and notwithstanding that we were viewed with marked disfavour by the other guests therein assembled in consequence of our moist and steamy condition, we seated ourselves and called for refreshment. The atmosphere in the stuffy den called the salon was a trifle pungent, and having contributed a little additional dampness to the apartment we set off again. That familiar old room with its odd collection of curiosities, in which the fare was on the whole more disproportionate to the price than at any other institution of a similar kind in the mountains, has ceased to exist long ago. I fancy that it did not require much pulling down. It is happily replaced now by one of the best managed and most comfortable mountain hotels to be found in the Alps, a sure sign of which attraction is to be found in the fact that it is, at any rate, spoken of with disfavour by the inhabitants of the village below or by such as do not hold shares. Another hour's descent and we passed through the few scattered houses just outside Chamouni. The attractions on the way down had not diverted us from our stern purpose of reaching Couttet's hotel as soon as possible. We had politely declined the invitation of a perennially knitting young woman to view a live chamois. The spasmodic smile called up by each approaching tourist faded from her countenance as we passed by. Four times did we decline the gentle refreshment of *limonade gazeuse*, once did we sternly refuse to partake of strawberries, and twice to purchase crystals. It was dark as we neared the town; it may have been my fancy, but I cannot help thinking that I perceived our old friend the blind beggar with the lugubrious expression which he wore when on duty, and with the tall hat which served the purpose of an alms'-box, and which he did not wear when on duty, enjoying himself in a very merry manner by the side of a blazing fire. Notwithstanding that night had fallen there was still a little group by the bridge round the one-armed telescope man, anxiously crowding to hear the last news of the two insane Englishmen who had without doubt perished that day miserably on the rocks of the Midi. A project had already been started to organise an expedition on the morrow to search for the bodies; and we might very possibly, if we had cared for the excitement, have been allowed to join the party.

As in a play the most striking situation is by the discreet author reserved to the conclusion, so in this contradictory chapter the most glaring deficiency comes now at the end. My readers, if they have generously followed me so far, will recognise that we not only went on something of a fool's errand, incurring considerable difficulty and perhaps risk in that mission, but that we never got up the mountain at all. The force of contradictoriness can no further go. Still, it may be pointed out that we did actually accomplish all that was novel in the expedition. Once on the ridge, the remaining portion of the climb is, in fine weather, easy and well known, so the fact that the Aiguille du Midi can be ascended by this line by any one consumed with an ambition to do so, is beyond doubt. We were not probably at one point more than twenty minutes or half an hour from the actual summit. I cannot honestly advise anybody to follow our tracks; but in all probability, if someone should desire to do so, he need not, under favourable conditions, contemplate meeting with any unsurmountable difficulties.

THE AIGUILLE DU DRU
FROM THE SOUTH

CHAPTER VI.

ASCENT OF THE AIGUILLE DU DRU

'*Decies repetita placebit*'

Disadvantages of narratives of personal adventure—Expeditions on the Aiguille du Dru in 1874—The ridge between the Aiguilles du Dru and Verte—' Défendu de passer par là '—Distance lends enchantment—Other climbers attack the peak—View of the mountain from the Col de Balme—We try the northern side, and fail more signally than usual—Showing that mountain fever is of the recurrent type—We take seats below, but have no opportunity of going up higher—The campaign opens—We go under canvas—A spasmodic start, and another failure—A change of tactics and a new leader—Our sixteenth attempt—Sports and pastimes at Chamouni—The art of cray-fishing—The apparel oft proclaims the man—A canine acquaintance—A new ally—The turning point of the expedition—A rehearsal for the final performance—A difficult descent—A blank in the narrative—A carriage misadventure—A penultimate failure—We start with two guides and finish with one—The rocks of the Dru—Maurer joins the party—Our nineteenth attempt—A narrow escape in the gully—The arête at last—The final scramble—Our foe is vanquished and decorated The return journey- Benighted—A moonlight descent—We are graciously received·· On 'fair' mountaineering—The prestige of new peaks—Chamouni becomes festive—' Heut' Abend grosses Feuerwerkfest '—Chamouni dances and shows hospitality—The scene closes in.

IT is to some extent an unfortunate circumstance that in a personal narrative of adventure the result is practically known from the very beginning. The only uncertainty that can exist is the actual pattern on which the links of the chain are united together, for the climax is from the outset a foregone conclusion. The descriptive account will inevitably conduct the reader along a more or less mazy path to an assured goal. There is certainly one other variety, but that takes the less satisfactory form of an obituary notice. Even in a thoroughly well-acted play a perceptible shudder runs through the audience when two actors select each a chair, draw them down to the footlights, and one announces ''Tis now some fourteen years ago.' The expression in its pristine dramatic simplicity may still be heard in transpontine theatres, but modern realism insists usually on a paraphrase. The audience cannot but feel, however thrilling the story to be told, that at any rate the two players have survived the adventures they have to narrate, and on the whole a good many wish they hadn't. There sit the heroes, and exert themselves as they will their recital is apt to fall somewhat flat. In like manner I will not attempt to conceal the fact that the ultimate result of our numerous attempts on the peak which forms the subject of this chapter was that we got up it, and the fact may also be divulged that we came down again, and in safety. Indeed, it seems difficult now to realise the length of time during which our ultimate success oscillated in the balance—at one time appearing hopeless, at another problematical, at times almost certain, and then again apparently out of our reach.

In 1874, with two guides, of whom Alexander Burgener was one, we started for the Montanvert with the intention of making for the ridge between the Aiguille du Dru and the Aiguille Verte, with the object of further investigating the route which Messrs. Pendlebury, Kennedy and Marshall had essayed on an occasion already described, when the bad condition of the rocks frustrated their hopes. The mountain was probably in a very different state on this occasion, and we experienced no very great difficulty in discovering a fairly easy route up the rocks. The chief trouble consisted in the fact that the rock gully by which the ascent is chiefly made was extensively plastered over with ice, a condition in which we nearly always found it. The last part of the climb up to the ridge affords a most splendid scramble. The face is so steep on either side that the climber comes quite suddenly to a position whence he overlooks the northern slope, if slope it may be called, and looks down on to the Glacier du Nant Blanc. Seen in grey shadow, or half shrouded in shifting mists and coloured only with half-tints, the precipice is magnificent; huge sheets of clear ice coat its flanks, and the almost unbroken descent of rock affords as striking a spectacle as the mountaineer fond of wild desolation can well picture.

If you would see this slope aright,
Look at it by the pale grey light.

On the left the mass of the Aiguille du Dru cuts off the view of the fertile regions; far away on the right the huge tapering towers of rock form a massive foreground stretching away to the base of the Aiguille Verte. The spectator too seems strangely shut off, so that, gazing around, on either side he can see but a narrow extent of the mountain. We looked down and did not like what we saw; we looked up and liked it less. The day was fine and the mountain in good condition. I can recall now that our eyes must have wandered over the very route that ultimately proved to be the right one, and yet to none of us that afternoon did it appear in the least degree possible. Unquestionably the crags of the Aiguille du Dru looked formidable enough from this point of view, and we could not but think that nature must have provided some easier mode of access to the summit than this face seemed to afford. We climbed along the ridge till we were almost against the face of the mountain, but then we had to turn our gaze so directly upwards that matters looked still worse. Then we faced about and climbed in the other direction. The rocks seemed to grow bigger and bigger the more we looked at them. What the guides actually thought I do not quite know, but at the moment my own impression was that it would be impossible to ascend more than two or three hundred feet: so we turned and came back. Even while we yet descended the thought came that this face of the mountain was perhaps not so utterly hopeless as it had appeared a few minutes previously, and in my own mind I decided that, should we fail in discovering some much more promising line from another point of view, we would at least return to the ridge often enough to familiarise ourselves with this aspect of the mountain, with the idea that such familiarity if it did not succeed in breeding contempt might at least give birth to a more sanguine frame of mind. The farther we got from our point of view the more hopeful did the mental impression seem to become, and by the time we reached Chamouni we had all separately arrived at the conclusion—somewhat selfish perhaps, but justifiable under the circumstances—that if asked what we thought of the possibility of ascending by the face we had tried, we would give honestly the opinion we had formed while on the ridge, and not the opinion at which we had arrived subsequently.

Other explorers were meanwhile at work on the mountain, but so far as I could learn all their attempts were made on the south-western peak. At any rate they followed more or less the line we had first struck out. Some thought that the lower peak alone was feasible, others that the higher peak was attainable only from the south-western side. So thought Mr. E. R. Whitwell; so again, Mr. J. Birkbeck, jun., both of whom reached probably a much higher point on the south-western face than we succeeded in obtaining in 1873.

In 1875 we were making our way once more by the Col de Balme to Chamouni, and being in somewhat of a reflective mood, induced by the consumption of a soup-tureen full of bread and milk at the hotel at the top of the pass, we sought a shady spot hard by whence a good view of the Aiguille du Dru could be obtained, and contemplated the precipices as seen from this point of view. The northern slope leading up to the ridge over which we had looked lay well before us. The upper part of the mountain looked distinctly different as far as accessibility was concerned. It seemed just possible, if a way could only be found up from the level of the ridge to a certain ledge some distance above, that the final mass might be feasible. There appeared to be a sort of gully sloping upwards in a direction curved away from us, in which the snow lay so thick that the rocks on either side could not, we thought, be very steep. At the least it seemed to be worth our while to make for this gully, which was obviously unattainable from the ridge itself, for it was here cut off by a belt of straight rock.

A few days later we carried the idea into effect. It was necessary to engage some one to carry the tent, and Burgener was deputed to search for a porter of a willing disposition and suitable physical conformation. Presently he came back in company with a shambling youth of great length of limb and somewhat lanky frame. We inquired if he were willing to come with us, whereupon the young man was seized with violent facial contortions, and we perceived that he suffered from an impediment in his speech. Not wishing to render him nervous by our presence, we took a short turn in the garden, leaving him where he stood. On our return the young man's efforts culminated in the remark, 'How much?' We said, 'Twenty-five francs,' and then started off to consult the barometer. On coming back after this interval we found that the young man had just previously succeeded in articulating 'Yes.' The practical result of this one-sided colloquy was that the next day the tall young man was laden with the tent, with directions to carry it up to a point immediately opposite the Montanvert below the Glacier du Nant Blanc. The tall young man shouldered his burden and started off with great activity. We followed him somewhat later under the rather transparent pretence of going to hunt for crystals next day. Making our way up by a long ridge lying between the Glacier du Nant Blanc and a little snow patch dignified in some maps by the appellation of the Glacier du Dru, we skirted round the base of the Aiguille looking constantly upwards to find some practicable line of ascent, and hoping that we might discover one which would conduct us up on to the main mass of the mountain before we had got opposite to the point by which we had made our ascent from the southern side. It soon became evident that we were very unlikely to find a way. Far above jutted out a little horizontal table of rock. Burgener observed that if we could only get there it would be something. So far his remarks did not appear inaccurate, but it was perfectly clear before long that there was no chance of getting any higher, supposing we could get on to this platform; yet a little further, and we perceived that we could not even get to it. Ultimately we discovered that the platform itself was an optical delusion. It did not seem worth while to make any attempt to reach the summit of the ridge from the side we were on, even if we could have done so, which I doubt. The day may come when the climber will seek to discover some variation to the route up the peak; but mountaineering skill will indeed have improved out of all knowledge if anyone ever succeeds in getting up this northern face. From every point of view we surveyed it, and from every point of view, in our opinion, it was equally impossible. So in the evening we came back once more to the tent, from the door of which protruded a pair of thick boots. These encased the feet articulated to the lanky legs of the tall young man, who had been enjoying a siesta of some ten or twelve hours' duration. Kicking gently at a prominent bulging of the canvas on the opposite side to the door had the effect of waking our slumbrous friend, who was exceedingly sarcastic at our want of success; so, at least, we judged by his expression of countenance. For a long while his efforts yielded no verbal result. But his words seemed as it were to stick fast in an endeavour to bring them out three or four abreast through a portal that was capable only of allowing egress to them in single file. Of a sudden the jostling syllables broke down the obstructing barrier, and he startled us by pouring forth a string of remarks with precipitate volubility. Knowing, however, that it would be some time before we could hope to try the peak again, we were not loth to leave him under the impression, to be communicated to his friends at Chamouni, that we had come to the conclusion that the mountain was inaccessible.

It was not till 1878 that we were able to revisit once more the scene of our many failures.

During the winter months, however, the thought of the stubborn Aiguille had been from time to time discussed, and when J. Oakley Maund and I came back to Chamouni we had very serious intentions. This time we were both possessed with one fixed determination with regard to the Aiguille. Either we would get up to the top or, at the worst, would, as far as lay in our power, prove that it was inaccessible by any line of attack. By my wish, our first attempts were to be made by the old route leading towards the

N

lower peak; not that we were very sanguine of succeeding by this line of ascent, but rather because we felt that no very great amount of exploration would be necessary to determine whether the higher point could or could not be reached from this side; but though our intentions were good we were scarcely prepared for the difficulties that met us from the beginning. The elements seemed to have set their faces against us. Time after time when all was ready for a start we were baulked by snow, wind, or rain. Day after day we sat waiting in vain for the favourable moment, sometimes at our bivouac high up above the Mer de Glace, by the side of the Glacier de la Charpoua, till hope deferred and a series of *table d'hôte* dinners combined with want of exercise to make the heart sick and the individual despondently dyspeptic. Perhaps the wind would shift round a point or two towards the north and a couple of fine days occur. Straightway we set off for the tent which we left concealed at the bivouac. Then came the rain again, and we had to return soaked and dejected. Sometimes it rained before we got to the Montanvert and sometimes after, and in fact we seemed to be making perpetually fitful excursions from the kitchen fire at the Montanvert to that at Couttet's hotel. On hydropathic principles we found the state of the elements no mean form of cure for the mountain fever. Still, like the hungry butler, we reflected that everything comes to him who waits, and seizing every possible opportunity did manage to achieve some climbing during the rare intervals of moderately favourable weather.

The campaign was opened with an attempt made with Jaun and Andreas Maurer as guides. A youth of hollow visage and weak joints (a relation, possibly, of our friend with the one defective articulation), who did not much enter into the spirit of the expedition, and who seemed by his expression to echo Hamlet's interrogation as to the necessity of bearing fardels, carried our tent up to the grass slopes by the Charpoua glacier. Here, on a smooth, level patch of turf surrounded on three sides by rocks, we established a little country seat, though we scarcely realised on this first occasion how often it would be our lot to run up and spend the night there, and to return to town the following morning. There are many and excellent camping places about these slopes; dry dwarf rhododendron bushes abound, and water is plentiful. There was no difficulty in rising early the next morning, for at some time in the small hours the spindle-legged porter was seized with terrible cramp. Under ordinary circumstances his lower limbs were imperfectly under his control, and when thus affected they became perfectly ungovernable, so that the neat order in which we had disposed ourselves overnight for slumber was rudely disarranged, and we were forced to rise and turn out till the spasms should have subsided. Under the influence of gentle friction the spasms quieted down, and when we left he was troubled only with a few twitching kicks, such as may be observed in a dreaming dog. At 2 A.M. we started and wended our way up the glacier, every step of which seemed familiar. To our surprise and delight the snow was in first-rate order, and our spirits rose at the prospect of a good climb; but the time had not yet come for success, and our hopes were soon to be dashed. There was still an immense amount of snow on the lower rock slopes over which access to the south-western peak is alone possible, and this snow was in a highly treacherous condition. Before we had ascended many feet the guides very properly refused to go on, a determination with which we felt ourselves bound to acquiesce. They pointed out that it would be unwarrantably dangerous to descend late in the afternoon over deep snow, soft, and but loosely adhering to the rocks. Under such conditions it is of course impossible to judge of the foothold, and there is nothing to hold on to with the hands. There was no other alternative, therefore, if we were to follow this route, than to wait till more of the snow should have melted, or else to find a track where the rocks were bare. As far as we could ascertain, however, there was no such track to be seen. We decided to go back, but still remained at

Chamouni, for we durst not lose a single favourable opportunity. With an imperturbability bred of long experience did we meet the sniggers and sneers of certain croakers below, who looked with an unfavourable eye on our proceedings.

Within the next fortnight we made two further attempts by much the same route and with the same guides, but only succeeded in going far enough to prove that the opinion of the guides was perfectly correct with regard to the state of the snow. Already matters seemed to justify some gloomy doubt as to whether we could carry out even the exploratory part of our programme, for Jaun was compelled to leave us in order to fulfil another engagement, and we scarcely knew where to turn to find another man capable of guiding us in the way we desired to go. Still our determination was unshaken by our run of ill-luck. We would not give it up. With no more definite object than that of justifying an impending *table d'hôte* dinner, I was walking up the Montanvert path one rainy afternoon, when a ray of sunlight suddenly burst upon me in the person of Alexander Burgener. He had come over the Col du Géant with a party of travellers, and to our delight was not only disengaged, but exceedingly anxious to attack once more, or, in fact, as often as we liked, the obstinate Aiguille. From the moment that he assumed the chief command matters began to wear a different complexion, for we learnt that he had taken every opportunity to consider and study the mountain. By his advice a complete change of tactics was adopted. We decided to abandon all idea of attacking the lower peak, and made up our minds to try the higher summit by the route we had first followed four years previously. We had often discussed together our chances of success on this peak, and had often come to the conclusion that its ascent was more than doubtful. But now Burgener was so positive of ultimate triumph, and so confident in his own powers, not only of getting up himself, but of getting us also to our goal, that the whole matter seemed placed before us in a different light. We might have to wait, we might have to try many times, but still we could not but believe the impression that now gradually formed that we must ultimately succeed. To the spirit which Burgener displayed that year, and which he imbued in us (at a time when it must be confessed that such a spirit was much wanted, for we were as downcast as water-cure patients during the process), and to his sagacity and great guiding qualities, the whole of our ultimate success was due. I knew that, as a guide, he was immeasurably superior to an amateur in his trained knack of finding the way, and that in quickness on rocks the two could hardly be compared. But previously it had always seemed to me that the amateur excelled in one great requisite, viz., pluck. Let this record show that in one instance at least this estimate was erroneous, for had it not been for Burgener's indomitable pluck we should never have succeeded in climbing the Aiguille du Dru.

Burgener was of opinion that from the summit of the actual ridge lying east of the higher peak, and between it and the Aiguille Verte, it was not feasible to ascend on to the face of the mountain, and he proposed accordingly that we should commence by making a study of the rocks lying to the left of the main gully running up to this same ridge, endeavouring if possible to discover some point where we could bear off to the left on to the real mass of the mountain. In addition he pointed out that the upper rocks might be very difficult and require much time (as we had already agreed together in previous years that they were altogether impossible, this remark seemed probable enough), and it was important therefore to discover the easiest and quickest way up the lower part of the rock slopes. Accordingly we departed—and this was our sixteenth attempt—from the Montanvert one morning at 1 A.M. We had long since cultivated a manner of going about our business in such a way as to avoid the gaze of the curious, and set forth on this occasion in much the same spirit that burglars adopt when on evil errands intent. The day was entirely spent as agreed in studying the lower rocks and working out accurately the most feasible line of assault. But though we ascended on this occasion to no very great height we were perpetually engaged in climbing, and the quantity of snow which still lay on the rocks rendered progress difficult and care necessary. Still it was no haphazard exploration that we were engaged in, and the spirit of deliberation in which we began begat a spirit of hopefulness as we went on. A fancied insufficiency of guiding strength, coupled with a decidedly insufficient supply of rope and an inherent idea that the new line of assault contemplated was not to be worked out to an end at the first attempt, all combined to drive us back to Chamouni late the same evening.

Après cela le déluge, and for a long time high mountaineering of any description was out of the question. Desperate were the attempts we made to amuse ourselves, and to while away the time. Sports and pastimes within the limited area of the hotel premises were the fashion for a time. The courtyard in front of Couttet's hotel was made into a lawn-tennis ground. The village stores being ransacked yielded a limited supply of parti-coloured india-rubber balls; the village carpenter constructed bats out of flat pieces of wood, and we sought to forget the unpropitious elements by playing morning, noon, and night. As a result several windows and a lamp were reduced to ruin. Then we went a-crayfishing. A basket carriage, which was constructed apparently of iron sheeting, but painted over with a wicker-work pattern in order to deceive a flea-bitten grey steed of great age with the impression that it was very light, conveyed us to Châtelard, which by a twofold inaccuracy was termed the fishing-ground, our object being to catch animals which were not fish and lived in water. There the sport began, and was conducted on this wise. Sticks with a cleft at the end, into which nondescript pieces of ill-smelling meat were wedged, were submerged in a little brook to tempt the prey, but the only bites we got were from the horse-flies and inflicted on our own persons; howbeit, one or two of the party when at a distance from their fellow-sportsmen averred that they had been on a point of catching monsters of the deep the size of lobsters. We did not discover till subsequently that, led astray by a plausible peasant possessed of riparian rights and untruthful propensities, we had been fishing (or 'crustaceaning,' to speak correctly) all day in a stream untenanted by any crayfish whatever, the result being that we caught a chill and nothing else. The ancient steed, moreover, though he bowled along merrily enough down the hill to Châtelard and required no more stimulus than an occasional chirrup from the driver afforded, was yet very loth to draw the party back up the hill at the same pace, and required such constant stimulation of a more active kind on the way back that it was found necessary before we reached the village to stop and smooth out the creases on his sides. The next day the report came that the spotted grey was 'très malade,' and the next day too my right arm was excessively stiff.

A subsequent sporting expedition yielded happier results. One of the party, gifted with diplomatic talents and a power of detecting the vulnerable points in the character of the natives, purchased, for the sum of one franc, information from a shockheaded juvenile suffering from a skin eruption as to the best stocked streams. Then did the deep yield up its carnivorous denizens. Artfully and in silence did the anglers wait for their prey to claw the reeking bait. Deftly and warily did they withdraw the rod, sometimes with two or three victims clinging in a bunch, and land the spoil on the bank. Then would the crayfish loosen their hold, roll over on their backs, flap their tails very briskly, and start off with amazing rapidity for short country walks, speedily to be captured and consigned to the recesses of a receptacle, bearing a suspicious resemblance to Madame Couttet's work-basket. Ultimately they formed the basis of a 'bisque' not unworthy of Brébant.

What time the india-rubber balls were all burst and the fishing-ground had lost its attraction, seated on a tilted chair beneath the verandah we fell a-musing and studied human nature, and the various types that presented day after day round and about the hotel.

Much was there to marvel at in many of the costumes, to many of which the late Mr. Planché himself would have been unable to assign a date. It has been noticed of course, times out of mind, as a characteristic of the Briton, that a costume in which he would not go coal-heaving at home is considered good enough for Sunday in the Alps. One gentleman indeed, whose own apparel would have been considered untidy even if he had been a member of a shipwrecked crew, had been enlarging on this topic with much fervour, to a select audience, dwelling especially on the discourtesy thus shown to the natives of the country. I looked, when Sunday came, that he should be clad in raiment of more than ordinary fitness and splendour, but the only changes that I could perceive from the week-day vesture consisted in a tall hat, which somebody had mistaken for an opera hat on some occasion, and a long strip of rag wound round a cut finger, while his wife, who had recently been on the glaciers, appeared in a low cut dress, so that she presented a curious piebald appearance. The lateness of the season may have accounted for the fact that many of the garments seemed rapidly to be resolving into their pristine condition of warp and woof, especially about the region where it is usual in the Alps to light the poison-darting lucifer matches of the country. There were flannel shirts with collars on some, and flannel shirts without them on others, while yet a third set wore white chokers round their necks made of vulcanite, so that they looked like favourite pug-dogs, or fashioned of a shiny paper, which obviously had no more to do with the garment with which they were temporarily associated than the label of an expensive wine at a second-rate restaurant has to do with the contents of the bottle. Then we fell to anatomical study, and marvelled at the various imperfections of development the muscle known to the learned as the gastrocnemius [1] could exhibit in the legs of our countrymen, and wondered why they took such pains in their costume to display its usually unsymmetrical proportions, and wondered too if they really believed that a double folding back of the upper part of the stocking below the knicker-bocker deceived anyone with an appearance of mighty thews. Then we went off and tapped the barometer, which was as devoid of principle as a bone setter, and kept on persistently rising. We made friends with a little stray waif of a dog of obsequious demeanour and cringing disposition, prone to roll over on its back when spoken to, thereby displaying a curiously speckled stomach, but which was withal inclined to be amiable, and wagged its tail so vigorously on being noticed that I quite feared it might sustain a sprain at the root of that appendage. But our friendship was short-lived. Before long our little friend found

---

[1] Described in anatomical text-books as forming the swelling of the calf.

an acquaintance in the shape of a small semi-shaved mongrel with a tail like a stalk of asparagus run to seed. After a little preliminary walking about on tiptoe, friendly overtures were made. The game commenced by the playmates licking each others' noses; next they ran round with surprising rapidity in very small circles, and then fell to wrestling in the middle of the courtyard. These canine acquaintance-ships always end in the same way. Before long a sudden, sharp squeak was heard, and the last I saw of my little friend was a vanishing form darting round the nearest corner, with his tail as much between his legs as the excessive shortness of that excrescence would permit. His playmate, somewhat disturbed for a moment by this abrupt termination of the acquaintanceship, gazed pensively, with ears erect, for a while in the direction in which his friend had vanished: then investigated two or three unimportant objects by the sense of smell, consumed a few blades of grass, yawned twice, stretched himself once, rolled on something which had puzzled him, and retired to repose at a little distance to await the expected medicinal effects of the herb of which he had partaken.

This is a true saying, that 'There's small choice in rotten apples,' and a description of boredom in one place is much like the same in another. Gradually, weariness of the flesh below in the valley became almost intolerable, while we were longing for an opportunity to weary the flesh, in another way, on the mountain. Ultimately, to my infinite regret, Maund found himself obliged to depart to fulfil an engagement elsewhere, but I still held on, though the conviction was daily becoming stronger that the rain would go on till the winter snows came.

On a mountain such as we knew the Aiguille du Dru to be it would not have been wise to make any attempt with a party of more than four. No doubt three—that is, an amateur with two guides—would have been better still, but I had, during the enforced inaction through which we had been passing, become so convinced of ultimate success that I was anxious to find a companion to share it. Fortunately, J. Walker Hartley, a highly skilful and practised mountaineer, was at Chamouni, and it required but little persuasion to induce him to join our party. Seizing an opportunity one August day when the rain had stopped for a short while, we decided to try once more, or at any rate to see what effects the climatic phases through which we had been passing had produced on the Aiguille. With Alexander Burgener and Andreas Maurer still as guides we ascended once again the slopes by the side of the Charpoua glacier, and succeeded in discovering a still more eligible site for a bivouac than on our previous attempts. A little before four the next morning we extracted each other from our respective sleeping bags, and made our way rapidly up the glacier. The snow still lay thick everywhere on the rocks, which were fearfully cold and glazed with thin layers of slippery ice; but our purpose was very serious that day, and we were not to be deterred by anything short of unwarrantable risk. We intended the climb to be merely one of exploration, but were resolved to make it as thorough as possible, and with the best results. From the middle of the slope leading up to the ridge the guides went on alone while we stayed to inspect and work out bit by bit the best routes over such parts of the mountain as lay within view. In an hour or two Burgener and Maurer came back to us, and the former invited me to go on with him back to the point from which he had just descended. His invitation was couched in gloomy terms, but there was a twinkle at the same time in his eye which it was easy to interpret—*ce n'est que l'œil qui rit*. We started off and climbed without the rope up the way which was now so familiar, but which on this occasion, in consequence of the glazed condition of the rocks, was as difficult as it could well be; but for a growing conviction that the upper crags were not so bad as they looked we should scarcely have persevered. 'Wait a little,' said Burgener, 'I will show you something presently.' We reached at last a great knob of rock close below the ridge, and for a long time sat a little distance apart silently staring at the precipices of the upper peak. I asked Burgener what it might be that he had to show me. He pointed to a little crack some way off, and begged that I would study it, and then fell again to gazing at it very hard himself. Though we scarcely knew it at the time, this was the turning point of our year's climbing. Up to that moment I had only felt doubts as to the inaccessibility of the mountain. Now a certain feeling of confident elation began to creep over me. The fact is, that we gradually worked ourselves up into the right mental condition, and the aspect of a mountain varies marvellously according to the beholder's frame of mind. These same crags had been by each of us independently, at one time or another, deliberately pronounced impossible. They were in no better condition that day than usual, in fact in much worse order than we had often seen them before. Yet, notwithstanding that good judges had ridiculed the idea of finding a way up the precipitous wall, the prospect looked different that day as turn by turn we screwed our determination up to the sticking point. Here and there we could clearly trace short bits of practicable rock ledges along which a man might walk, or over which at any rate he might transport himself, while cracks and irregularities seemed to develop as we looked. Gradually, uniting and communicating passages appeared to form. Faster and faster did our thoughts travel, and at last we rose and turned to each other. The same train of ideas had independently been passing through our minds. Burgener's face flushed, his eyes brightened, and he struck a great blow with his axe as we exclaimed almost together, 'It must, and it shall be done!'

The rest of the day was devoted to bringing down the long ladder, which had previously been deposited close below the summit of the ridge, to a point much lower and nearer to the main peak. This ladder had not hitherto been of the slightest assistance on the rocks, and had indeed proved a source of constant anxiety and worry, for it was ever prone to precipitate its lumbering form headlong down the slope. We had, it is true, used it occasionally on the glacier to bridge over the crevasses, and had saved some time thereby. Still we were loth to discard its aid altogether, and accordingly devoted much time and no little exertion to hauling it about and fixing it in a place of security. It was late in the evening before we had made all our preparations for the next assault and turned to the descent, which proved to be exceedingly difficult on this occasion. The snow had become very soft during the day; the late hour and the melting above caused the stones to fall so freely down the gully that we gave up that line of descent and made our way over the face. Often, in travelling down, we were buried up to the waist in

o

soft snow overlying rock slabs, of which we knew no more than that they were very smooth and inclined at a highly inconvenient angle. It was imperative for one only to move at a time, and the perpetual roping and unroping was most wearisome. In one place it was necessary to pay out 150 feet of rope between one position of comparative security and the one next below it, till the individual who was thus lowered looked like a bait at the end of a deep sea line. One step and the snow would crunch up in a wholesome manner and yield firm support. The next, and the leg plunged in as far as it could reach, while the submerged climber would, literally, struggle in vain to collect himself. Of course those above, to whom the duty of paying out the rope was entrusted, would seize the occasion to jerk as violently at the cord as a cabman does at his horse's mouth when he has misguided the animal round a corner. Now another step and a layer of snow not more than a foot deep would slide off with a gentle hiss, exposing bare, black ice beneath, or treacherous loose stones. Nor were our difficulties at an end when we reached the foot of the rocks, for the head of the glacier had fallen away from the main mass of the mountain, even as an ill-constructed bow window occasionally dissociates itself from the façade of a jerry-built villa, and some very complicated manœuvring was necessary in order to reach the snow slopes. It was not till late in the evening that we reached Chamouni; but it would have mattered nothing to us even had we been benighted, for we had seen all that we had wanted to see, and I would have staked my existence now on the possibility of ascending the peak. But the moment was not yet at hand, and our fortress held out against surrender to the very last by calling in its old allies, sou'westerly winds and rainy weather. The whirligig of time had not yet revolved so as to bring us in our revenge.

. . . .

Perhaps the monotonous repetition of failures on the peak influences my recollection of what took place subsequently to the expedition last mentioned. Perhaps (as I sometimes think even now) an intense desire to accomplish our ambition ripened into a realisation of actual occurrences which really were only efforts of imagination. This much I know, that when on September 7 we sat once more round a blazing wood fire at the familiar bivouac gazing pensively at the crackling fuel, it seemed hard to persuade one's-self that so much had taken place since our last attempt. Leaning back against the rock and closing the eyes for a moment it seemed but a dream, whose reality could be disproved by an effort of the will, that we had gone to Zermatt in a storm and hurried back again in a drizzle on hearing that some other climbers were intent on our peak; that we had left

Chamouni in rain and tried, for the seventeenth time, in a tempest; that matters had seemed so utterly hopeless, seeing that the season was far advanced and the days but short, as to induce me to return to England, leaving minute directions that if the snow should chance to melt and the weather to mend I might be summoned back at once; that after eight-and-forty hours of sojourn in the fogs of my native land an intimation had come by telegraph of glad tidings; that I had posted off straightway by *grande vitesse* back to Chamouni; that I had arrived there at four in the morning, in consequence of a little misadventure, which may be here parenthetically narrated.

The afternoon diligence from Geneva did not go beyond Sallanches. However, an ingenious young man of low commercial morality, who said that he had a remarkable horse and a super-excellent carriage, was persuaded to drive me on the remainder of the way to Chamouni. The young man, observing that he had been very busy of late and had not been to bed for two nights (nor had he, as might be judged, washed or tidied himself since last he sought repose), took a very hearty drink out of a tumbler and climbed on to an eminence like a long-legged footstool, which it appeared was the box seat. With much cracking of whips and various ill-tempered remarks to his horse we started with success, aided by the efforts of a well-meaning person (judging by the way in which he wore his braces loosely encircling his waist, devoted to the tending of horses), who, to oblige his friend the driver, ran suddenly at the slothful animal in the shafts and punched the beast very heartily in the ribs with his fist. Before we had gone a mile our troubles began. The coachman's ill-humour subsided, it is true, but only in consequence of Nature's soft nurse weighing his eyelids down. Accordingly I got out my axe and poked him in the back when he curled up under the influence of his fatigue. This made him swear a good deal, but for a time the device was successful enough. Gradually the monotonous jangling of the harness bells induced a somnolent disposition in me too, and I conceived then the brilliant idea, as we were ascending the long hill near St. Gervais at a walk, of planting the head of the axe against my own chest and arranging the weapon in such a way that the spike was in close contact with the small of the driver's back, so that when he fell back it would run into him. Of a sudden I opened my eyes to find that the jangling had ceased and the carriage stopped. We were undoubtedly at Chamouni, and the journey was at an end. Such, however, was not quite the case. As a matter of fact, we were not 200 yards further up the hill, the horse was peacefully grazing by the roadside, and the young man had eluded my artful contrivance by falling forwards off the box, where he lay crumpled up into a shapeless heap, peacefully asleep, entangled between the shafts, the traces, the splinter bar, and the horse's tail.

I rubbed my eyes and forced away by an effort the confused jumble and whirl of thoughts that were crowding through the brain. It was not the sound of the parting farewell as the diligence lumbered away from Chamouni, nor the slow heavy clank of the railway carriages as they entered the station, nor the voices of the railway porters that rang in my ears. Voices there were, but they were familiar. I started up and looked around. Surely that was the familiar outline of the Aiguille du Dru clear and bright above; surely that was Hartley (occupied for the moment in mollifying the effects of sunburn by anointing his face with the contents of a little squeeze-bottle), and there was Burgener; but what was this untidy, sleeping mass at our feet? Gradually it dawned upon me that I was but inverting a psychological process and trying to make a dream out of a reality. Hartley was there; Burgener was there; and the uncomely bundle was the outward form of the most incompetent guide in all the Alps. It was not till next day that we learnt that this creature had previously distinguished himself by utter imbecility in a difficult ascent up the north face of the Zermatt Breithorn, nor did we till the next day fully realise how bad a guide a man ranking as such might be. We kicked him in a suitable place and he awoke; then he made the one true remark that during our acquaintance with him he was heard to utter. He said he had been drunk the day before; with this he relapsed, and during the remainder of the time he was with us gave expression to nothing but whining complaints and inaccurate statements.

From four in the morning of the next day till seven in the evening, when we reached our bivouac again, we were climbing without intermission; not that our imbecile friend took any very active share in the day's amusement. He was roped as last man in the caravan, and Hartley had to drag him up the glacier. He was as slow of foot as he was of understanding, and took no interest in the expedition. Twice we pointed out to him half-hidden crevasses and begged that he would be careful. Twice did he acknowledge our courtesy by disappearing abruptly into the snowy depths. Then he favoured us with a short biographical sketch of his wife, her attributes, and her affection for himself: he narrated the chief characteristics of his children, and dilated on the responsible position that as father of a family (probably all crétins, if there be any truth in the hereditary transmission of parental qualities) he considered that he occupied. Finally, as he appeared disposed to give us at length a memoir of his grandfather deceased, we decided to unrope him and let him have his own way in peace. For seven hours did he crouch under a little rock, not daring to move either up or down, or even to take the knapsack off his back.

For the first time on this occasion did we succeed in climbing on to the main peak well above the level of the ridge we had so often reached, by means of leaving the gully at a much earlier point than usual. We followed the exact line that we had marked out mentally on the last occasion. At first progress was easy, but we could only make our way very slowly, seeing that we had but one short rope and only one guide; for we had injudiciously left the longer spare rope with our feeble-minded guide below, and no shouts or implorations could induce him to make his way up to us, nor had we leisure to go down to him; so we had to make the best of matters as they were. We soon found a place where the ladder might be of service, and spent some time in placing it in a position in which it remains I believe till this day.

Now, personal considerations had to a great extent to be lost sight of in the desire to make the most of the day, and the result was that Hartley must have had a very bad time of it. Unfortunately perhaps for him he was by far the lightest member of the party; accordingly we argued that he was far less likely to break the rickety old ladder than we were. Again, as the lightest weight, he was most conveniently lowered down first over awkward places when they occurred.

In the times which are spoken of as old, and which have also, for some not very definable reason, the prefix good, if you wanted your chimneys swept you did not employ an individual now dignified by the title of a Ramoneur, but you adopted the simpler plan of calling in a master sweep. This person would come attended by a satellite, who wore the outward form of a boy and was gifted with certain special physical attributes. Especially was it necessary that the boy should be of such a size and shape as to fit nicely to the chimney, not so loosely on the one hand as to have any difficulty in ascending by means of his knees and elbows, nor so tightly on the other as to run any peril of being wedged in. The boy was then inserted into the chimney and did all the work, while the master remained below or sat expectant on the roof to encourage, to preside over, and subsequently to profit by, his apprentice's exertions. We adopted much the same principle. Hartley, as the lightest, was cast for the *rôle* of the 'jeune premier' or boy, while Burgener and I on physical grounds alone filled the part, however unworthily, of the master sweep. As a play not infrequently owes its success to one actor, so did our 'jeune premier,' sometimes very literally, pull us through on the present occasion. Gallantly indeed did he fulfil his duty. Whether climbing up a ladder slightly out of the perpendicular, leaning against nothing in particular and with overhanging rocks above; whether let down by a rope tied round his waist, so that he dangled like the sign of the 'Golden Fleece' outside a haberdasher's shop, or hauled up smooth slabs of rock with his raiment in an untidy heap around his neck; in each and all of these exercises he was equally at home, and would be let down or would come up smiling. One place gave us great difficulty. An excessively steep wall of rock presented itself and seemed to bar the way to a higher level. A narrow crack ran some little way up the face, but above the rock was slightly overhanging, and the water trickling from some higher point had led to the formation of a huge bunch of gigantic icicles, which hung down from above. It was necessary to get past these, but impossible to cut them away, as they would have fallen on us below. Burgener climbed a little way up the face, planted his back against it, and held on to the ladder in front of him, while I did the same just below: by this means we kept the ladder almost perpendicular, but feared to press the highest rung heavily against the icicles above lest we should break them off. We now invited Hartley to mount up. For the first few steps it was easy enough; but the leverage was more and more against us as he climbed higher, seeing that he could not touch the rock, and the strain on our arms below was very severe. However, he got safely to the top and disappeared from view. The performance was a brilliant one, but, fortunately, had not to be repeated; as on a subsequent occasion, by a deviation of about fifteen or twenty feet, we climbed to the same spot in a few minutes with perfect ease and without using any ladder at all. On this occasion, however, we must have spent fully an hour while Hartley performed his feats, which were not unworthy of a Japanese acrobat. Every few feet of the mountain at this part gave us difficulty, and it was curious to notice how, on this the first occasion of travelling over the rock face, we often selected the wrong route in points of detail. We ascended from twenty to fifty feet, then surveyed right and left, up and down, before going any further. The minutes slipped by fast, but I have no doubt now that if we had had time we might have ascended to the final arête on this occasion. We had often to retrace our steps, and whenever we did so found some slightly different line by which time could have been saved. Though the way was always difficult nothing was impossible, and when the word at last was given, owing to the failing light, to descend, we had every reason to be satisfied with the result of the day's exploration. There seemed to be little doubt that we had traversed the most difficult part of the mountain, and, indeed, we found on a later occasion, with one or two notable exceptions, that such was the case.

However, at the time we did not think that, even if it were possible, it would be at all advisable to make our next attempt without a second guide. A telegram had been sent to Kaspar Maurer, instructing him to join us at the bivouac with all possible expedition. The excitement was thus kept up to the very last, for we knew not whether the message might have reached him, and the days of fine weather were precious.

It was late in the evening when we reached again the head of the glacier, and the point where we had left the feeble creature who had started with us as a second guide. On beholding us once more he wept copiously, but whether his tears were those of gratitude for release from the cramped position in which he had spent his entire day, or of joy at seeing us safe again, or whether they were the natural overflow of an imbecile intellect stirred by any emotion whatever, it were hard to say; at any rate he wept, and then fell to a description of some interesting details concerning the proper mode of bringing up infants, and the duties of parents towards their children: the most important of which, in his estimation, was that the father of a family should run no risk whatever on a mountain. Reaching our bivouac, we looked anxiously down over the glacier for any signs of Kaspar Maurer. Two or three parties were seen crawling homewards towards the Montanvert over the ice-fields, but no signs of our guide were visible. As the shades of night, however, were falling, we were able indistinctly to see in the far-off distance a little black dot skipping over the Mer de Glace with great activity. Most eagerly did we watch the apparition, and when finally it headed in our direction and all doubt was removed as to the personality, we felt that our constant ill-luck was at last on the eve of changing. However, it was not till two days later that we left Chamouni once more for the nineteenth and, as it proved, for the last time to try the peak.

On September 11, we sat on the rocks a few feet above the camping-place. Never before had we been so confident of success. The next day's climb was no longer to be one of exploration. We were to start as early as the light would permit, and we were to go up and always up, if necessary till the light should fail. Possibly we might have succeeded long before if we had had the same amount of determination to do so that we were possessed with on this occasion. We had made up our minds to succeed, and felt as if all our previous attempts had been but a sort of training for this special occasion. We had gone so far as to instruct our friends below to look

out for us on the summit between twelve and two the next day. We had even gone to the length of bringing a stick wherewith to make a flag-staff on the top. Still one, and that a very familiar source of disquietude, harassed us as our eyes turned anxiously to the west. A single huge band of cloud hung heavily right across the sky, and looked like a harbinger of evil, for it was of a livid colour above, and tinged with a deep crimson red below. My companion was despondent at the prospect it suggested, and the guides tapped their teeth with their forefingers when they looked in that direction; but it was suggested by a more sanguine person that its form and very watery look suggested a Band of Hope. An insinuating smell of savoury soup was wafted up gently from below—
Stealing and giving odour.

We took courage; then descended to the tent, and took sustenance.

There was no difficulty experienced in making an early start the next day, and the moment the grey light allowed us to see our way we set off. On such occasions, when the mind is strung up to a high pitch of excitement, odd and trivial little details and incidents fix themselves indelibly on the memory. I can recall as distinctly now, as if it had only happened a moment ago, the exact tone of voice in which Burgener, on looking out of the tent, announced that the weather would do. Burgener and Kaspar Maurer were now our guides, for our old enemy with the family ties had been paid off and sent away with a flea in his ear—an almost unnecessary adjunct, as anyone who had slept in the same tent with him could testify. Notwithstanding that Maurer was far from well, and rather weak, we mounted rapidly at first, for the way was by this time familiar enough, and we all meant business.

Our position now was this. By our exploration on the last occasion we had ascertained that it was possible to ascend to a great height on the main mass of the mountain. From the slope of the rocks, and from the shape of the mountain, we felt sure that the final crest would be easy enough. We had then to find a way still up the face, from the point where we had turned back on our last attempt, to some point on the final ridge of the mountain. The rocks on this part we had never been able to examine very closely, for it is necessary to cross well over to the south-eastern face while ascending from the ridge between the Aiguille du Dru and the Aiguille Verte. A great projecting buttress of rock, some two or three hundred feet in height, cuts off the view of that part of the mountain over which we now hoped to make our way. By turning up straight behind this buttress, we hoped to hit off and reach the final crest just above the point where it merges into the precipitous north-eastern wall visible from the Chapeau. This part of the mountain can only be seen from the very head of the Glacier de la Charpoua just under the mass of the Aiguille Verte. But this point of view is too far off for accurate observations, and the strip of mountain was practically, therefore, a *terra incognita* to us.

We followed the gully running up from the head of the glacier towards the ridge above mentioned, keeping well to the left. Before long it was necessary to cross the gully on to the main peak. To make the topography clearer a somewhat prosaic and domestic simile may be employed. The Aiguille du Dru and the Aiguille Verte are connected by a long sharp ridge, towards which we were now climbing; and this ridge is let in as it were into the south-eastern side of the Aiguille du Dru, much as a comb may be stuck into the middle of a hairbrush, the latter article representing the main peak. Here we employed the ladder which had been placed in the right position the day previously. Right glad were we to see the rickety old structure which had now spent four years on the mountain, and was much the worse for it. It creaked and groaned dismally under our weight and ran sharp splinters into us at all points of contact, but yet there was a certain companionship about the old ladder, and we seemed almost to regret that it was not destined to share more in our prospective success. A few steps on and we came to a rough cleft some five-and-twenty feet in depth, which had to be descended. A double rope was fastened to a projecting crag, and we swung ourselves down as if we were barrels of split peas going into a ship's hold; then to the ascent again, and the excitement waxed stronger as we drew nearer to the doubtful part of the mountain. Still, we did not anticipate insuperable obstacles; for I think we were possessed with a determination to succeed, which is a sensation often spoken of as a presentiment of success. A short climb up an easy broken gully, and of a sudden we seemed to be brought to a standstill. A little ledge at our feet curled round a projecting crag on the left. 'What are we to do now?' said Burgener, but with a smile on his face that left no doubt as to the answer. He lay flat down on the ledge and wriggled round the projection, disappearing suddenly from view as if the rock had swallowed him up. A shout proclaimed that his expectations had not been deceived, and we were bidden to follow; and follow we did, sticking to the flat face of the rock with all our power, and progressing like the skates down the glass sides of an aquarium tank. When the last man joined us we found ourselves all huddled together on a very little ledge indeed, while an overhanging rock above compelled us to assume the anomalous attitude enforced on the occupant of a little-ease dungeon. What next? An eager look up solved part of the doubt. 'There is the way,' said Burgener, leaning

P

back to get a view. 'Oh, indeed,' we answered. No doubt there was a way, and we were glad to hear that it was possible to get up it. The attractions of the route consisted of a narrow flat gully plastered up with ice, exceeding straight and steep and crowned at the top with a pendulous mass of enormous icicles. The gully resembled a half-open book standing up on end. Enthusiasts in rock-climbing who have ascended the Riffelhorn from the Görner Glacier side will have met with a similar gully, but, as a rule, free from ice, which, in the present instance, constituted the chief difficulty. The ice, filling up the receding angle from top to bottom, rendered it impossible to find hand-hold on the rocks, and it was exceedingly difficult to cut steps in such a place, for the slabs of ice were prone to break away entire. However, the guides said they could get up, and asked us to keep out of the way of chance fragments of ice which might fall down as they ascended. So we tucked ourselves away on one side, and they fell to as difficult a business as could well be imagined. The rope was discarded, and slowly they worked up, their backs and elbows against one sloping wall, their feet against the other. But the angle was too wide to give security to this position, the more especially that with shortened axes they were compelled to hack out enough of the ice to reveal the rock below. In such places the ice is but loosely adherent, being raised up from the face much as pie-crust dissociates itself from the fruit beneath under the influence of the oven. Strike lightly with the axe, and a hollow sound is yielded without much impression on the ice; strike hard, and the whole mass breaks away. But the latter method is the right one to adopt, though it necessitates very hard work. No steps are really reliable when cut in ice of this description.

The masses of ice, coming down harder and harder as they ascended without intermission, showed how they were working, and the only consolation that we had during a time that we felt to be critical, was that the guides were not likely to expend so much labour unless they thought that some good result would come of it. Suddenly there came a sharp shout and cry; then a crash as a great slab of ice, falling from above, was dashed into pieces at our feet and leaped into the air; then a brief pause, and we knew not what would happen next. Either the gully had been ascended or the guides had been pounded, and failure here might be failure altogether. It is true that Hartley and I had urged the guides to find a way some little distance to the right of the line on which they were now working; but they had reported that, though easy below, the route we had pointed out was impossible above.[1] A faint scratching noise close above

---

[1] It has transpired since that our judgment happened to be right in this matter, and we might probably have saved an hour or more at this part of the ascent.

us, as of a mouse perambulating behind a wainscot. We look up. It is the end of a rope. We seize it, and our pull from below is answered by a triumphant yell from above as the line is drawn taut. Fastening the end around my waist, I started forth. The gully was a scene of ruin, and I could hardly have believed that two axes in so short a time could have dealt so much destruction. Nowhere were the guides visible, and in another moment there was a curious sense of solitariness as I battled with the obstacles, aided in no small degree by the rope. The top of the gully was blocked up by a great cube of rock, dripping still where the icicles had just been broken off. The situation appeared to me to demand deliberation, though it was not accorded. 'Come on,' said voices from above. 'Up you go,' said a voice from below. I leaned as far back as I could, and felt about for a hand-hold. There was none. Everything seemed smooth. Then right, then left; still none. So I smiled feebly to myself, and called out, 'Wait a minute.' This was of course taken as an invitation to pull vigorously, and, struggling and kicking like a spider irritated by tobacco smoke, I topped the rock and lent a hand on the rope for Hartley to follow. Then we learnt that a great mass of ice had broken away under Maurer's feet while they were in the gully, and that he must have fallen had not Burgener pinned him to the rock with one hand. From the number of times that this escape was described to us during that day and the next, I am inclined to think that it was rather a near thing. At the time, and often since, I have questioned myself as to whether we could have got up this passage without the rope let down from above. I think either of us could have done it in time with a companion. It was necessary for two to be in the gully at the same time, to assist each other. It was necessary also to discard the rope, which in such a place could only be a source of danger. But no amateur should have tried the passage on that occasion without confidence in his own powers, and without absolute knowledge of the limit of his own powers. If the gully had been free from ice it would have been much easier.

'The worst is over now,' said Burgener. I was glad to hear it, but, looking upwards, had my doubts. The higher we went the bigger the rocks seemed to be. Still there was a way, and it was not so very unlike what I had, times out of mind, pictured to myself in imagination. Another tough scramble and we stood on a comparatively extensive ledge. With elation we observed that we had now climbed more than half of the only part of the mountain of the nature of which we were uncertain. A few steps on and Burgener grasped me suddenly by the arm. 'Do you see the great red rock up yonder?' he whispered, hoarse with excitement—' in ten minutes we shall be there and on the arête, and then——' Nothing could stop us now; but a feverish anxiety to see what lay beyond, to look on the final slope which we knew must be easy, impelled us on, and we worked harder than ever to overcome the last few obstacles. The ten minutes expanded into something like thirty before we really reached the rock. Of a sudden the mountain seemed to change its form. For hours we had been climbing the hard, dry rocks. Now these appeared suddenly to vanish from under our feet, and once again our eyes fell on snow which lay thick, half hiding, half revealing, the final slope of the ridge. A glance along it showed that we had not misjudged. Even the cautious Maurer admitted that, as far as we could see, all appeared promising. And now, with the prize almost within our grasp, a strange desire to halt and hang back came on. Burgener tapped the rock with his axe, and we seemed somehow to regret that the way in front of us must prove comparatively easy. Our foe had almost yielded, and it appeared something like cruelty to administer the final *coup de grâce*. We could already anticipate the half-sad feeling with which we should reach the top itself. It needed but little to make the feeling give way. Some one cried 'Forwards,' and instantly we were all in our places again, and the leader's axe crashed through the layers of snow into the hard blue ice beneath. A dozen steps, and then a short bit of rock scramble;

then more steps along the south side of the ridge, followed by more rock, and the ridge beyond, which had been hidden for a minute or two, stretched out before us again as we topped the first eminence. Better and better it looked as we went on. 'See there,' cried Burgener suddenly, 'the actual top!'

There was no possibility of mistaking the two huge stones we had so often looked at from below. They seemed, in the excitement of the moment, misty and blurred for a brief space, but grew clear again as I passed my hand over my eyes and seemed to swallow something. A few feet below the pinnacles and on the left was one of those strange arches formed by a great transverse boulder, so common near the summits of these aiguilles, and through the hole we could see blue sky. Nothing could lay beyond, and, still better, nothing could be above. On again, while we could scarcely stand still in the great steps the leader set his teeth to hack out. Then there came a short troublesome bit of snow scramble, where the heaped-up cornice had fallen back from the final rock. There we paused for a moment, for the summit was but a few feet from us, and Hartley, who was ahead, courteously allowed me to unrope and go on first. In a few seconds I clutched at the last broken rocks, and hauled myself up on to the sloping summit. There for a moment I stood alone gazing down on Chamouni. The holiday dream of five years was accomplished;

the Aiguille du Dru was climbed. Where in the wide world will you find a sport able to yield pleasure like this?

Mountaineers are often asked, 'What did you do when you got to the top?' With regard to this peak the same question has often been put to me, and I have often answered it, but, it must be confessed, always suppressing one or two facts. I do not know why I should conceal them now any longer, the more especially as I think there is a moral to be drawn from my experience, or I would still keep it locked up. I had tried so hard and so long to get up this little peak, that some reaction of mind was not improbable; but it took a turn which I had never before and have never since experienced in the slightest degree. For a second or two—it cannot have been longer—all the past seemed blotted out, all consciousness of self, all desire of life was lost, and I was seized with an impulse almost incontrollable to throw myself down the vertical precipice which lay immediately at my feet. I know not now, though the feeling is still and always will be intensely vivid, how it was resisted, but at the sound of the voices below the faculties seemed to return each to its proper place, and with the restoration of the menta balance the momentary idea of violently overturning the physical balance vanished. What has happened to one may have happened to others. It appeared to me quite different from what is known as mountain vertigo. In fact, I never moved at all from where I stood, and awoke, as it were, to find myself looking calmly down the identical place. It may be that the mental equilibrium under similar circumstances has not always been so fortunately restored, and that thus calamities on the mountains may have taken place. In another minute the rest of the party ascended, and we were all reposing on the hard-won summit.

Far below a little white speck representing Couttet's Hotel was well in view, and towards this we directed our telescope. We could make out a few individuals wandering listlessly about, but there did not seem to be much excitement; in front of the Imperial Hotel, however, we were pleased to imagine that we saw somebody gazing in our direction. Accordingly, with much pomp and ceremony, the stick—which it may be stated was borrowed without leave—was fixed into a little cleft and tightly wedged in; then, to my horror, Burgener, with many chuckles at his own foresight and at the completeness of his equipment, produced from a concealed pocket a piece of scarlet flannel strongly suggestive of a baby's under garment, and tied it on to the stick. I protested in vain; in a moment the objectionable rag was floating proudly in the breeze. However, it seemed to want airing. Determined that our ascent should be placed beyond doubt in the eyes of any subsequent visitors, we ransacked our stores, and were enabled to leave the following articles:—One half-pint bottle containing our names, preserved by a paper stopper from the inclemency of the weather; two wooden wedges of unknown use, two ends of string, three burnt fusees, divers chips, one stone man of dwarf proportions, the tenpenny stick, and the infant's petticoat.

There is a popular belief that the main object of climbing up a mountain is to get a view from the top. It may therefore be a matter of regret to some, but it will certainly be a matter of great congratulation to many others, that of the view obtained I can say but little. Chamouni looked very nice, however, from this distance. Turning towards the Aiguille Verte we were astonished to notice that this great mass appeared to tower far less above us than might have been expected from its much greater height and close proximity. On the other hand, the lower south-eastern peak of the Aiguille du Dru seemed much more below us than we had imagined would be the case. It is a moot point in mountaineering circles how much difference between two closely contiguous points is necessary in order that they may be rated as individual peaks. At the time we estimated the difference between the two peaks of our Aiguille to be about 80 feet, but Hartley, who has since climbed the lower point, estimates that the difference between the two must be at the very least 120 feet. Still, the comparative meagreness of the panorama did not affect our spirits, nor detract in any appreciable degree from the completeness of the expedition. The Aiguille du Dru is essentially an expedition only for those who love a good climb for climbing's sake. Every step, every bit of scrambling, was—and is still—a pleasure.

We had reached the top at half-past twelve, so that our estimate of the time required had been a very accurate one. After spending three-quarters of an hour on the summit we turned to the descent with regret, and possessed with much the same feeling as a schoolboy on Black Monday, who takes an affectionate farewell of all sorts of inanimate objects. Very difficult the descent proved to be. We were so anxious, now that our efforts had been finally crowned with success, that the whole expedition should pass off without the least misadventure, that we went much more slowly, and took more elaborate precautions than under ordinary circumstances would have been deemed necessary. From the start we had agreed that, whatever the hour, nothing should persuade us to hurry the least in the descent. On such mountains, however, as the Aiguille du Dru it is easier on the whole to get down than to get up, especially if a good supply of spare rope be included in the equipment. At three places we found it advisable to fix ropes in order to assist our progress. It was curious to observe how marvellously the aspect of the mountain was changed as we looked down the places up which we had climbed so recently; and there were so many deviations from the straight line, that the way was very difficult to find at all. Indeed, Burgener alone could hit it off with certainty, and, though last on the rope, directed the way without ever making the slightest mistake at any part. We followed precisely the same route as in ascending, and noticed few if any places where this route was capable of improvement, or even of alteration.

Not till nearly five o'clock did we regain our abandoned store of provisions; the sight of the little white packets, and especially of a certain can of tinned meat, seen at a considerable distance below, incited us to great exertions, for since ten in the morning we had partaken of nothing but a sandwich crushed out of all recognisable shape. Ignoring the probability of being benighted on the rocks, we caroused merrily on seltzer water and the contents of the tin can. It seemed almost a pity to quit for good these familiar rocks on which we had spent such a glorious time, and the sun was sinking low behind the Brévent range, and the rocks were all darkened in the grey shadows, before the guides could persuade us to pack up and resume our journey. Very little time was lost in descending when we had once started, but before we had reached a certain little sloping ledge furnished with a collection of little pointed stones, and known as the breakfast place, the darkness had overtaken us. The glacier lay only a few feet below, when the mist which had been long threatening swept up and closed in around us. The crevasses at the head of the glacier were so complicated, and the snow bridges so fragile, that we thought it wiser not to go on at once, but to wait till the snow should have had time to harden. So we sat down under an overhanging rock, and made believe that we enjoyed the fun. Hartley wedged a stone under his waist, as if he were the hind wheel of a waggon going uphill, and imitated the inaction and attitude of a person going to sleep. The guides retired to a little distance and, as is their wont when inactive, fell to a warm discussion over the dimensions of the different chamois they had shot, each of course outvying the other in turn. The game has this merit at least, when there is plenty of spare time at disposal, that if the players only begin low enough down in the animal scale it is practically unlimited.

Before long the situation ceased to be amusing, as we found that we had managed to get wet through in the gully, and that the slowly falling temperature was exceedingly unpleasant. I converted a cowhide knapsack into a temporary foot-warmer, much to the detriment of such articles of food as were still stored in its recesses, and tucked a boot under each arm to keep the leather from hardening. Then we fell to discussing what we would have next day for breakfast, and for some two hours found a certain amount of solace in disputing over the merits of divers dainty dishes. Even this fertile subject failed at length to give adequate satisfaction. The ledge became colder and colder, and new spiky little points appeared to develop every moment. The argument of the sportsmen grew fainter, and we became slowly chilled through. For a while the mind became more active, but less logical, and fanciful visions crowded thickly through it. On such occasions it is seldom possible to fix the thoughts on events immediately past. To my drowsy gaze the mist seemed to take the form of our native fogs, while the condition of the ledge suggested obtrusively a newly macadamised road. Almost at will I could transport myself in imagination to the metropolis I had so recently left, or back again to the wild little ledge on which we were stranded. Following up the train of sensations, it was easy to conceive how reason might fail altogether, and how gradually, as the senses became numbed one by one, delirium might supervene from cold and exposure—as has often happened to arctic travellers. The thoughts flew off far afield, and pictured the exact contrast of the immediate surroundings. I saw a brilliantly lighted street with long rows of flaming lamps. The windows of the clubhouses shone out as great red and orange squares and oblongs. Carriages dashed by, cabs oscillated down the roads. Elegantly attired youths about to commence their wakeful period (why are men who only know the seamy side of life called 'men of the world'? Is it so bad a world, my masters?) were strolling off to places of entertainment. A feeble, ragged creature crept along in the shadows. A worn, bright-eyed girl, just free from work which had begun at early dawn, dragged her aching limbs homewards, but stopped a moment to glance with envy at a mamma and two fair daughters crossing the pavement to their carriage; light, life, bustle, crowding everywhere. Faster and faster follow the shifting scenes till the visions jostle and become confused——A crack, a distant sound of a falling shower of stones, a hiss as they fall on to the snow slopes below. The eyes open, but the mind only half awakes, and almost immediately dreams again, with changed visions of comfortable rooms, in which the flickering light of a coal fire now throws up, now half conceals the close-drawn curtains, or the familiar form of books and pictures; visions of some formless individual with slippered feet disposed at judicious distance from the blazing coals, of soft carpets and deep arm-chairs moulded by long use into the precise intaglio adapted to the human frame; visions of a warm flood of subdued light, of things steaming gently with curling wreaths of vapour. All these passed in order before the mind, called up by the incantation of discomfort out of the cauldron of misery, like unto the regal display manifested to that impulsive and somewhat over-married individual, Macbeth.

But before long it was most difficult to picture these pleasant sights so vividly as to become altogether oblivious of an exceedingly chilly personality, and ultimately human nature triumphed, and the *ego* in a rather frozen state became again paramount. I had begun to calculate the number of hours we might have to remain where we were, and the probable state in which we should be next morning, when of a sudden the mist lifted, and disclosed the glacier just below feebly lit up by the rising moon. We sprang instantly to our feet, almost as instantaneously returning to our former positions by reason of the exceeding stiffness and cramp begotten of the cold. The guides, leaving their discussion at a point where the last speaker had, in imagination, shot a chamois about the size of an elephant, descended to inspect the ice. The snow bridges were pronounced secure, and we were soon across the crevasses, but found to our disgust that we had rather overdone the waiting. The slope was hard frozen, and in the dim light it was found necessary to cut steps nearly the whole way down the glacier. For five hours and a half were we thus engaged, and did not reach our camp till 2.30 A.M. Never did the tent look so comfortable as on that morning. If, as was remarked of Mrs. Gamp's apartment in Kingsgate Street, High Holborn, to the contented mind a cottage is a palace, so to the weary frame may a tent be a luxurious hotel. We rushed over the loose rocks by the snout of the glacier, and ran helter-skelter for our bivouac. From the circumstance that the invariable struggle for the best pillow was usually brief, and that one of the party was discovered next morning wrong end foremost in his sleeping bag with his boots still on his feet, I am disposed to think that we were not long in dropping off to sleep; but the unstudied attitudes of the party suggested rather four revellers returning from a Greenwich dinner in a four-wheeled cab over a cobbled road than a company of sober mountaineers. By seven o'clock, however, the predominant thought of breakfast so asserted itself that we woke up and looked out.

The first object that met our gaze was a large sheet of paper, affixed to the rock just in front of the tent, and bearing the simple inscription 'Hooray!' This led us to surmise that our success was already known below; for the author of the legend had returned to Chamouni the previous evening, after having seen us on the summit. To each man was apportioned the burden he should bear of the camp equipage. Such a collection of pots and pans and other paraphernalia had we amassed gradually during our stay, that our appearance as we crossed the glacier

Q

suggested rather that of certain inhabitants of Lagado mentioned in Gulliver's voyage to Laputa. By nine o'clock we had deposited our burdens at the Montanvert and, disregarding the principles of the sages above referred to, ventured to corrode our lungs by articulating our wants to the landlord. This worthy received us with more than his usual affability, for the tidings of our success had in truth already reached the inn. A bottle of conical form was produced, the cork drawn with a monstrous explosion, and some very indifferent fluid poured out as a token of congratulation. In spite of, perhaps in consequence of, these early libations, we skipped down the well-worn and somewhat unsavoury path with great nimbleness, and in an hour or so found ourselves on the level path leading along the valley to Chamouni by the English church. There, I am pleased to record, the first man to congratulate us was our old friend M. Gabriel Loppé, without whose kindly sympathy and constant encouragement I doubt if we should have ever persevered to our successful end. It mattered little to us that but few of the Chamouni guides gave us credit for having really ascended the peak, for most of them maintained that we had merely reached a point on the south-east face of the lower summit; indeed, to those not so familiar with the details of the mountain as we were, it might well seem hard to realise that the crag jutting out on the right, as seen from Chamouni, is really the actual summit.

Such is the record of the most fascinating rock climb with which I am acquainted. From beginning to end it is interesting. There is no wearisome tramping over loose moraine and no great extent of snow-field to traverse. The rocks are wondrously firm and big, and peculiarly unlike those on other mountains, even on many of the aiguilles about Chamouni.

An odd code of mountaineering morality has gradually sprung into existence, and ideas as to what is fair and sportsmanlike in mountain climbing are somewhat peculiar. People speak somewhat vaguely of 'artificial aid,' and are wont to criticise in very severe language the employment of such assistance, at the same time finding it rather hard, if driven into a corner, to define what they mean by the term. It would seem that artificial aid may signify the driving of iron pegs into rocks when nature has provided insufficient hand or foot-hold. Such a proceeding is considered highly improper. To cut a step in ice is right, but to chisel out a step on rock is in the highest degree unjustifiable. Again, a ladder may be used without critical animadversion to bridge a crevasse, but its employment over a rock cleft is tabooed. A certain amount of mountaineering equipment is not only considered proper, but those who go on the mountains without it are spoken of with great asperity, and called very hard names; but the equipment must not include anything beyond hobnails, rope, axes, and possibly a ladder for a crevasse; any other contrivance is sniffed at contemptuously as artificial aid. Rockets and such like are usually only mentioned in order to be condemned; while grapnels, chains, and crampons are held to be the inventions of the fiend. Why these unwritten laws should exist in such an imaginary code it is hard to see. Perhaps we must not consider too curiously on the matter. For my own part, if it could be proved that by no possible means could a given bad passage be traversed without some such aid, nor turned by another route, I should not hesitate to adopt any mechanical means to the desired end. As a matter of fact, in the Alps scarcely any such places exist for those who have taken the trouble to learn how to climb, and there are none on the Aiguille du Dru. We used our ladder often enough in exploring the mountain, but when we actually ascended it we employed it in one place only, saving thereby at least an hour of invaluable time. Indeed, subsequent explorers have found such to be the case; and Mr. W. E. Davidson, in a recent ascent of the mountain, was able to find his way without invoking the assistance of either ladder or fixed ropes. In a marvellously short space of time, too, did he get up and down the peak on which we had spent hours without number. Still, this is the fate of all mountains. The mountaineers who make the third ascent are, usually, able to sweep away the blushing honours that the first climbers might fondly hope they had invested the mountain with. A word, a stroke of the pen, will do it. The peaks do not yield gradually from their high estate, but fall, like Lucifer, from summit to ultimate destination, and are suddenly converted from 'the most difficult mountain in the Alps' to 'Oh yes; a fine peak, but not a patch upon Mount So-and-so.' It is but with the mountains as with other matters of this life, save in this respect, that once deposed they never can hope to reign again supreme. Statements concerning our fellow-creatures when of a depreciatory, and still more when of a scandal-flavoured, nature, are always believed by nine people out of ten to be, if not absolutely true, at any rate well-founded enough for repetition. A different estimate of the standard of veracity to be met with in this world is assumed when the remarks are favourable. Even so may it be, in some instances, with the mountains. The prestige that clings to a maiden peak is like the bark on a wand: peel it off, and it cannot be replaced; the bough withers, and is cast to one side, its character permanently altered.

We would fain have rested that evening, but the edict went forth that festivities were to take place in honour of the ascent, and, to tell the truth, that evening was not the least fatiguing part of the whole affair. The opportunity was too good to be lost, especially as the customary mode of testifying congratulations by firing off divers podgy little cannons had been omitted. Preparations were made for a display of fireworks on a large scale. Some six rockets of moderately soaring ambition were placed in order on the grass-plot in front of the hotel. A skilful pyrotechnist, who knew the right end to which to apply the match, was placed in charge, and fussed about a great deal. A very little table covered with a white cloth, and on which were displayed several bottles, reminded the crowd of loafers who assembled expectant as the darkness came on, that a carousal was meditated. At last the word was given, and the pyrotechnist, beaming with pride, advanced bearing a lighted taper attached to the end of a stick of judicious length. A hush of expectancy followed, and experienced persons retired to sheltered corners. The fireworks behaved as they usually do. They fizzed prodigiously, and went off in the most unexpected directions. One rocket, rather weak in the waist, described, after a little preliminary spluttering, an exceedingly sharp, corkscrew-like series of curves, and then turned head-over-heels with astounding rapidity on the lawn, like a rabbit shot through the head, and there lay flat, spluttering out its gunpowdery vitals. Another was perfectly unmoved at the initial application of the kindling flame, but then suddenly began to swell up in an alarming way, causing the pyrotechnist, who had no previous experience of this phenomenon, to retreat somewhat hastily. However, one of the rockets rose to a height of some five-and-twenty feet, much to the operator's satisfaction, and we were all able to congratulate him warmly on his contribution to our entertainment as we emerged from our places of security.

A series of smaller explosions, resulting from the drawing of corks, was the next item in the programme, and appeared to give more general satisfaction. Then the bell rang, and the master of the ceremonies announced that the ball was about to commence. Some over-zealous person had unfortunately sought to improve the condition of the floor for dancing, by tracing an arabesque pattern on the boards with water, using for the purpose a tin pot with a convenient leak at the bottom. It followed that the exercise of waltzing in thick boots was more laborious than graceful. Without, the villagers crowded at the windows to gaze upon our fantastic gyrations. But little formality had been observed in organising the ball; in fact, the ceremony of issuing cards of invitation had been replaced by ringing a bell and displaying a placard on which it was announced that the dance would commence at nine o'clock. However, the enjoyment appeared to be none the less keen, for all that the dancers were breathing fairly pure air, taking no champagne, and not fulfilling any social duty. But for the costumes the gathering might

have been mistaken for a fashionable entertainment.
All the recognised types to be met with in a London
ball-room were there. The conversation, judging from
the fragments overheard, did not appear to be below the
average standard of intellectuality. The ladies, who
came from the various hotels of Chamouni, displayed, as
most English girls do—*pace* the jealous criticism of certain French writers, more smart than observant—their
curious faculty of improvising ball costume exactly
suitable to the occasion. There was a young man who
had a pair of white gloves, and was looked upon
with awe in consequence, and who, in the intervals of
the dances, slid about in an elegant manner instead
of walking. There was a middle-aged person of
energetic temperament who skipped and hopped like
the little hills, and kept everything going—including
the refreshments. There was a captious and cynical
person, who frowned horribly, and sat in a corner
in the verandah with an altogether superior air, and
who, in support of the character, smoked a cigar of uncertain botanical pedigree provided by the hotel, which
disagreed with him and increased his splenetic mood.
Elsewhere, at more fashionable gatherings, he would
have leaned against doorposts, cultivated a dejected
demeanour, and got very much in other people's way.
There was a pianist who was a very clever artist, and
found out at once the notes that yielded no response
on the instrument, and who, like his more fashionable

analogue, regularly required stimulants after playing a waltz. It mattered little what he played—polka, waltz, galop, or mazurka—whatever the tune, the couples all rotated more or less slowly about; so it was evidently an English gathering. At such impromptu dances there is always a strong desire to show off musical talent. No sooner did the hireling pianist desist than a little cluster gathered around the instrument, assured him that he must be tired, and volunteered to play. Finally he was induced to rest, and a young lady who knew 'Rousseau's Dream,' or some tune very like it, triumphantly seated herself and favoured the company with that air in waltz time, whereat the unsuccessful candidates for the seat smiled scornfully at each other, and rolled up their eyes, and would not dance. So they, in turn, triumphed, and the young lady blushed, and said she had never seen such a stupid set of people, and went away and sat by her parents, and thought the world was indeed hollow. The hireling came back, and all went on merrily again.

In the yard outside the crowd increased. In the midst of the throng could be seen Maurer, resplendent in a shirt the front of which was like unto a petrified bath-towel, wearing a coat many sizes too large, his face beaming with smiles and shining from the effects of drinks offered in the spirit of good fellowship on all sides. Close by stood Burgener, displaying similar physiognomical phenomena, his natural free movements hampered by the excessive tightness of some garments with which an admirer of smaller girth had presented him. Let us do justice to the guides of Chamouni, who might not unnaturally have found some cause for disappointment that the peak had been captured by strangers in the land. On this occasion, at any rate, they offered the hand of good fellowship, and listened with admiring attention while our guides, in an unknown tongue, expatiated on the difficulties and dangers they had successfully overcome—difficulties which did not appear to become less by frequent repetition. Let us leave them there. They did their work thoroughly well, and might be pardoned, under all the circumstances, for a little swagger.

The days grow shorter apace. The sun has barely time to make the ice peaks glisten, ere the cold shadows creep over again. Snow lies thick on ledge and cranny, and only the steepest mountain faces show dark through the powdery veil. Bleak night winds whistle around the beetling crags and whirl and chevy the wreathing snow-clouds, making weird music in these desolate fastnesses, while the glaciers and snow-fields collect fresh strength against the time when their relentless destroyer shall attack them once again at an advantage. The scene is changed. The clear air, the delicate purity of the Alpine tints are but recollections, and have given way to fog, mist, slush, and smoke-laden atmosphere. Would you recall these mountain pictures? Draw close the curtains, stir the coals into an indignant crackling blaze, and fashion, in the rising smoke, the mountain vista. How easy it is to unlock the storehouse of the mind where these images are stowed away! how these scenes crowd back into the mind! What keener charm than to pass in review the memories of these simple, wholesome pleasures; to see again, as clear as in the reality, every ledge, every hand and foot-hold; to feel the fingers tingle and the muscles instinctively contract at the recollection of some tough scramble on rock or glacier? The pleasures of the Alps endure long after the actual experience, and are but invested; whether the interest can be derived by any one but the actual investor is a matter for others to decide. For my own part, I can only wish that any one could possibly derive a hundredth part of the pleasure in reading, that I have had in writing, of our adventures.

CHAPTER VII.

BYE-DAYS IN ALPINE MIDLANDS

1. *A Pardonable Digression.*

On well-ordered intellects—The drawbacks of accurate memory—Sub-Alpine walks: their admirers and their recommendations—The 'High Level Route'—The Ruinette—An infallible prescription for ill-humour—A climb and a meditation on grass slopes—The agile person's acrobatic feats—The psychological effects of sunrise—The ascent of the Ruinette—We return to our mutton at Arolla—A vision on the hill-side.

2. *A Little Maiden.*

Saas in the olden days—A neglected valley—The mountains drained dry—A curious omission—The Portienhorn, and its good points as a mountain—The chef produces a masterpiece—An undesirable tenement to be let unfurnished—An evicted family—A rapid act of mountaineering—On the pleasures of little climbs—The various methods of making new expeditions on one mountain—On the mountaineer who has nothing to learn, and his consequent ignorance.

1. *A Pardonable Digression.*

THERE are some, and they are considered, on the whole, fortunate by less highly gifted individuals, who possess minds as accurately divided up into receptacles for the storage of valuable material as a honeycomb. Every scrap of information acquired by the owner of such a well-ordered intellect is duly sifted, purged, ticketed, and finally pigeon-holed in its proper cell, whence it could undoubtedly be drawn out at any future time for reference, were it not for the fact that the pigeon-holes are all so very much alike that the geometrically minded man commonly forgets the number of the shelf to which he has relegated his item of knowledge. He need not really regret that this should be the case; persons with this exceedingly well-ordered form of mind are apt to be a little too precise for ordinary folk, and may even by the captious be rated as dull creatures. A love for the beautiful is not usually associated with excessively tidy habits of mind. An artist's studio in apple-pie order would seem as unnatural as a legal document drawn up on æsthetic principles. If the truth be told, the picturesque is always associated with—not to mince matters—the dirty; and the city of Hygeia, however commendably free from the latter quality, would be but a dreary and unattractive town. Nor would it, as seems to be sometimes supposed, be quite a paradise to that terrible and minatory person, the sanitarian. On the contrary, he would probably be found dining with the undertaker—off approved viands—and the pair would be bewailing the hard times.

I knew a man once who was marvellously proud of a certain little cabinet, devoted to the reception of keys, all of which were arranged in a remarkably orderly manner. He was fond of demonstrating the system, which seemed, in truth, highly business-like; but I lost faith one day in his method, on finding that he did not know the locks which the several keys were constructed respectively to open. It is with the mind's eye as with the bodily eye. We are able only to focus sharply one thing at a time, and the beauty of a given view, from the physiological standpoint, consists in the softened indistinctness of all objects out of the range of absolute focus—a fact of which the early Florentine artists evinced a curious disregard, and which their modern imitators, who, at least in our scientific age, ought to know something of the elementary laws of optics, render themselves somewhat ridiculous by servilely copying. So is it also with the memory. A certain indistinctness of detail often renders the recollection even more pleasing; we may be able only to reproduce from the pigeon-hole, as it were, a rather indistinct, blotted-in impression, but as the artist would be fully justified in working up such a study into a finished picture, so may the writer be allowed also to elaborate from his mental sketch a complete work. Now, in wandering in those numerous districts in the mountains of Switzerland which cannot properly be classed as sub-Alpine, and yet are not lofty enough to warrant their explorer in dignifying his rambles by the term 'climbing,' one great charm consists in the fact that, while everything is pleasing, there is no distinct objective point that we are bidden to admire. The critical tendency is a very constant factor in human character, and the chief business the professional critic has to learn consists in finding out how far he may legitimately go, and how he may best say what he is called upon to express. Now even the least critical of our race, the gushing section of humanity, feel irresistibly disposed to cavil at anything they are told they must admire. Perhaps, though, it is not the critical attributes which come out on such occasions in them. Possibly it is but an example of that still more uniformly found characteristic of man and woman, a quality which, in the process of the descent of our species, has been handed down without the least alteration from such lower animals as the mule for instance, and for which, oddly enough, we have no proper term in our language this side of the water, but know it as 'cussedness.'

Most travellers hear with a slight feeling of relief, on arriving at their destination and inquiring what there is to be seen, that there is nothing in particular, and the sub-Alpine walker has this charm perpetually with him. His expedition cannot fail, for it does not aim at any particular object on the attainment of which it depends whether he considers himself successful or not. These sub-Alpine walks and rambles form the background, the setting, the frame, and the surrounding of the more sharply defined and more memorable high expeditions. Perhaps these are but the sentiments of advancing mountaineering age; certainly they may be heard most often from those who have reached that period of life when they no longer pay heed to wrinkles in their trousers, when they are somewhat exacting in the matter of club dinners, and when they object strongly to receiving assistance from younger folk in putting on their overcoats. Howbeit, as we may recall the statement made in the 'Delectus,'—

> Neque semper arcum
> Tendit Apollo,

even so does the mountaineer occasionally relax his muscles, and find pleasure in the Alpine midlands. Moreover, the writer feels that the perpetual breathing of rarefied air may be apt to induce too great a strain on his readers, and recollects that a piano always tuned to concert pitch is not so harmonious an instrument as one occasionally unstrung; so some relief is at times necessary. Contrast, inasmuch as nature provides it on every hand, we may be sure is a thing for which man has an instinctive craving; and to my mind, at least, a picture in which rich colouring is introduced, and where the result of the blending is harmonious, is more satisfactory than the work which appeals by what I believe artists would call 'tone.' The principle applies rather widely. We may have observed that young ladies of prepossessing appearance love to be accompanied by dogs of repulsive mien. The costermonger, again, if possessed, as he always is, of a hoarse voice, is not completely equipped unless provided with a boy companion capable of sending forth in alternate measure the shrillest cries which the human larynx is capable of emitting. Thus may the pair better vaunt their wares, compel attention, and attract notice. The same objects, at any rate the latter two, influence an author, and not only in all cases, it would seem, when he is actually engaged in writing. So our expeditions, now to be described, may be looked upon as material for contrast, and may be skipped if thought fit—at any rate by purchasers—without risk of wounding the writer's feelings.

Some years ago we were travelling over that district of the Alps which to the true lover of mountain scenery can never become hackneyed—that is, the stretch of glacier land between Chamouni and Zermatt, first made known by Messrs. Foster, Jacomb, Winkfield, and others, and known to mountaineers as the 'high-level route.' We had reached Monvoisin, then, possibly still, one of the cosiest and most comfortable little inns to be found among the mountains. An immense variety of first-rate glacier passes of moderate difficulty lie between this Val de Bagne and the Arolla valley; the Col de la Serpentine, the Col Gétroz, the

Col de Brency, the Col Chermontane, and others, all of high interest and varied scenery, tempt the walker according to his powers. We selected on this occasion the Col du Mont Rouge, having a design on the bold little peak towering just above the Col, and known as the Ruinette. This peak, it may be at once mentioned, was ascended for the first time in 1865 by Mr. Edward Whymper, a mountaineer who has never ceased happily to add to his spoils and trophies since in all parts of the globe, and who, unlike most of the clan, has kept in the front rank from the day he first climbed an Alpine slope.

We arrived soaked through, and with deplorably short tempers, at the hotel at Monvoisin. Now tobacco has been vaunted as a palliative to persons in this emotional state. Liquid remedies, described by the vulgar-minded as 'a drop of something short,' or, more tersely, 'a wet,' have been recommended as tending to induce a healthier state of mind. But there is one specific remedy which never fails, and to this by tacit consent we at once resorted.

Even as one touch of nature has been stated, on reliable authority, to make the whole world kin, so may one touch of a lucifer match, if discreetly applied beneath well-seasoned logs, induce even in the most irritable and wearied individual a change of feeling and a calm contentment. As the logs crackled and spluttered, hissing like angry cats, so did the prescription purge away, if not the evil humours, at any rate the ill-humour engendered by sore feet and damp raiment, till it vanished with the smoke up the chimney. As a matter of actual fact, however, it ought to be stated that the greater part of the smoke at first made its way into the room. Before long, assisted by a passable dinner, which acts on such conditions of mind as do the remedies known to the learned in medicine as 'derivatives,' we waxed monstrous merry. We laughed heartily at our own jokes, and with almost equal fervour at those of other people—a very creditable state of feeling, as any who have associated much with facetiously disposed folk will be ready to acknowledge. As the evening wore on, and the fire burnt lower, we became more silent and thoughtful, watching the pale blue and green tongues of flame licking round the charred logs. There is a pleasure, too, in this state. No one felt disposed to break the charm of thoughtfulness in the company by throwing on fresh fuel. The fire had done its work, had helped matters on, had left things a little better than it found them—an epitome of a good and useful life. The embers fell together at last, throwing up but a few short-lived sparks; nothing remained but the recollection of what had been once so bright, and a heap of ashes—a fit emblem; for one of the party who was the life and soul of the expedition can never again join in body with us in the Alps, or revisit those Alpine midlands he loved so keenly. We rose from our seats and threw back the curtains from the window. The mists had vanished, and with them all doubt and all uncertainty, while the stream of light from the full moon seemed a promise of peace and rest from elsewhere.

At an early period of a walk there is always the greatest objection to putting forth exertion, the result of which has almost immediately to be undone. That man is indeed robust, and possessed of three times the ordinary amount of brass, if he fails not to find it distasteful to walk up a hill at the end of an expedition, or down one at the commencement. The drawback to the commanding position of the hotel at Monvoisin lies in the fact that it is absolutely necessary to descend the hill to begin with, which always seems a sinful waste of energy, seeing that the grass slopes opposite, which are steep, have immediately afterwards to be climbed. The natural grass steps looked inviting, but in the language of the Portuguese dialogue book we found them all either ' too long or much short.' One ascent over a grass slope is very much like another, and description in detail would be as wearisome as the slopes themselves often prove. Yet it is worthy of notice that there is an art to be acquired even in climbing grass slopes. We had more than one opportunity on the present occasion of seeing that persons look supremely ridiculous if they stumble about, and we noticed also that, like a bowler when he has delivered a long hop to the off for the third time in one over, the stumbler invariably inspects the nails in his boots, a proceeding which deceives no one. It is quite easy to judge of a man's real mountaineering capacity by the way in which he attacks a steep grass slope. The unskilful person, who fancies himself perfectly at home amongst the intricacies of an ice-fall, will often candidly admit that he never can walk with well-balanced equilibrium on grass, a form of vegetable which, it might be thought in many instances of self-sufficient mountaineers, would naturally suit them. There is often real danger in such places, and not infrequently the wise man will demand the use of the rope, especially when there are any tired members among the party. There is no better way of learning how to preserve a proper balance on a slope than by practising on declivities of moderate steepness, and it is astonishing to find how often those who think they have little to learn, or, still worse, believe that there is nothing to learn, will find themselves in difficulties on a mountain-side, and forced to realise that they have got themselves into a rather humiliating position. We may have seen before now, all of us, distinguished cragsmen to whom an ascent of the Weisshorn or Matterhorn was but a mere stroll, utterly pounded in botanical expeditions after Edelweiss, and compelled to regain a position of security by very ungraceful sprawls, or, worse still, have to resort to the unpardonable alternative of asking for assistance. It is on such places that the skill born of constant practice is best shown in the peasant as contrasted with the amateur; but the latter could easily acquire the art, were he not, as a rule, too high and mighty to do so. It is a great point, too, if the expedition is to be thoroughly enjoyed, to transport one's self over the earlier part of the day's climb with the least possible amount of exertion. The art possibly resembles that which, I am told, is acquired by those of ill-regulated minds, whom the force of circumstances and the interests of society compel to exercise themselves for a certain number of hours daily in that form of unproductive labour exemplified in the machine known as the treadmill. No doubt the very ardent mountaineer might find that facilities would be accorded to him during such time as he cannot visit the Alps of practising this art in the manner indicated.

Before long, the smooth unbroken snow slope leading up to the Col du Mont Rouge, glistening like a sheet of amber-coloured satin in the light of early dawn, came into sight. One of the party, who had complained throughout of the slow pace at which he had been going, and who was already far ahead, now went through a singular performance. Conceiving that he would stimulate us to greater exertion by displaying his own agility, he suddenly shot forth, as an arrow from the bow, and ran at great speed on to the snow slope. But he had misjudged the hardness of the snow. It fell out, therefore, that after two or three curious flounders his limbs suddenly shot out to all points of the compass. A desperate effort to recall his members under control resulted only in his suddenly coiling up into a little round ball, like a spider in a state of nervousness, and in that shape descending with considerable momentum, and not a few bumps, down the slope over some knobby stones and on to a fortunately placed little grass ledge. When we joined him a few minutes later, he observed unblushingly that he had found a capital place for breakfast. So have I seen a skater, after performing a few exercises of a somewhat violent nature, resembling the dances performed by nigger minstrels wearing excessively long boots, suddenly sit down and instantly adjust a perfectly correctly applied strap. On resuming our journey the agile member was firmly secured with a rope, for fear, as we told him, that he should become possessed with a sudden idea to hunt for a suitable place for luncheon by resorting to his previous tactics. Somewhat crestfallen, he took a place in the rear of the caravan, and condescended to make use of the little notches scraped out by the leader in the hard snow.

A few minutes later the full sunlight of early morning burst upon us, and produced, as it always does on such occasions, a feeling of supreme contempt for those slothful individuals who had not got up as early as we had. This moment of exhilaration is often the very best of a whole expedition, and is apt to lead, I know not why, to an ebullition of feeling, which usually takes the form of horse-play and practical joking. A series of gentle slopes led us up to the Col. Our ascent took us gradually round the base of the Ruinette, and we cast anxious glances to our right to see if any practicable line of rocks could be made out. The mountain is tolerably steep from this side, but the rocks are broken and were bare of snow. On the summit of the Col the party divided, the agile person and some of the others deciding that they would go straight on to Arolla, while Burgener and I bespoke the services of the porter, and made straight for the long buttress of rock running down almost directly to the Col on the north-west face of the mountain. Half an hour's complicated scrambling resulted in our attaining a little level plateau of rock on the ridge. As we looked down on to the great snow-field from which the Gétroz glacier takes its origin, we perceived, far away, the forms of our companions looking like a flight of driven grouse about a quarter of a minute after the sportsman has missed them with both barrels. No doubt they were enjoying themselves thoroughly, but from our point of view the sight of some four or five individuals walking along at ten-foot intervals with bowed heads and plodding gait did not suggest any very consummate pleasure. Rejoicing, therefore, that they were making nice tracks for us to follow later in the day, we turned again to the rocks above. Following always the ridge, we clambered straight up, and found opportunities for very pretty gymnastics (that is, from our own point of view) on this part of the mountain. Our object was to select rocks that would give good practice in climbing, rather than to pick out the easiest possible line, and as a result we got into more than one difficult place, difficult enough at any rate to demand much conversation on the part of the guides. In about three hours from the Col we found ourselves looking over the arête on to the southern side of the mountain with a very compact and varied view in all directions. Close by, the long ridge of the Serpentine formed a fine foreground, and a wide expanse of glacier district made up a tolerably wild panorama. A few minutes' climbing along the crest landed us above a deep notch filled in with soft snow. Into this we plunged, and in another minute or two stood on the summit of the Ruinette. So far as we knew at the time, the mountain had not previously been ascended from the northern side, and, indeed, the peak does not appear to be visited nearly so often as it deserves. Following for the most part the same line as that taken during the ascent, we regained, in about a couple of hours, the Col. Here we hunted diligently, seeking what we might devour, and feeling sure that our friends would have left us something as a reward for our energy. It transpired, however, subsequently, that the agile person's exertions had provoked in him such an appetite that there was little if anything to leave, so we followed the tracks laid out in the snow, noticing with some concern that one member of the previous party had sunk at every step some eighteen inches deeper into the soft compound than anybody else. By the marks on the snow we perceived, also, that he had trailed his axe along by his side, a sure sign of weariness. By sunset we had gained the Pas de Chévres, and ran gaily down the gentle slope towards the hotel. A little distance from the building we came so suddenly upon a manly form, outstretched, like a stranded star-fish, on a mossy bank, that we almost leaped upon his stomach. Yet he moved not, and was apparently wrapped in slumber. We stopped and crept cautiously up to survey him more closely. It was the agile person.

2. *A Little Maiden.*

In the old days of mountaineering, Saas was a place more often talked about than visited. The beauty of the scenery around was indeed unquestionable, the number of expeditions of every degree of difficulty seemed almost without limit, first-rate guides could be obtained with ease, and yet there was never any difficulty in finding quarters in the hotels. In ascending the main valley from Visp the great stream of travellers divided at Stalden into a large stream that made its way to Zermatt and a little rivulet that meandered along the much finer valley towards Saas and the Mattmark. It thus fell out that, notwithstanding a small body of indefatigable mountaineers had explored the higher peaks and passes on both sides of the valley with tolerable completeness, there was left a considerable number of smaller expeditions capable of providing good amusement for the climber desirous of acquiring fame or of exploring the less known districts. In these days, when the soaring ambition of mountaineers has led them to climb heights far greater than any found in the Alps, an account of an expedition of an unimportant peak may seem out of place. Indeed, its details were so devoid of sensational incident that the recital may be dull; but, as will appear directly, that is not the writer's fault; at any rate, he ventures to give it, for the same reason that invariably prompts youthful authors to write unnecessary books ; that is, as they say in their preface, to supply a want long felt—a want, it may be stated, usually felt in their own pockets and nowhere else.

With every respect to the older generation of mountaineers, they are much to blame in one matter. The stock of Alpine jokes is scanty; indeed, a well-read author can get them all, with a little arrangement, into the compass of one short description of a day in the mountains. Again, the number of Alpine subjects lending themselves to facetiousness is but small. The supply has been proved beyond question entirely inadequate to meet the demand, but former writers have recklessly drawn on this limited stock and entirely exhausted the topics, if not the readers. Some allowance may therefore be made when the position is considered, and it is realised that the writer is endeavouring to patch together a fabric with materials almost too threadbare for use, and that he is compelled wholly to pass by such attractive topics as the early start and consequent ill-temper, the dirty porter, the bergschrund, the use of tobacco, or the flea. The last-mentioned beast is in fact now universally prohibited from intrusion into polite Alpine literature; he has had his day. But why? he has surely some right to the place. An eminent French composer[1] has written a ballad in his honour; but though, as old Hans Andersen wrote, he was much thought of at one time, and occupied a high position, seeing that he was in the habit of mixing with the human race, and might even have royal blood in his veins, yet he is now deposed. I cannot forbear from paying a last tribute to the memory of a departing, though formerly constant, companion. To find oneself obliged to cut the acquaintance of a friend whom I have fed with my own hand must give rise to some qualms.

Unfortunately, too, the older writings are too well known of many to be dished up again in altered form, like a Sunday dinner in the suburbs; so that even the most common form of originality, videlicet, forgetfulness of the source from which you are borrowing, is forbidden. Plagiarism is a crime that seldom is allowed to pass undetected. There are many people in this world possessed of such a small amount of originality themselves, that they spend their whole time in searching for the want of that quality in others. The human inhabitants of the ark, unless they made the most of their unexampled opportunities for the study of natural history, must have become desperately bored with each other, and no doubt, when set free, said all the good things, each in their own independent nucleus of commencing society, which they had heard while immured. On the whole, it is

[1] Hector Berlioz.

fortunate for writers that the period known as the dark ages came to pass; it allowed those who commenced their career on this side of the hiatus to make, on the old lines, a perfectly fresh start.

Perhaps no country in the world has had the minute topography of its uninhabited districts so thoroughly worked out as Switzerland. Beyond question the orography is more accurately given than anywhere else; in this respect, indeed, no other country can compare with it. It might seem, even to those who have studied the matter, almost impossible to find any corner of the Alps that has not been described; and the discovery that a few superficial square yards of Swiss territory, arranged on an incline, had not been discussed in detail came upon the writer with somewhat of a shock. It was clearly somebody's duty to rectify the omission and fill the gap; whether the expedition was of importance from any point of view, or whether any one in the wide world had the smallest desire to read a description of it, was a matter of no moment whatever. There was a vacuum, and it was a thing abhorrent. The mountain, to which reference is made above, lies east of Saas, and is known to such of the inhabitants as have any knowledge of geography as the Portienhorn. Substantially this peak is the highest point of a long rocky ridge running north and south, and called the Portien Grat.

One fine evening we sat outside the inn at Saas just before dinner, seriously discussing the prospect of climbing this mountain. The guides were of opinion that we ought to sleep out, and surmised that the rocks might be found much more difficult than they looked. With some reluctance on our part thier views were allowed to prevail on the point, and they started off in triumph, promising to return and report when all the necessary preparations for starting should be completed, while we went in to prepare ourselves for the next day by an early dinner. The inn in those days was somewhat rude, and the cuisine was not remarkable save for the extraordinary faculty possessed by the chef for cooking anything that happened to come in his way, and reducing it all to the same level of tastelessness. On the present occasion, however, stimulated, no doubt, by certain critical rebukes, he had determined to surpass himself. Towards the end of the repast, as we sat chewing some little wooden toothpicks, which were found to have more flavour than anything else placed on the table, we heard the chef cross the yard and go into a certain little outhouse. A few minutes later a subtle and delicate aroma made its way into the apartment, leading us, after a few interrogative sniffs, to get up and close the window. Gradually the savour became more pronounced, and one of the party gave expression to his opinion that there was now satisfactory proof of the accuracy of his constant statement that the drains were out of order. Gradually intensifying, the savour assumed the decided character of a smell, and we looked out of window to see in which direction the cemetery lay. Stronger and stronger grew the perception as steps came mounting up the stairs; the door opened, and all doubt was set at rest as the chef entered, bearing proudly a large cheese. In a moment, to his dismay, he was left undisputed master of the apartment.

We left Saas equipped as for a serious expedition. A stout rustic, who was the most preternaturally ugly man I ever saw, led the way; he had a very large mouth and an odd-shaped face, so that he resembled a frog with a skewer wedged across inside his cheeks. On his back he bore a bag full of very spiky straw, which the guides said was a mattress. In about an hour's time we arrived at a carelessly built chalet on the Almagel Alp, of which the outside was repulsive and the inside revolting. But the experienced mountaineer, on such occasions, is not easily put out, and exhibits very little astonishment at anything he may see, and none at anything that he may smell. The hut consisted of a single apartment, furnished with a fireplace and a bed. The fireplace was situated in the centre of the room; the couch was separated by a dilapidated hoarding from a shed tenanted by a cow of insatiable appetite—indeed, it may have been originally designed as a manger. The bed, which accommodated apparently the family of the tenant, was found on actual measurement to be forty-eight inches in length and twenty in width; nevertheless the two guides packed themselves into it, adopting in their recumbent position the theory that if you keep your head and your feet warm you are all right. By the flickering gleams of firelight it could be perceived through the smoke that these were the only portions of their frames actually in the bed owing to its excessive shortness; but guides share, with babies in perambulators, a happy faculty of being able to sleep peacefully whatever be the position of their heads. The dispossessed family of the tenant would not submit, notwithstanding strong remarks, to summary eviction, and watched our proceedings with much interest. It was pointed out to them that curiosity was a vicious quality, that it had been defined as looking over other people's affairs and overlooking one's own, and that, on the whole, they had better retire, which they did reluctantly, to a little shed in which was a large copper pot with other cheese-making accessories. Apparently they spent the night in scouring the copper pot.

The mattress proved to be so tightly packed that it was easier, on the whole, to lie awake under it than to sleep on the top of it, and less painful. About 4 A.M. one of the guides incautiously moved his head, and having thus disturbed his equilibrium fell heavily on to the floor. Thereupon he woke up and said it was time to start. We bade a cheerful adieu to our host, who was obtaining such repose as could be got by the process of leaning against the doorpost, and made our way upwards.

On the south side of the Portienhorn a long and rough rocky ridge, preserving a tolerably uniform height, extends as far as the Sonnighorn. Ultimately the ridge, still running in a southerly direction, curves slightly round to the west up to the Monte Moro, and thus forms the head of the Saas valley. There are several unimportant peaks in this ridge perhaps equally worthy, with the Portienhorn, of a place in literature; but of all the points south of the Weissmies this Portienhorn is perhaps the most considerable, and certainly the most difficult of access. At any rate, we climbed the peak, and this is how we did it.

It was clear that the southern ridge was more feasible than the northern one, which drops to a col known as the Zwischbergen Pass, and then rises again to merge into the mass of the Weissmies. The whole of the western slope of the Portienhorn is covered by the Rothblatt Glacier, the ice of which is plastered up against its sides. We kept to the left of the termination of this glacier, and after a brief look round turned our steps away from the rock buttress forming the northern boundary of the glacier, though we were of opinion that we might by this line ascend the mountain; but we nevertheless selected the southern ridge, on the same principle that the sportsman, perfectly capable of flying across any obstacle, however high, sometimes, out of consideration no doubt for his horse, elects to follow somebody else through a gap. In good time we reached a point about halfway up the side of the mountain, and halted at the upper edge of a sloping patch of snow. It was fortunate that we had ample time to spare, for considerable delay was experienced here. Burgener had become newly possessed of a remarkable knife, which he was perpetually taking out of his pocket and admiring fondly; in fact, it provided material for conversation to the guides for the whole day. The knife was an intricate article, and strikingly useless, being weak in the joints; but nevertheless Burgener was vastly proud of the weapon, and valued it as much as an ugly man does a compliment. In the middle of breakfast the treasure suddenly slipped out of his hand, and started off down the slope. With a yell of anguish he bounded off after it, and went down the rocks in a manner and at a pace that only a guide in a state of excitement can exhibit. The incident was trivial, but it impressed on me the extraordinary powers of sure-footedness and quickness on rocks that a good guide possesses. An amateur might have climbed after these men the whole day, and have thought that he was nearly as good as they, but he could no more have gone down a couple of hundred feet as this guide did without committing suicide, than he could have performed a double-three backwards the first time he put on skates. He might, indeed, have gone backwards, but he would not have achieved his double-three. Turning northwards the moment we were on the arête, we made our way, with a good deal of scrambling, upwards. The rocks were firm and good, and, being dry, gave no great difficulty. Still they were far from easy, and now and again there were short passages sufficiently troublesome to yield the needed charm to a mountain climb, difficult enough at any rate to make us leave our axes behind and move one at a time. But how have the times altered since our expedition was made! Nowadays such a climb would be more fitly mentioned casually after dinner as 'a nice little walk before church,' 'a capital after-breakfast scramble,' 'a stroll strongly recommended to persons of an obese habit,' and so forth. Nevertheless, there is a very distinct pleasure in climbing up a peak of this sort—greater, perhaps, than may be found on many of the more highly rated, formidable, and, if the truth be told, fashionable mountains; for the expedition was throughout interesting, and the contrast between the view to the west where the Mischabelhörner reared up their massive forms, and to the east looking towards Domo d'Ossola and the Italian lake district, was one to repay a climber who has eyes as well as limbs. The crest was in places tolerably sharp, and we were forced at times to adopt the expedient, conventionally supposed to be the only safe one in such cases, of bestriding the rock edge. It should be stated, however, that, as usual on such occasions, when we desired to progress we discarded this position, and made our way onwards in the graceful attitude observed at the seaside in those who are hunting on the sand for marine specimens. And thus we arrived ultimately at the top, where we gave way to a properly regulated amount of subdued enthusiasm, proportionate to the difficulty and height of the vanquished mountain. No trace of previous travellers could be found on the summit. It was a maiden ascent. Doubtless the mythical and ubiquitous chamois-hunter had been up before us, for at the time I write of the district was noted for chamois; but even if he had, it makes no difference. We have found it long since necessary to look upon ascents stated to have been made by chamois-hunters as counting for nothing, and in the dearth of new peaks in the Alps, have to resort to strange devices and strained ideas for novelty. Thus, a mountain in the present day can be the means of bringing glory and honour to many climbers. For instance :—

A climbs it	First ascent.
B ascends it	First recorded ascent.
C goes up it	First ascent from the other side.
D combines A and C's expedition	First time that the peak has been 'colled.'
E scrambles up the wrong way	First ascent by the E.N.E. arête.
F climbs it in the ordinary way	First ascent by an Englishman, or first ascent without guides.
G is dragged up by his guides	First real ascent; because all the others were ignorant of the topographical details, and G's peak is nearly three feet higher than any other point.

Many more might be added; probably in the future many more will, for, in modern mountaineering phrase, the Portienhorn 'goes all over.' By 4 P.M. we were back again in the Saas valley.

It seems, as I write, only yesterday that all this happened. But a regular revolution has really taken place. There can be no question, I think, that fewer real mountaineers are to be found in the old 'playground' than formerly. Still, there are not wanting climbers, all of them apparently of the first rank. For among the high Alps now, even as on the dramatic stage of to-day, there are no amateurs.

A curious human fungus that has grown up

suddenly of late is the emancipated schoolboy spoken of by a certain, principally feminine, clique of admirers as 'such a wonderful actor, you know.' Very learned is he in the technicalities of the stage. The perspiring audience in the main drawing-room he alludes to as 'those in front.' He knows what 'battens' are, and 'flies,' and 'tormentors,' and 'spider-traps.' He endeavours to imitate well-known actors, but does not imitate the laborious process by which these same artists arrive at successful results. But we all know him, and are aware also, at any rate by report, of his overweening vanity, and the manner in which he intrudes his conception of 'Hamlet' or 'Richelieu' on a longsuffering public. Without the slightest knowledge technically of how to walk, talk, sit down, go off, or come on, he rushes on the boards possessed solely of such qualifications for his task as may arise in a brain fermenting with conceit. Critics he regards as persons existing solely for the purpose of crushing him, and showing ill-tempered hostility born of envy. The judicious, if they accept and weakly avail themselves of orders, can but grieve and marvel that there should exist that curious state of folly which prompts a man to exhibit it before the world, or even to thrust it upon his fellow-creatures. Some men are born foolish—a pity, no doubt, but the circumstances are beyond their own control; some achieve a reputation for lack of wisdom, and even make it pay; but some thrust their folly on others, and to such no quarter need be given. The self-constituted exponent of a most difficult art is not a whit more ridiculous than the boy or man who rushes at a difficult peak before he has learnt the elements of mountaineering science. A man may become a good amateur actor if he will consent to devote his leisure to ascertaining what there is to learn, and trying to learn it; and a man may become a good mountaineer by adopting the same line of action. But this is rarely the case. Too often they forget that, as a late president of the Alpine Club remarked, 'life is a great opportunity, not to be thrown away lightly.' It is said sometimes by unreflecting persons that such institutions as the Alpine Club are responsible for the misfortunes and calamities that have arisen from time to time, and may still arise. But there has been a good example set if recruits would only turn to it; for the mountaineers in the old style, speaking of a generation that climbs but little in these days, did what it is the fashion now to call their 'work' thoroughly—too thoroughly and completely, perhaps, to please altogether their successors. Novelty in the mountains of Switzerland may be exhausted, but there are still too many expeditions of which, because they have been done once or twice, the danger is not adequately recognised. If these remarks, written in no captious spirit, but rather with the strongest desire to lay stress on truths that are too often ignored, should lead any aspiring but unpractised mountaineer to pause and reflect before he tries something beyond his strength and capabilities, some little good will at least have been done. It is not that the rules are unknown; they are simple, short, ready to hand, and intelligible; but the penalty that may be exacted for breaking any of them is a terribly heavy one—*absit omen.*

CHAPTER VIII.

A SENTIMENTAL ALPINE JOURNEY

Long 'waits' and entr'actes—The Mont Buet as an unknown mountain—We hire carriages—A digression on a stationary vehicle—A straggling start—The incomplete moralist—The niece to the moralist—A discourse on gourmets—An artistic interlude—We become thoughtful, and reach the height of sentiment and the top of the Mont Buet—Some other members of the party—The mountaineers perform—How glissading ambition did o'erleap itself—A vision on the summit—The moralist leaves us for a while—Entertainment at the Bérard Chalet—View of the Aiguille Verte—The end of the journey.

A FAIR critic—in the matter of sex—discussing a recently published work with the author, remarked that it was the most charming book she had ever read. 'I was told it would not interest me,' she remarked most seriously to him, 'but really I found it delightful: there are such lovely wide margins to the pages, you know.' On much the same principle a highly intelligent lady, noted for her theatrical discrimination, once remarked that she liked those theatres best which afforded the longest entr'actes. So in the Alps we felt from time to time the necessity, between the more stirring episodes resulting from higher mountaineering, to interpose minor expeditions, on which no less care and thought was often lavished to make them worthy of pursuit. These were our entr'actes. Of such expeditions it is customary to say that they are the most enjoyable of any undertaken. Without going so far as this, it may be conceded that they have a pleasure of their own, and it is at least no more difficult to discover a novel form of sub-Alpine expedition than to vary the details of a big climb. One of these episodes, undertaken while we were barred from the higher mountains by a fall of snow, consisted in a night attack on the Mont Buet.

Now the Mont Buet, although it lies close to the regular highway to Chamouni from the Rhone valley, is a peak but rarely even seen of the ordinary tourist; and, considering the numbers of our countrymen that flock to the village whence they imagine that they see the summit of Mont Blanc, the English folk who make the ascent are strangely few. Yet the walk is not a laborious one; not more fatiguing, for example, than the tramp from Martigny to Chamouni over the Col de Balme on a hot day. Fashion in the mountains is very conservative, and probably it is too late in the day now to hope that this mountain will ever gain all the reputation it deserves, for, though comparatively unknown, its praises have been by no means left unsung. Possibly the lowness of the guides' tariff for the peak may have something to do with the matter, and may serve to explain why it is so much left out in the cold; for this is a very potent agent in determining the attractiveness of special localities. How many go to Chamouni, and never wander along one of the most beautiful sylvan paths in the Alps, that leads to the Glacier des Bossons through the woods, where the view, as the spectator suddenly finds himself confronted with the huge stream of pure glacier, topped by a most magnificent ice-fall, and backed by the crags of the Aiguille du Midi, compares by no means unfavourably with the more frequently photographed panorama from the Montanvert. Ask a dozen persons at haphazard who are staying at Chamouni where the Mont Buet is, and ten out of the number will be unable to answer you. But the pictures hung on the line are not invariably the best in an exhibition; and the Mont Buet is a masterpiece, so to speak, 'skied.'

Our party that summer at Chamouni was a large one, for we had stayed a long time in the hotel, and knew, as the phrase goes, a great many to speak to—quite a different thing to answering for them. We conceived the plan of so timing our modest expedition as to arrive on the summit of the Mont Buet about sunset. It was agreed by some members of the party that it would be 'such fun, you know,' to come down in the dark. The inference to be gathered from this is that the party was not exclusively composed of the male sex. Two of us, reputed to be good at a bargain, were deputed to charter carriages to convey the members of the expedition up to Argentière, where the ascent commenced. The carriages of Chamouni, though no doubt practical and well suited to the mountain roads, were not found to be of uniform excellence. Availing ourselves of a proper in roduction, we made the temporary acquaintance of an individual interested officially in vehicular traffic, who possessed that remarkable insight into character noticeable in all who are concerned with horses, and knew exactly what we wanted without any preliminary explanation on our part. 'Voilà votre affaire,' he said, and indicated a machine that would have been out of date when the first *char-à-banc* was constructed. We inquired if the somewhat unsavoury load (it had, apparently, been in recent requisition for farming purposes) which the cart contained might be removed, and he said there was no objection to this. 'See,' said the proprietor, 'the seats have backs.' 'But they tip up,' we remonstrated. 'That is nothing,' rejoined the proprietor; 'they can be tied down: the carriage is good, and has gone many miles. However, Monsieur is evidently particular; he shall be satisfied. Behold!' and the proprietor threw open the creaking door of a shed, and revealed to our gaze a pretentious landau with faded linings and wheels which did not seem to be circular. This 'machine,' he assured us, it would be hard to equal for locomotive purposes. Two strange beasts were connected to it, chiefly, as it seemed, by bits of string. One of the animals was supported on two very puffy hind legs and two very tremulous fore-legs, and seemed perpetually on the point of going down on its knees to supplicate that it might be allowed to go no further. Its companion was a horse of the most gloomy nature, that no amount of chastisement could stir from a despondent and pensive frame of mind. Both these treasures had a capacity for detecting an upward incline that was marvellously acute. Then there was a structure like a magnified perambulator, of which one wheel was afflicted with a chronic propensity for squeaking, while the other described a curious serpentine track as it rolled along. Not being, however, in any particular hurry, we decided to avail ourselves of such assistance as these vehicles might afford, and did, as a matter of fact, ultimately reach our destination, if not in, at least with them.

From Argentière we followed the familiar track of the Tête Noire for some little distance, and then bore away to the left up the valley leading towards the Bérard Chalet. The party, which had kept well together for the first few minutes after parting with the carriages, were soon straggling off in every direction, and the chief organiser of the expedition, desperately anxious lest some should go astray and be no more found, ran to and fro from one little group to another, and got into a highly excitable frame of mind, like a busily minded little dog when first taken out for a walk. Chief among the more erratic members was an elderly person who had, unwisely, been asked to join the party for no very definite reason, but because some one had said that it would be obviously incomplete without him. The old gentleman had no previous experience of mountain walks, but had very complete theories on the subject. He had made great preparations for his day's climb, had carefully dieted himself the day previously, and was not a little proud of his equipment and attire. He was furnished with a spiked umbrella, a green tin box, and a particularly thin pair of boots; for he wished to prove the accuracy of a theory that man, being descended from the apes, might properly use his feet as prehensile members, and he held that this additional aid would prove valuable on rocks. It was currently reported, notwithstanding his loquacity, that he was a very wise person, and indeed he dropped hints himself, which he was much annoyed if we did not take, on the subject of a projected literary work. We were given to understand that the publishers were all hankering after the same, and he had a manner in conversation of tentatively quoting passages and watching eagerly for the effects. He was known to us as the incomplete moralist, and proved to be a very didactic person.

But this was not all; there was one other member of the party, who may be described, as in the old-fashioned list of the 'Dramatis Personæ,' as 'niece to the moralist.' Somehow or another, she seemed to lead everything; instinctively all gave way to her wishes, and even the chief organiser looked to her for confirmation of his opinions before enunciating them with decision. Bright, impulsive, wilful, she led the moralist, subjectively speaking, whither she would, and he had no chance at all. 'She ought not to have come at all on such an expedition,' he said, looking at the light, fragile form ahead; 'but you know you can't persuade a butterfly to take systematic exercise, and everything seems to give her so much pleasure;' and here the moralist looked rather wistful, and somehow the artificiality seemed to fade away from him for the moment. 'Such of us,' he resumed, 'as stay long enough in this world cease to have much hopefulness; and when that quality shows up too strong in the young, such as that child yonder, somehow I don't think they often——' Here he paused abruptly, and, selecting a meat lozenge from a store in his tin box, put it into his mouth and apparently swallowed it at once; at any rate, he gulped down something. It must be allowed that the moralist had done his best to prevent his charge from accompanying the party.

She had been reminded of what learned doctors had said, that she was not to exert herself; that certain persons, vaguely alluded to, would be very angry, and so forth. The moralist had been talked down in two minutes. He might as well have pointed out to the little budding leaflets the unwisdom of mistaking warm days in March for commencing summer; and, finally, he had surrendered at discretion, fencing himself in with some stipulations as to warm cloaks, 'this once only,' and the like, which he knew would not be attended to. So she came, and her eager brightness shed a radiance over the most commonplace objects, and infected the most prosaic of the party, even a young lady of varied accomplishments, who distinguished herself later on. After all, if the flame burned a little more brightly at the expense of a limited stock of fuel, was there anything to regret? Tone down such brightness as hers was, and you have but an uncut diamond, or a plant that may possibly last a little longer because its blossom, its fruit, and with them its beauties, have been cut off to preserve the dull stem to the utmost. Check the natural characteristics and outflow of such natures, and you force them to the contemplation of what is painful and gloomy. You bring them back fully to this world, and it is their greatest privilege to be but half in it, and to have eyes blind to the seamy side. The Alpine rose-glow owes its fascination to the fact that

T

we know it will soon fade. So is it with these natures. They are to be envied. We may hold it truth with him who sings, 'Better fifty years of Europe than a cycle of Cathay.' But the parallel is not strictly true: the brightness will not fade, but will be there to the end, and the streak of sadness running through it all gives the fascination. So the wit that approaches nearest to pathos touches us most deeply, and is one of the rarest of intellectual talents. With what a thrill of mixed, but yet pleasurable, sensation do we recall the timely jest of a lost friend. But all this has nothing to do with a holiday expedition in the Alps. Still, it must be remembered, we were on a sentimental journey in the mountains.

Before long the chief organiser, seizing an opportunity when most of the stragglers were within earshot, announced at the top of his voice that luncheon would be served on certain flat rocks. This had the immediate effect of uniting our scattered forces. The first to arrive (the moralist was slow of foot) were some gallant members of the high mountaineering fraternity, who throughout the day evinced astounding activity, and an unwonted desire to carry burdens on their backs. Secretly they were burning with an ambition to display their prowess on some 'mauvais pas,' or glissade, an ambition rewarded later on in a somewhat remarkable manner. The rock was spread, the moralist selected a comfortable place, and, stimulated by the appearance of the viands, favoured us with certain extracts.

'There are many,' he observed, holding a large piece of pie to his mouth and eyeing it to select an appropriate place for the next bite, 'who hold that the sense of taste is not one to which we should much minister. I do not hold with such;' and here he found the right spot, and for a minute or two the thread of his discourse was broken off. 'The painter blends colours to please the sense of sight; the musician studies harmonics of sound to please the ear; each appeals to but one of our imperfect senses, and yet we think much of them for so doing; we compliment them, and give them the appellation of artists. Now the worthy person who dexterously compounded this article, of which, alas! I hold now but little in my hand, appeals not to a single but to a twofold sense; he ministers alike to taste and to smell, and I must own, after a toilsome walk, with commendable results. He is an artist in the highest sense of the word; his merits, to my thinking, are but inadequately recognised in this world. I am convinced that they will be more so in another. The gourmet's paradise shall provide for him a cherubic state of existence; then shall he have all the pleasure that the palate can afford without any ill-omened presage of subsequent discomfort; for, thrice happy that he will be, digestion will be an anatomical impossibility.' It may be remarked parenthetically that the possession of a gigantic brain had not obviated, in the case of the moralist, the deleterious effects of sour wine. But the moralist was not, as yet, much of a cherub.

As the speaker showed unmistakable signs of continuing his discourse, which had been chiefly directed at a youth of whom we only knew that he was some one's brother, if the opportunity were afforded, a sudden and general move was made, and the proposal that a short adjournment should take place previous to resuming our upward journey found instant favour. The chief organiser was by common consent left to pack up. Straightway the ladies all produced little sketch-books, and fell very vigorously to recording their impressions of the scenery around; whilst the moralist, already somewhat stiff, wandered from one group to the other and favoured them with his suggestions. The result of half an hour's work with pencil and brush was to produce diagrams of certain objects which looked uncommonly like telegraph poles with cross bars attached, but which were coloured of a vivid green, and were thus obviously intended for fir trees. The moralist, not finding that his remarks were met with much favour by the artists, selected an ascetic who sat apart from the others, and delivered his next discourse into his inattentive but uncomplaining ear.

'It seems strange to me,' he remarked, 'that those who are wholly unable to depict, even in the most elementary manner, the commonplace objects around them, are for ever seen in the Alps striving after the most impossible art problems. If so great a stimulus is needed, a poor result may be confidently anticipated.' (Here the moralist made a fourth attempt to light a very curious native cigar.) 'If it takes the sight of Nature in her sublimest phase, as seen in the Alps, to stimulate our friends here to show their art, why, then they haven't much of it. A milestone should be sufficient for the purpose, but it seems that they require a Matterhorn; and it may be gathered, from what I have heard you and your companions say, that what is true of Alpine art is true also of Alpine climbing, and that the *dilettanti* will never take the trouble to learn how much there is to learn. Our friends here try to paint a glacier, and have not the most elementary idea of its anatomy. They represent vast panoramas, and know nothing of distance; they——' But here the moralist, in the excitement of his discourse, turned a little white, probably from the depth of his feelings; and, throwing away his cigar, walked off alone, and was discovered shortly after perspiring a good deal, and crumpled up in a somewhat limp and helpless state.

The books were packed up, for the sun was setting low, and the party wended their way up the steep grass slope till the first great dome of the Mont Buet came well into sight. Far ahead was the niece, seemingly unconscious of the effects that the exertion of climbing told on her slight frame. She was apparently unaware of any companions around, though watchful eyes and strong hands were always near lest any mischance should befall. She spoke to no one. Nature absorbed all her faculties as she went on with cheeks rather flushed, and bright, dilated eyes drinking in every object and every point of beauty. As an artist in the exercise of his craft makes the outside world acquainted with beauties ever present to his eyes, so did the effect on her of the wondrous lights and shades and colours around call up new thoughts and reveal fresh marvels in the panorama to others, though well acquainted with such Alpine scenes. The spell caught one after another, till the whole party, all held by the same unsuspected fascination, walked silently on, while the majestic splendour around inspired an awe in the mind that even those most familiar with the marvels of nature in the mountains had never felt before. The mere recognition of the fact that the same thought or emotion is passing simultaneously through the minds of many is in itself so striking, that the impression so caused will not ever be effaced from the mind. A crowded hall is waiting for the advent of the orator of the occasion, and there enters an old man whose name and work were familiar to all. Instantly, and as if by magic, all present rose to their feet in token of respect. No word was spoken, no signal given. The matter may seem slight, but the scene was one that those present will never forget. The most hideous part of the punishment in the old days to the criminal must have been the moment when, as he stepped through the last door, the sea of faces below him upturned simultaneously with a howl of execration. And all these thoughts were called up by the fact that one consumptive girl was a member of our mountain party. Well, such was the case, and it made the expedition different in many ways from any that we had ever undertaken, but not perhaps the less worthy of remembrance.

'It looks a long way off,' observed the moralist, gazing despondently upwards. 'Do you say that the object of our expedition is to climb up to that eminence yonder? I fear lest some of the weaker members of the party should fail.' (The moralist was now the penultimate member of the party, the absolute rear being brought up by one of the guides, who was pushing him up with the head of his axe. The youth to whom he was in the habit of addressing his discourses had in a revengeful mood offered similar assistance; but the youth wore such a saturnine look when he made the suggestion, that it was declined hastily with thanks.) 'I think that if I took a little wine'—here he took all that was left—'this feeling of disinclination to move might conceivably pass off, and I could then encourage some of the others on what is clearly to them an arduous expedition. Ah me! but these little stones are excessively sharp to the feet; let us turn off on to the snow. I have heard that it is possible to walk uphill on such a medium, and yet scarce recognise the fact.' By this time most of the party were well on to the first summit, and the glories of the sunset, from a point of view which it would be hard to match in all the mountains, were beginning to display themselves to the full. The higher we ascended the more did the eternal mass of white snow on the other side of the valley develop and tower above us. Two or three of the more active members were floundering in the deep snow along the ridge uniting the two summits, and finding it, if the truth be told, no small matter to keep pace with the niece, who skimmed lightly over the surface. Gallantry and the desire to keep up their reputation forbade that they should fall to the rear, or allow the rope to tighten unduly; but their superior mountaineering experience seemed not a little in danger of being counterbalanced by their superior weight. All over the rocks on the Sixt side a thin grey veil of mist seemed to hang, making the cliffs appear still more vertical than nature had moulded them, and tinting the crags at the same time with a deep purple colour.

In the foreground, looking south, the long jagged line of the Aiguilles Rouges cut off the view into the Chamouni valley, and threw up still higher and more into relief the minor peaks of the Mont Blanc chain. We huddled together on the summit, while there seemed hardly time to turn to all points of the compass to survey the effects. The emotional members of the party came out strong, and the young lady of varied accomplishments, who was adjudged by the others to be of poetic temperament, as she was fond of alluding rather vaguely to unknown Italian geniuses, burst forth into ecstasies. However, one or two of us had rather lost faith in her historical knowledge and her profound acquaintance with mediæval art on hearing her discourse learnedly to the vacuous youth on Savonarola as an artist of great repute, and on discovering that in the family circle she was held in submission by an Italianised English governess —discreetly left at the hotel. A formidable person, this preceptress, of austere demeanour, with a dyspeptic habit, highly pomatumed ringlets, and evangelistic tendencies—a triple combination not infrequently met with. Still, no one paid any attention to the accomplished young lady, for an object in the foreground of the great picture riveted the gaze of most of us. The niece had advanced a few steps from the rest of the party, and stood a little apart on the summit ridge of the mountain, her slight form brought out in strong relief against the many-tinted sky. The folds of her dress fluttered back in the light breeze, and the night wind as it came sighing over the crest had loosened her veil and tossed it upwards. Mechanically as she raised her hand to draw it back, the thin arm and hand seemed to point upwards to something beyond what we could see. Instinctively the others all drew back a few paces, and closed in together as they watched the motionless form. The sunset glories were more than we could realise, but somehow we felt that she was gazing with fixed eyes far, far beyond these—into a pure and passionless region, beyond the mental grasp of the profoundest theologian depending on his own acquired knowledge. As we looked, though she moved no limb, her breath came faster and faster. One or two of us made a start forwards, but at that moment the last red glow vanished from the belt of fleecy cloud hanging in mid-sky. Lower down, the limestone cliffs seemed strangely desolate as the icy hand of night spread over them. The breeze suddenly dropped and died away. She stamped her foot on the snow, and with a quick movement of the head seemed to come back again to the scene around. 'Let us go,' she said, half petulantly. Silently the party arranged themselves in order as we wended our way back along the ridge. We had seen a sight that lingered in the mind, and that was not easily to be erased from the memory. As we walked along we gradually drew closer and closer together, prompted by some feeling that all seemed to share alike—as if the recollection of what we had just seen had dazed the mind, and brought us face to face with some influence beyond our ordinary thoughts, and as if with nearer union we should not feel so powerless and insignificant. But the glories of that sunset from the Mont Buet, a scene within the reach of all of very moderate walking ability, were far beyond the power of any language to describe, and beyond the province of any discreet writer to attempt. The twilight gathered in fast, and the snow already felt more crisp under foot. The roll-call was held, and it was discovered that the only absentees were the moralist and his propelling companion. At this point two of the skilled mountaineers of the party recognised their opportunity, and were not slow to seize it. Secretly they had felt that no suitable occasion had hitherto offered of displaying their prowess, so they volunteered to perform a glissade for the amusement and instruction of the others. The ladies clapped their hands gleefully, and the youth, who did not know how to glissade, looked sinister. Accordingly the skilful ones made their way to a steep snow slope, and started off with great speed and dexterity, amidst the admiring plaudits of the less acrobatically minded members. But the course of their true descent did not run entirely smooth, for before half the downward journey was accomplished the foremost member was observed suddenly to propel himself wildly into the air, performing a remarkable antic—similar to those known of street Arabs as cart-wheels—and the remainder of the journey to the foot of the slope was performed with about the grace of a floating log descending a mountain torrent. Nor was this all; the rearmost man, apparently also possessed by an identical frenzy, leaped forth into the air at precisely the same spot and in precisely the same manner. Had it not been that they were known to be highly skilful and adroit mountaineers the impression might have gained ground that the circumstances of this part of the descent were not wholly under their own control. Ever anxious to investigate the true cause of strange occurrences, to their credit be it said that when they had collected their wits and emptied their pockets of snow, they mounted up again to the scene of the disaster, and discovered the explanation in an entirely imaginary stone, which had, beyond doubt, tripped them up.

Somewhat crestfallen, the energetic pair rejoined the rest of the troupe and a search was instituted for the moralist. This worthy was discovered, astonishingly weary of body but surprisingly active of mind, wedged in a narrow rocky niche, so that he looked like the figure of a little 'Joss' in the carved model of a Japanese temple. It was found necessary to pull him vigorously by the legs, in order to straighten out those members sufficiently for him to progress upon them. However, he seemed to have more to say about the sunset than anybody else, and his description of the beauties thereof was so glowing and eloquent, that the idea crossed our minds that possibly some of the descriptions we had read in Alpine writings of similar scenes might be as authentic as that with which he favoured us. 'A great point in the Alps,' remarked the moralist, after he had been securely fastened by a rope to a guide for fear we should lose him again, so that he looked like a dancing bear—'a great point in walking amongst the Alps is that we learn to use our eyes and look around us. I have observed that those who perambulate our native flagstones appear perpetually to be absorbed in the contemplation of what lies at their feet. Now here, stimulated by the beauties around, man holds, as he should do, his head erect, and steps out boldly.' At this point a little delay was occasioned owing to the abrupt disappearance of the speaker through a crust of snow. Some curious rumblings below our feet seemed to imply that he had descended to a considerable depth, and was in great personal discomfort. In the dim light we could scarcely see what had actually happened, but concluded to pull vigorously at the rope as the best means of getting our temporarily absent friend out of his difficulties. This we succeeded in doing, and a strenuous haul on the cord was rewarded by the sudden appearance of two boots through the snow-crust at our feet—a phenomenon so unexpected that we relaxed our efforts, with the result that the boots immediately disappeared again. A second attempt was more successful; an arm and a leg this time came to the surface simultaneously, and the moralist was delivered from the snowy recesses broadside on. We rearranged his raiment, shook the snow out of the creases of his clothes, tied a bath towel round his head, which, for some obscure reason, he had brought with him—the towel, not his head—and harnessed him this time securely between two members of the party. Possibly from the effects of his misadventure, he remained silent for some time, or his flow of conversation may have been hindered by the fact that his supporters ran him violently down steep places whenever he showed symptoms of commencing a fresh dissertation. It was no easy task to find the little hut in the darkness, and it was not until after we had blundered about a good deal that we caught sight of the beacon light, consisting of a very cheap dip exhibited in the window, as a sign that entertainment for man and beast might be found within. The moralist, who was always to the fore when the subject of refreshment was mentioned, discovered a milking-stool, and drawing it in great triumph to the best place in front of the stove, sat down on it, with the immediate result that he was precipitated backwards into the ash-pan. There we left him, as being a suitable place for repentance.

The rest of the party gathered for supper round the festive board, which was rather uncertain on its legs, and inclined to tip up. Owing to some miscarriage, the larder of the cabane was not well stocked, and all the entertainment that could be furnished consisted of one bent-up little sausage, exceeding black and dry, and a very large teapot. However, there was plenty of fresh milk provided after a short interval, though the latter article was not obtained without considerable difficulty, and remonstrances proceeding from an adjoining shed, probably due to somnolence on the part of the animal from which the supply was drawn. Presently a great commotion, as of numerous bodies rolling down a steep ladder, was heard, and there appeared at the door a large collection of small shock-headed children, who gaped at us in silent wonder. Anxious to ascertain the physical effects that might be induced by the consumption of the sausage, the moralist, who amongst his many talents had apparently a turn for experimental physiology, cut off a block and placed it in the open mouth of the eldest of the children. This unexpected favour led to the boy's swallowing the morsel whole, and he shortly afterwards retired with a somewhat pained expression of countenance; the other members of the family followed shortly after in tears, in consequence of the Italianised young lady, who possessed a strong fund of human sympathy and a love for the picturesque, having made an attempt to conciliate their good-will by patting their respective heads, and asking them their names in a conjectural *patois*. We were now ready to start again, and demanded of our hostess what there was to pay. This request led her to go to the foot of the ladder, which represented a staircase, and call out for the proprietor. A little black-headed man in response instantly precipitated himself down the steps, shot into the apartment, and, without any preliminary calculation, named the exact price. On receiving his money he scuttled away again like a frightened rabbit, brought the change, jerked it down on the table, and darted off again to his slumbers. The whole transaction occupied some five-and-twenty seconds.

Part of the programme consisted in descending back to Argentière by lantern-light, but the resources of the establishment could only produce one battered machine, and it was no easy task with this illumination to keep the members of the party from straying away from the narrow path. Indeed, several members did part from the rest, curiously enough in pairs; but before long we left the narrow defile, and as we passed from under the shelter of the slope on our right, and could see across the Chamouni valley, we came suddenly in view of the great mass of the Aiguille Verte, so suddenly, indeed, that it made us start back for the moment; for, illumined by a grey ghostly light, the mountain seemed at first to hang right over us. There is, perhaps, no finer view of the Aiguille Verte to be obtained than from this point; certainly no finer effects of light and shade than were granted by the conditions under which we saw it, could have been devised to show the peak off to the best advantage. So long did we delay to dwell on the fairy-like scene, that the vacuous youth, accompanied by the young lady of varied accomplishments, caught us up and joined us quite suddenly, to their exceeding confusion. The youth, without being invited to do so, explained, blushing violently the while, that they had lost the path in the darkness, and had only been able to regain the track by lighting a series of lucifer matches—an entire fiction on his part, but condoned, as evincing more readiness of wit than we had previously given him credit for. We heard also that their way had been barred by a swamp and a mountain stream, which, like gossip, can have had no particular origin. The young lady, mindful of the absence of her preceptress and consequently heedless of grammar, described the situation neatly as being 'awfully bogs.'

If the expedition had shown us no more than this moonlight effect, the reward would have been ample.

In truth, from first to last the expedition was one which it would be hard to match for variety of interest in all the sub-Alpine district. At Argentière we rejoined the carriages, and found the horses just a little more inclined for exertion than they had been in the morning; their joy at going home seemed to be tempered by the fact that they recognised that they would inevitably be called upon to start from the same point at no very distant period; and that to return home was but to go back to the starting-point for further laborious excursions. But their equine tempers seemed thoroughly soured. The Italianised young lady was taken in charge by her elder sister, who had completed her education, and knew consequently the hollowness of the world and the folly of younger sisters' flirtations, and securely lodged in the landau. The youth, after an ineffectual attempt to find a place in the same carriage, climbed to the box seat of the other vehicle, and relieved his feelings by cracking the driver's whip with great dexterity; in fact, we discovered that this was one of his principal accomplishments. Not the least satisfactory part of the climb, in the estimation of some members of the party, was the fact that the moralist had lost his note-book during his imprisonment in the crevasse.

CHAPTER IX.

A FRAGMENT

An unauthentic MS.—Solitude on the mountain: its advantages to the historian of the Alps—A rope walk The crossing of the Schrund—A novel form of avalanche and an airy situation—A towering obstacle—The issue of the expedition in the balance—A very narrow escape—The final rush—Victory!—The perils of the descent—I plunge *in medias res* A flying descent.

THE following account is somewhat of a puzzle. It appears to contain certain facts of so startling a nature, that the ascent to which they refer must unquestionably have been of a very exciting character. The details are not so wholly unlike descriptions which have passed the searching discrimination of editors, in publications relating more or less to Alpine matters, as to warrant the assumption that they are fabrications. They do not appear, as far as the writer can ascertain, to have been seen in print hitherto; but as all Alpine writings relate but rigid matters of fact and actual occurrences, there seems no objection to publishing the manuscript, notwithstanding that its authorship is only conjectural. It is unfortunate that its fragmentary nature leaves one somewhat in doubt as to the actual peak to which the description refers.

It has been suggested by a plausible commentator, judging from internal evidence and the style of writing, that the manuscript of which the fragment consists formed part of an account originally intended for some work not published in this country, or even, possibly, was primarily designed to fill the columns of one of our own daily newspapers during the silly season.

'. . . . The day was cloudless, serene, and bright. Only in the immediate foreground did the heavy banks, betokening a *tourmente*, sweep around with relentless fury. Far above, the towering crags of the majestic peak pierced the sky. How to get there! And alone! The situation was sublime; yet more, it was fascinating; once again, it was enthralling. Far below lay the prostrate bodies of my companions, worn out, wearied, gorged with *petit vin* and sardines. A thought flashed across my mind. Why should I not scale alone these heights which had hitherto defied the most consummate *intrépides* ? In a moment the resolution was taken. For me, for me alone, should the laurel wreaths be twined. For me should the booming cannon, charged with fifty centimes' worth of uncertain powder, betoken victory. For me alone should the assortment of cheap flags which had done duty on many previous occasions of rejoicing, be dragged forth. What was the expense to a hero when the glow of so magnificent an achievement should swell his heart and loosen his purse-strings? The account might reach a sum of two and a half, nay, even five francs; but what of that? I girded myself with the trusty rope, and, attaching one end lightly to a projecting crag twenty feet above, hauled myself in a moment on to the eminence. Involuntarily I shot a glance downwards. The scene was fearful—one to make the most resolute quail. But there was no time for thought, still less for accurate description. A fearfully steep couloir, flanked by two yawning bergschrunds, stretched away horizontally right and left. How to cross them! It was the work of a moment. Unfastening the knot in the rope above me, I threw myself, heart and soul, into the work. Where heart and soul are, there must, in the ante-mortem state, be the body also. This is logic. Thus I entered the chasm. Battling desperately with the huge icicles that threatened me at every step, I forced my way through the snow bridge and breathed again. The first schrund was accomplished. Next the rope was fastened to my trusty axe, and with an herculean effort I threw it far above me; fortunately it caught in a notch, and in a few seconds I had climbed, with the agility of a monkey, up the tightened cord. Goodness gracious! (*sapristi!*) what do I hear? A sudden roar below betokened an immediate danger. Horror! sweeping and roaring up the slope from the glacier beneath, I beheld a huge avalanche. I will conceal nothing. I own that the appalling situation and its terribly dramatic nature forced me to ejaculate a cry. I do not claim originality for it. I said, "Oh! my mother!" (*Oh! ma mère!*) This relieved me. Now was the time indeed for coolness. Fortunate, most fortunate, that I was alone. Thrusting the spike of the axe into the solid rock face like the spear of Ithuriel, in the twinkling of an eye I had fastened one end of the rope to the projecting head of the axe, and the other to my waist, and launched myself over the ridge into space. Fortunate, most fortunate again, as in the hurry of the moment I had attached the rope below my own centre of gravity, that I was light-headed. Had this not been the case, assuredly I should have dangled feet uppermost over the abyss. Not a moment too soon. The avalanche dashed up the slope, grinding the axe to powder, but by good luck entangling the rope between the massive blocks and carrying it up, with myself attached, nearly 100 metres—I should say 300 feet—above where I had previously stood. I had accomplished in a moment what might have cost hours of toil. Again it was sublime. The thought crossed my mind that the sublime often approaches the ridiculous. But the rocks, previously broken up, had been ground by the sweeping avalanche into a surface smooth as polished steel. How to descend these again! Banish the thought! The mountain was not yet climbed. Upwards, past yawning séracs, towering bergschrunds, slippery crevasses, gaping arêtes, I made my way. For a few hundred feet I bounded upwards with great rapidity. Despite the rugged nature of the rocks everything went smoothly. Of a sudden a terrible obstacle was presented to my gaze. I felt that all my hopes seemingly were dashed. A stupendous cleft, riving the mountain's side to an unfathomable depth, barred further progress. From top to bottom both sides of the chasm overhung; and far below, where they joined, the angle of meeting was so sharp that I felt that I must infallibly be wedged in without hope of extrication if I fell. For a few moments I hesitated, but only for a few. Close by was a tower of rock, smooth and vertical, some twelve feet high—the height of two men, in fact. No handhold save on the top. This was but a simple matter. Had any one else been with me, I should have stood on his shoulders; as it was I stood on my own head. Thus I climbed to the summit of the pointed obelisk of rock. Exactly opposite, on the farther side of the cleft, was a similar rock cone, but the distance was too great to spring across. I was in a dilemma—on one horn of it, in fact; how to get to the other! I adopted an ingenious plan. Taking my trusty axe, I placed the pointed end in a little notch in the rock, and then, with herculean strength, bent the staff and wedged the head also into a notch. The trusty axe was now bent like a bow. Again I hesitated before trusting myself to the bow; in fact, it was long before I drew it. But a former experience stood me in good stead. Once before, driven by a less powerful impetus—merely that of a human leg—I had flown through a greater distance. I made up my mind, and, summoning all my fortitude, placed my back against the arc and, lightly touching one end, released the spring. Instantly I felt myself propelled straight into mid-air, and before I had time to realise the success of my scheme, was flung against the pinnacle on the opposite side and embraced it. What were my feelings on finding that this huge pinnacle had no more stability than a ninepin, and as my weight came on to it slowly heeled over! Nor was this all. Slowly, like the pendulum of a metronome, it rolled back again, and I found to my horror that I was clinging to the apex of the rock, and dangling right over the chasm! I cannot recall that in all my adventures I had ever been in a precisely similar situation. However, a hasty calculation satisfied me that the rocking crag must again right itself. As I expected, it did so, and as the pinnacle of rock swung back once more to the perpendicular I sprang from it with all my force. The impetus landed me safe, but the crag toppled over into the abyss. Here I noted an interesting scientific fact. Taking out my watch,

I was able to estimate, by the depth of the cleft, the height I had already climbed. *The boulder took a minute and a half in falling before it reached anywhere.* I own that the escape was a narrow one, and even my unblushing cheek paled a little at the thought of it. But I could not be far now, I hoped, from the summit; and, indeed, the condition of a dead bird which it so happened lay on the rocks—in a passive sense—convinced me that the summit of the lofty peak was close at hand. But few obstacles now remained. Another step or two revealed a glassy unbroken rock cone leading to the summit. It seemed impossible at first to surmount it, but my resources were not yet at an end. Dragging off my boots, I tore out with my teeth the long nails and drove them in one after another. By this means I ascended the first half of the final peak; but then the supply of nails was exhausted, and I felt that time would not permit me to draw out the lower nails and place them in succession above the others. Luckily I still carried with me a flask of the execrable *petit vin* supplied by Mons. —— of the inn below. I applied a little to the rock. The effect was magical. In a moment the hard face was softened to the consistence of cheese, and with my trusty axe I had no difficulty in scraping out small steps. The worst was now over. Just as the shades of night were gathering softly around, I stepped with the proud consciousness of victory on to the very highest point. This indeed was sublime. The toil of years was accomplished; it seemed almost a dream. Nerved to frenzy, with a mighty sweep of the axe I struck off a huge block from the summit to carry away as a token of conquest, and planting the weapon in the hole, tore off garment after garment to make a suitable flag; only did I desist on reflecting that it would become barely possible for me to descend if I acted thus. Intoxicated with victory, I shouted and sang for a while, and then turned to the descent. The night was fast closing in, but this mattered not, for I made light of all the obstacles, and they were so numerous that I succeeded perfectly by this means in seeing my way. Faster and faster I sped along, descending with ease over the blocks and fragments of the morning's avalanche. Now and again the descent was assisted by fastening the rope securely to projecting crags, and then allowing myself to slide down to its full length. Then I went up again, untied the rope, fastened it anew below, and repeated the manœuvre. Thus at midnight I reached the edge of the cliff, at the foot of which my companions had been left in the morning. I feared they might be anxious for my safety, the more especially that I had not yet paid them for their services. Peering over the edge of the vertical precipice into the murky darkness, I called out. There was no response. Then I said "Pst," and tapped the glassy slope with my pocket knife. Even this plan failed to attract their attention. I shouted with still more force. Finally, standing up on the edge of the cliff, I sent forth a shout so terribly loud that it must have waked even a sleeping adder. A fatal error! for the reverberation of my voice was echoed back with such fearful force from a neighbouring crag that the shock struck me backwards, and in a moment I was flying through mid-air—to annihilation.'

. . . . . .

'There is a blank in this narrative which I can never fill up. This only do I know; that when I came again to my senses, I was warmly ensconced in a blanket, whilst my companions stood around in a circle shivering, as they gazed at me with amazement. Their account, which I can scarcely credit, was that as they were engaged in stretching out and shaking a blanket preparatory to spreading their bed for the night, an apparently heaven-sent form had descended from above into the very middle of it; the shock tore the blanket from their grasp, and in a twinkling I lay wrapt up safe and comfortable at their feet.'

Such is the fragment. It has been thought better to present it as far as possible in its original form, and without any editing. That the account is a little highly coloured perhaps in parts may be allowed, but some licence may legitimately be accorded to an author who is no empty dreamer, but has evidently experienced some rather exciting episodes.

CHAPTER X.

THE FUTURE OF MOUNTAINEERING

Mountaineers and their critics—The early days of the Alpine Club—The founders of mountaineering—The growth of the amusement—Novelty and exploration—The formation of centres—Narrowing of the field of mountaineering—The upward limit of mountaineering—De Saussure's experience—Modern development of climbing—Mr. Whymper's experience—Mr. Graham's experience—The ascent of great heights—Mr. Grove's views—Messrs. Coxwell and Glaisher's balloon experiences—Reasons for dissenting from Mr. Glaisher's views—The possibility of ascending Mount Everest—Physiological aspect of the question—Acclimatisation to great heights—The direction in which mountaineering should be developed—The results that may be obtained—Chamouni a century hence—A Rip van Winkle in the Pennine Alps—The dangers of mountaineering—Conclusion.

FROM time to time, when some accident has happened in the Alps, the press and the public have been pleased to take such unfortunate occurrence as a text, and to preach serious sermons to mountaineers. We have been called hard names in our time; we have been accused of fostering an amusement of no earthly practical good, and one which has led to 'miserable' waste of valuable life. Gentle expressions of animadversion, such as 'criminal folly,' 'reckless venture, which has no better purpose than the gratification of a caprice or the indulgence of a small ambition,' 'a subject of humiliating interest,' and the like, have at times been freely used. But it is well known to authors and to dramatists that criticisms of a nature known as 'smashing' are not, on the whole, always to be deplored, and are occasionally the best to enhance the success of the work. The novel or play, however unreservedly condemned by the reviewer, has got some chance of living if it be hinted that some of the situations in it are a little *risquées*; and to a great many the idea seems constantly present that mountaineering owes its principal attraction to the element of risk inseparable from its pursuit. As an absolute matter of fact such is not the case. Apart from this, however, mountaineers may be thankful that the critics in question have, when they noticed our doings at all, condemned us very heartily indeed, and thundered forth their own strictures on our folly in sonorous terms; in fact, attacks of this nature have by no means impaired the vitality of such associations as Alpine clubs, but rather, like attacks of distemper in dogs, have increased their value.

It would be easy enough, from the mountaineer's point of view, and in a work which, at the best, can interest only those who have some sympathy with climbing as a pure pastime, to pass over these hard words, and to reckon them as merely the vapourings of envious mortals not initiated into the mysteries of the mountaineering craft; but such criticisms may lead or perhaps reflect public opinion, and are not, therefore, to be treated lightly. It might be held that for any notice to be taken at all is complimentary, and we might seek shelter in the epigrammatic saying that he who has no enemies has no character; that though hope may spring eternal in the human breast, jealousy is a trait still more constantly found. But this line of argument is not one to be adopted. The *tu quoque* style of defence is not one well calculated to gain a verdict. No doubt the question has been treated often enough before, and in discussing it the writer may seem but to be doing what nowadays the climber is forced to do in the Alps —namely, wander again, perhaps ramble, over ground that has been well trodden many times before. But the conditions have changed greatly since mountaineering first became a popular pastime, and since the first editions of ' Peaks, Passes, and Glaciers ' were rapidly sold out. It is, the writer fears, only too true in these latter days that mountaineers may be classified as Past and Present. Whether a third class may be added of ' the Future ' is a question—to be answered, I hope, in the affirmative.

The Alpine Club was founded in 1857 by a few ardent devotees to what was then an entirely new form of pastime. The original members of that club could never have even dreamed of the wide popularity mountaineering was destined to acquire, or the influence that the establishment of the Alpine Club was to have on it; and, like the fish in an aquarium, they can hardly have known what they were in for. In the present day there are Alpine clubs in almost every country in Europe, and in some countries there are several, numbering their members in some cases by thousands. Nor is it only on the continent of Europe that there are mountaineering clubs. Not that the writer ventures to assert that every member of this multitude is devoted to the high Alps, or that it is in the least degree essential to climb high and difficult mountains in order to learn the fascination of their natural beauties. It may be pointed out, however, that the 'miserable waste of valuable life' is in the greatest part not on the great peaks and passes, but on little hills. Every year we read of accidents on mountains such as the Faulhorn, the Monte Salvatore in the Alps, or Snowdon, Helvellyn and the like in our own country. Possibly these disasters might never have taken place had the experience of mountaineering craft gained in high regions been properly appreciated and utilised. The good surgeon is he who, utilising all his own and all his predecessors' experience, recognises, and makes provision against, all the risks that may conceivably be involved in the most trifling operation he may be called upon to perform; and holiday ramblers in our own land and in sub-Alpine regions might, not without advantage, profit by the example.

Five-and-twenty years ago in Switzerland there were numberless heights untrodden, passes uncrossed, and regions unexplored. Then, moreover, there were comparatively but few to cross the passes or climb the mountains; but those few did mighty deeds. Peak after peak fell before them, while slowly but surely they opened up new regions and brought unexpected beauties to light. In those days climbing as an art was but in its infancy, restricted to a few amateurs specially qualified to pursue it, and to a very limited number of guides—merely those, in fact (not such a numerous class as people seem generally to imagine), who had made chamois-hunting one of the principal objects of their lives. Gradually the art became more developed, and with the increase of power thus acquired came increase of confidence. From the fact that the training in the mountaineering art was gradual, it was necessarily thorough—a fact that a good many climbers would do well to bear in mind in these latter days. Then, of course, the charm of novelty, so dear to the mountaineer, was seldom absent; he could strike out right or left and find virgin soil; but in quest of novelty search had to be made before long in remote regions. It followed that exploration was not limited, and the early pioneers of mountaineering could, and did learn more of the geography and varied beauties of the Alps in a single season than their followers do, in the present day, in five or six.

After a while the fashion of mountaineering altered sensibly, and a strong conservatism sprang up. Certain districts became more and more frequented; certain peaks acquired special popularity, either because they were conveniently placed and ready of access; or because there was a certain touch of romance about them, as in the case of the Matterhorn; or because they had acquired the reputation of being difficult, and it was thought that a successful ascent would stamp the climber at once as a skilful person and a very daring creature. Thus places like Zermatt, Grindelwald, Chamouni, and the Æggischhorn became the great centres of mountaineering, and have remained so ever since. Independent exploration gradually gave way to the charm of meeting others bent on the same pursuit of climbing; but this feeling was not without its drawbacks, and tended to check what has been called cosmopolitanism in mountaineering. How few, even among those who visit the Alps regularly, know anything whatever of such large, important, and interesting districts as the Silvretta group, the Rheinwald group, or the Lepontine Alps! while districts like Zermatt are thronged and crowded, and the mountains absolutely done to death. Not that it is hard to understand how this narrowing of the field of mountaineering has been brought about. There comes a time of life to most men when they find more pleasure in meeting old friends than in making new acquaintances; and the same feeling would appear to extend to the mountains.

It must be confessed here that the writer is disposed to look upon mountaineering in the Alps, in the sense in which it has hitherto been known, as a pastime that will before long become extinct. In some soils trees grow with extraordinary rapidity and vigour, but do not strike their roots very deep, and so are prone to early decay. Still, it does not follow that, even should these pessimist forebodings prove true, and climbing be relegated to the limbo of archaic pursuits, the Alps will not attract their thousands as they have done for many years. The dearth of novelty is sometimes held to be the principal cause that will eventually lead to the decay of mountaineering. There is a reasonable probability, however, to judge from the Registrar-General's reports, that the world will still be peopled some time hence, and possibly a generation will then arise of mountaineering revivalists who, never having tasted the flavour of novelty in Alpine climbing, will not perceive that its absence is any loss. Yet in the Alps alone many seem to forget that, while they are exhausting in every detail a few spots, there are numerous and varied expeditions of similar nature still to be accomplished, the scenes of which lie within a few hours of London. It is of course only to mountaineering as a semi-fashionable craze that these remarks apply. The knowledge of the art, acquired primarily in the Alps, which has led to the development of mountaineering as a science will not be wasted, and the training acquired in holiday expeditions, when amusement or the regaining of health was the principal object, can be turned to valuable practical account elsewhere. So shall there be a future for mountaineering. No doubt but few may be able to find the opportunity, unless indeed they make it somewhat of a profession, of exploring the great mountainous districts still almost untouched—such, for instance, as the Himalayas. But it is in some such direction as this that the force of the stream, somewhat tending to dry up in its original channel, will, it may be hoped, spread in the future.

It has already been shown, by the results of many modern expeditions, that the old views that obtained with respect to the upward limit of mountaineering must, to say the least, be considerably modified. From early times the question of the effects of rarefied air in high regions on mountaineers has attracted attention. As a matter of fact the subject is still barely in its infancy. A few remarks on this point may not perhaps be thought too technical, for they bear, I hope, on the mountaineering of the future.

It is matter of notoriety that in these days travellers seem less subject to discomfort in the high Alps than in former times. De Saussure, for instance, in the account of his famous ascent of Mont Blanc in 1787, speaks a good deal of the difficulty of respiration. At his bivouac on the Plateau, at an elevation of 13,300 feet, the effects of the rarefied air were much commented on; and these remarks are the more valuable, inasmuch as De Saussure was a man of science and a most acute observer; while his account, a thing too rare in these days, is characterised by extreme modesty of description. The frequency of the respirations, he observed, which ensued on any exertion caused great fatigue. Nowadays, however, pedestrians, often untrained, may be seen daily ascending at a very much faster pace than De Saussure seems to have gone, and yet the effects are scarcely felt. No one now expects much to suffer from this cause, and no one does. In recent times we hear accounts of ascents of mountains like Elbruz, 18,526 feet, by Mr. Grove and others; of Cotopaxi, 19,735 feet, and Chimborazo, 20,517[1] feet, by Mr. Whymper; and the most recent, and by far the most remarkable, of

---

[1] This is Mr. Edward Whymper's measurement. Humboldt, as quoted by Mr. Whymper, gave 21,460 feet as the height. (*Alpine Journal*, vol. x. p. 442.)

Kabru in the Himalayas, about 24,000 feet, by Mr. Graham. In all these expeditions the travellers spent nights in bivouacs far above the level of the Grand Plateau where De Saussure encamped. We cannot suppose that in the Caucasus, the Andes, or the Himalayas the air differs much from that of the Alps with regard to its rarefaction effects on travellers. In fact, the Alpine traveller would in this respect probably be much better off, for the general conditions surrounding him would be more like those to which he was accustomed. He would not have, for instance, to contend with the effects of changed or meagre diet or unaccustomed climate.

Mr. F. C. Grove, a very high authority on such a point, in his description of the ascent of Elbruz, in the course of some remarks on the rarity of the air, states his belief that at some height or another, less than that of the loftiest mountain, there must be a limit at which no amount of training and good condition will enable a man to live; and he says, 'It may be taken for granted that no human being could walk to the top of Mount Everest.'[1] This was written in 1875; but a great deal has happened since then, though the same opinion is still very generally entertained. But with this opinion I cannot coincide at all, for reasons that appear to me logically conclusive. In the first place, a party of three, composed of Mr. Graham,

[1] *The Frosty Caucasus*, by F. C. Grove, p. 236.

Herr Emil Boss, and the Swiss guide Kauffman, have ascended more than 5,000 feet higher than the top of Elbruz, and none of the party experienced any serious effect, or, indeed, apparently any effect at all other than those naturally incidental to severe exertion. It must be admitted that one result of their expedition was to prove, tolerably conclusively, that Mount Everest is not the highest mountain in the world. Still, until it is officially deposed, it may be taken, for argument's sake, as the ultimate point. Now, it would seem to be beyond doubt that a man, being transported to a height much greater than Mount Everest, can still live. In Messrs. Coxwell and Glaisher's famous balloon ascent from Wolverhampton on September 5, 1862, described in 'Travels in the Air,' it was computed that the travellers reached a height of nearly 37,000 feet,[1] and this in less than an hour from the time of leaving the earth. Deduct 5,000 feet from this computation, to allow for possible error, and we still have a height left of 32,000 feet, an elevation, that is, very considerably greater than the summit of Mount Everest—possibly a greater elevation than the summit of any mountain. Life then, it is proved, can be sustained at such a height, and the point that remains for consideration is whether the necessary exertion of walking or climbing to the same height would render the actual ascent impossible.

[1] *Travels in the Air*, edited by James Glaisher, F.R.S., p. 57 2nd ed.).

Since the days of De Saussure some 8,000 feet have been added to the height to which the possibility of ascending has been proved. It seems to me unreasonable to assume that another 5,000 feet may not yet be added, and arbitrary to conclude that at some point higher than Kabru but lower than Mount Everest the limit of human endurance must necessarily be reached. Mr. Glaisher himself does not appear to think that, from his experience, any such ascent as that we have been considering would be possible for an Alpine traveller (*op. cit.* p. 21 and elsewhere). But, with every deference to so great an authority, a few considerations may be submitted which tend most seriously to invalidate his conclusions and opinions, and which may serve to show also that the effects of rarefied air probably differ more widely in the two cases of the aëronaut and the mountaineer than is generally supposed. Writing in 1871, Mr. Glaisher says,[1] 'At a height of three miles I never experienced any annoyance or discomfort; yet there is no ascent I think of Mont Blanc in which great inconvenience and severe *pain* have not been felt at a height of 13,000 feet; but then, as before remarked, this is an elevation attained only after two days of excessive toil.' Mr. Glaisher is here referring chiefly to Dr. Hamel's ascent of Mont Blanc, and would seem apparently to be unaware that, long before he wrote, the ascent of Mont Blanc, from Chamouni and

[1] *Op. cit.* p. 9.

back to the same place, had been accomplished within twenty-four hours. In 1873, if my memory serves me right, Mr. Passingham started from Chamouni, ascended the mountain, and returned to his hotel in a little less than twenty hours.¹ Compare such an ascent as this — not by any means an isolated instance — with De Saussure's experience, and when we consider how remarkable has been the developmen of mountaineering in this direction, we may surely hold that to fix at present any absolute limit is unduly arbitrary. Further, the ascents of Chimborazo and the other mountains named above have all been accomplished since Mr. Glaisher wrote. Mr. Glaisher states that the aëronaut may acclimatise himself to great heights by repeated ascents; but how much more may the mountaineer then hope to do so! The aëronaut necessarily makes ascents rapidly ² and at rare intervals. The mountaineer can acclimatise himself to high regions by a constant and gradua process, a method obviously better calculated to extend the limits of his endurance.

Of course I am only discussing the actual possibility, not entering into the question for a moment of whether it is worth while to do it. It may be that

¹ I understand that the expedition has since been accomplished in a much shorter time.
² In Messrs. Coxwell and Glaisher's ascent from Wolverhampton the balloon when at the height of 29,000 feet was mounting at the rate of 1,000 feet a minute.

to attempt an ascent of Mount Everest would prove almost as rash an undertaking as an endeavour to swim through the Niagara rapids—that is, if the mountaineering difficulties are so great as to make the two instances parallel. Two points have to be considered: one, that, granted the desirability of making such an ascent, we do not yet fully know the best manner of undertaking it; and another, that we are still very ignorant as to the physiological effects of rarefied air on the human frame.[1]

With regard to the first point, we know indeed this much—that, granted good condition, a man can 'acclimatise' himself to great heights, and when so acclimatised he can undergo much more exertion in very high regions with much less effect. The experience of Mr. Whymper in the Andes, and of Mr. Graham and others in the Himalayas, has shown this conclusively enough. Let a man sleep at a height, say, of 18,000 feet, and then ascend from that point another 3,000 or 4,000 feet; he may possibly feel the effects to be so great that an attempt to sleep again at the latter height would render him incapable of exertion the next day, as far as an ascent is concerned. Let him descend till he can bivouac, say at 20,000 feet, and then again try, starting afresh. After a while he would be able to

---

[1] I am aware of M. Paul Bert's researches; but these questions are not to be settled in the laboratory.

accomplish still more than at his first attempt; and so on, until he reached the summit. But even supposing that no amount of acclimatisation enables him to accomplish his end, he has other weapons in his armoury.

The second point mentioned above is that the physiological effects of rarefied air on the human economy are but little known; were these understood the resources of science might be called in to obviate them. It may be said that no amount of science will obviate the very simple fact that exertion causes fatigue, but the answer is that we have no real idea of all the causes which lead to this fatigue. This is not the place to speculate on a somewhat abstruse and unquestionably complicated physiological problem, but the direction in which the question may be approached from the scientific side is worthy of being pointed out. This much may be said, however, that when we talk of strong heart and strong lungs in connection with the question of the possibility of ascending on foot to the greatest altitudes, we are only, from the physiological point of view, taking into account one or two factors, and perhaps not the most important ones. The cavillers may be reminded that physiology is not and never will become a finite science. To my mind at least, as far as human endurance is concerned, it would be no more surprising to me to hear that a man had succeeded in walking up Mount Everest than to know that a man can succeed in standing an arctic climate while on a sledging expedition. Objections like the difficulty of arranging for a supply of food, of expense, of risk, and so forth, are not taken into account—they are really beside the question: they have not proved insuperable obstacles in the case of arctic exploration; they will not prove insurmountable to the ambitious mountaineer we are contemplating. I do not for a moment say that it would be wise to ascend Mount Everest, but I believe most firmly that it is humanly possible to do so; and, further, I feel sure that, even in our own time, perhaps, the truth of these views will receive material corroboration. Mount Everest itself may offer insuperable mountaineering obstacles, but in the unknown, unseen district to the north there may be peaks of equal height presenting no more technical difficulties than Mont Blanc or Elbruz.

From the purely athletic point of view, then, the mountaineering experience which has been gained almost exclusively in the Alps may, by a still further development in the future, enable the climber so to develop the art that he may reach the highest elevation on this world's crust; and he may do this without running undue risk. *Cui bono?* it may be asked; and it is nearly as hard to answer the question as it is to explain to the supine and unaspiring person the good that may be expected to accrue to humanity by reaching the North Pole; yet the latter project, albeit to some it seems like a struggle of man against physical forces which make or mar worlds, is one that is held to be right and proper to be followed. At the least an observer, even of limited powers, may reasonably be expected, supposing he accomplished such a feat as the ascent of Mount Everest, to bring back results of equal scientific value with the arctic traveller, while the purely geographical information he should gain would have fiftyfold greater practical value. The art and science of mountaineering has been learned and developed in the Alps, and the acquirement of this learning has been a pleasure to many. If the holiday nature of mountaineering should in the future be somewhat dropped, and if a few of those who follow should take up the more serious side, and make what has been a pastime into a profession (and why should not some do so? That which is worth doing at all is worth developing to the utmost possible limit), good will come, unless it be argued that there is no gain in extending geographical knowledge; and no advantage in rectifying surveys and rendering them as accurate as possible. As has been remarked by Mr. Douglas Freshfield, the advantage of including in survey parties, such as are still engaged on our Indian frontier, the services of some who have made mountaineering a branch to be learnt in their profession, would be very distinct. Work done in the Alps would, in this direction, perhaps, bear the best fruit and reap the highest practical value which it might be hoped to attain. The value would be real. The search after truth, whether it be in the fields of natural science, of geography, or its to-be-adopted sister orography, can never fail to be right and good and beneficial. Enthusiasm all this! you say. Granted freely. Without some enthusiasm and energy the world would cease to turn, and the retarding section of mankind would be triumphant, save that they would be too languid to realise the victory of their principles.

But still, if properly qualified men are to be forthcoming to meet such a want, which undoubtedly seems to exist, the old training-ground must not be deserted; the playground of Europe must be regarded in relation to serious work in the same light that the playing-fields of Eton were regarded by one who was somewhat of an authority. The Great Duke's remark is too well known to need quotation. English folk may find it hard to hold their own against their near relations in athletic pursuits, such as cricket and sculling, but in mountaineering they undoubtedly lead, and will continue to do so. In one phase indeed of the pursuit their supremacy is menaced. In the matter of recognising the practical value to be obtained from mountaineering in surveying and the like, they are already behind other countries. The roll of honorary members of the Alpine Club comprises a list of men, most of whom have utilised their mountaineering experience to good purpose in advancing scientific exploration. In this department it is to be hoped that we shall not suffer ourselves to be outstripped, nor allow a store of valuable and laboriously acquired experience to remain wasted. The threatening cloud may pass off; the future of Alpine mountaineering may not prove to be so gloomy as it sometimes seems to the writer in danger of gradually becoming. The depression is, possibly, only temporary, and a natural consequence of reaction; and the zigzagging line on the chart, though it may never perhaps rise again to the point it once marked, yet may keep well at the normal—better, perhaps, at such a level than at fever heat. The old cry that we know so well on the mountains, that meets always with a ready thrill of response, may acquire a wider significance, and men will be found to answer to the familiar call of 'Vorwärts, immer vorwärts!'

After all, a century hence the mountaineering centres of to-day will perhaps still attract as they do now. It may be possible to get to Chamouni without submitting to the elaborately devised discomfort of the present Channel passage, and without the terrors of asphyxiation in the carriages of the Chemin de Fer du Nord. Surely the charm of the mountains must always draw men to the Alps, even though the glaciers may have shrunk up and sunk down, though places like Arolla and the Grimsel may have become thriving towns, or radical changes such as a drainage system at Chamouni have been instituted. If the glaciers do shrink, there will be all the more scope for the rock climber and the more opportunity of perfecting an art which has already been so much developed.

A Rip van Winkle of our day, waking up in that epoch of the future, would for certain find much that was unaltered. The same types of humanity would be around him. Conceive this somnolent hero of fiction, clad in a felt wideawake that had once been white, in knickerbockers and Norfolk jacket, of which the seams had at one time held together, supporting his bent frame and creaking joints on a staff with rusted spike and pick. He descends laboriously from a vehicle that had jolted impartially generations before him (for the carriages of the valley are as little liable to wear out, in the eyes of their proprietors, as the 'wonderful one-hoss shay'). He finds himself on a summer evening by the Hôtel de Ville at Chamouni, and facing the newly erected Opera-house. He looks with wondering eyes around. A youth (great-great-great-great-grandson of Jacques Balmat) approaches and waits respectfully by his side, ready to furnish information.

'Why these flags and these rejoicings?' the old man asks.

'To celebrate the tercentenary of the first ascent of Mont Blanc,' the boy answers.

The veteran gazes around, shading his eyes with his shrivelled hand. The travellers come in. First a triumphal procession of successful and intrepid mountaineers. Banners wave, cannon go off—or more probably miss fire—bouquets are displayed, champagne and compliments are poured out; both the latter expressions of congratulation equally gassy, and both about equally genuine.

'Who are these?' the old man inquires.

'Do you not see the number on their banner?' answers the youth; 'they are the heroes of the forty-fifth section of the tenth branch of the northern division of the Savoy Alpine Club.'

'Ah!' the old man murmurs to himself, with a sigh of recollection, 'I can remember that they were numerous even in my day.'

Then follows a sad-looking, dejected creature, stealing back to his hotel by byways, but with face bronzed from exposure on rocks, not scorched by sun-reflecting snow; his boots scored with multitudinous little cuts and scratches telling of difficult climbing; his hands as brown as his face; his finger-nails, it must be admitted, seriously impaired in their symmetry.

'And who is this? Has he been guilty of some crime?' the old man asks.

'Not so,' the answer comes; 'he has just completed the thousandth ascent of the Aiguille . . . . ; he comes of a curious race which, history relates, at one time much frequented these districts; but that was a great while ago—long before the monarchy was re-established. You do well to look at him; that is the last of the climbing Englishmen. They always seem depressed when they have succeeded in achieving their ambition of the moment; it is a characteristic of their now almost extinct race.'

'And what about the perils of the expedition?' the old man asks, brightening up a little as if some old ideas had suddenly flashed across his mind. 'I would fain know whether the journey is different now from what it was formerly; yet the heroes would mock me, perchance, if I were to interrogate them.'

'Not at all,' the youth replies. 'There are but few of the first party who would not vouchsafe to give you a full account, and might even in their courtesy embellish the narrative with flowers of rhetoric. But it is unnecessary. They will print a detailed and full description of their exploits. It has all been said before, but so has everything else, I think.'

'That is true,' the old man murmurs to himself; 'it was even so in my time, and two hundred years before I lived a French writer commenced his book with the remark, "*Tout est dit*." But what of the other, the dejected survivor? does he not too write?'

'Yes, indeed, but not in the same strain; he will

but pour out a little gentle sarcasm and native spleen, in mild criticism of the fulsome periods he peruses in other tongues.'

'Ah me!' thinks the old man, 'in one respect then I need not prove so much behind the time. If the memory of the Alpine literature of my day were still fresh, I could hold mine own with those I see around.'

May I be permitted, in conclusion, to come back to our own day, and to say a very few words on the subject of mountaineering accidents? Most heartily would I concur with any one who raised the objection that such remarks are out of place in a chapter on the mountaineering of the future. But perhaps we have been looking too far ahead, and there may be a period to follow between this our time and the future to be hoped for.

It has sometimes been stated and written that no one desires to remove from mountaineering all danger. The dangers of mountaineering have been divided by a well-known authority into real and imaginary. The supposed existence of the latter is, I grant, desirable, especially to the inexperienced climber; but I shall always contend that it ought to be the great object of every votary of the pursuit to minimise the former to the utmost of his ability. Now, it is only by true experience—that is, by learning gradually the art of mountaineering—that the climber will achieve this result. Few of those unacquainted with the subject can have any idea of the extraordinary difference between the risk run on a difficult expedition (that is, on one where difficulties occur : the name of the peak or pass has little to do with the matter) by a practised mountaineer who has learned something of the art, and an inexperienced climber who has nothing but the best intentions to assist his steps. The man of experience bears always in mind the simple axioms and rules of his craft; if he does not he is a bad mountaineer. If the plain truth be told, accidents in the Alps have almost invariably, to whomsoever they befell, been due to breaking one or more of these same well-known rules, or, in other words, to bad mountaineering. That such is no more than a simple statement of fact a former president of the Alpine Club, Mr. C. E. Mathews, has abundantly proved.[1] Numbers of our countrymen, young and old, annually rush out to the Alps for the first time. Fired with ambition, or led on by the fascination of the pastime, with scarcely any preliminary training and no preliminary study of the subject, they at once begin to attack the more difficult peaks and passes. Success perhaps attends their efforts. Unfit, they go up a difficult mountain, trusting practically to the ability of the guides to do their employers' share of the work as well as their own. They descend, and think to gauge

[1] Vide *Alpine Journal*, vol. xi. p. 78. 'The Alpine Obituary,' by C. E. Mathews.

their skill by the name of the expedition undertaken. The state of the weather and of the mountain determine whether such a performance be an act of simple or of culpable folly. For such the imaginary dangers are the most formidable. If they had taken the trouble to begin at the beginning, to learn the difference between the stem and stern of a boat before attempting to navigate an ironclad, they would have recognised, and profited by, the true risks run. As it is, they are probably inflated with conceit at overcoming visionary difficulties. They may make, indeed, in this way what in Alpine slang is called a good 'book;' but by far the greater number fail to perceive that there is anything to learn. It is a pastime —an amusement; they do not look beyond this. But these same climbers would admit that in other forms of sport, such as cricket or rowing, proficiency is not found in beginners. It is in the study and development of the amusement that the true and deeper pleasure is to be found. A tyro in cricket would make himself an object of ridicule in a high-class match; the novice in the art of rowing would be loth to display his feeble powers if thrust into a racing four with three tried oarsmen; and yet the embryo climber can see nothing absurd in attacking mountains of recognised difficulty. Inexperience in the former instances at least could cause no harm, while ignorance of the elementary principles of mountaineering renders the climber a serious source of danger not only to himself but to others. There is no royal road to the acquirement of mountaineering knowledge. It is just as difficult to use the axe or alpenstock properly as the oar or the racquet; just as much patient, persevering practice is needed; but it is not on difficult expeditions that such inexperience can be best overcome.

A man of average activity could, probably, actually climb, without any particular experience, most of, or all, the more difficult rock peaks under good conditions of weather and the like. But how different from the really practical mountaineer, who strives to make an art of his pastime. Watch the latter. First and foremost, he knows when to turn back, and does not hesitate to act as his judgment directs. He bears in mind that there is pleasure to be obtained from mountaineering even though the programme may not be carried out in its entirety as planned, and realises to the full that

> 'Tis better to have climbed and failed
> Than never to have climbed at all.

His companions are always safe with him, his climbing unselfish; he never dislodges a loose stone—except purposely—either with hands, feet, or the loose rope; he is always as firm as circumstances will permit, prepared to withstand any sudden slip; he never puts forth more strength at each step than is necessary, thus saving his powers, being always ready in an emergency, and never degenerating into that most dangerous of encumbrances, a tired member of a united party: not, of course, that the vast majority of amateurs can ever hope, with their imperfect practice, to attain to the level of even a second-rate guide; still, by bringing his intelligence to bear on this, as he does on any other amusement, the amateur can render himself something more than a thoroughly reliable companion on any justifiable expedition.

Let the spirit of competition lead young climbers to strive after excellence in this direction, rather than, as is too commonly the case, induce them to take 'Times' as the criterion of mountaineering proficiency. There are instructors enough. Even from an inferior guide an infinite amount may be learnt; at the least such a one can recognise the real danger of the Alps, and in this respect possesses a faculty which is one of the chief the mountaineer has to acquire. Let the spirit in which the Alps are climbed be of some such nature as that I have attempted to indicate, and accidents such as those recorded in Mr. C. E. Mathews' grim list will be of such rare occurrence that they will never be called up to discredit mountaineering. If, perchance, any words here written shall prompt in the future the climber to perfect his art more and more while frequenting the old haunts, and to extend and utilise mountaineering still more, then at least the writer may feel, like the mountain when it had brought forth the ridiculous mouse, that his labour has not been wholly in vain. Yet more: his gloomy forebodings shall be falsified, and with respect to the future of mountaineering the outlook will be bright enough.

www.ingramcontent.com/pod-product-compliance
Lightning Source LLC
Chambersburg PA
CBHW030325240426
43673CB00040B/1275